More Praise for *The Ritual Effect*

"An endlessly fascinating exploration of the rituals all around us, and the remarkable power they have to shape our moods, identities, and performance. *The Ritual Effect* will stir you to see your beliefs and relationships with fresh eyes—and spur you to transform ordinary activities into sources of wonder and delight."

—Daniel H. Pink, #1 *New York Times* bestselling author of
The Power of Regret, Drive, and *When*

"Norton gives the reader a witty, thought-provoking guide to some of our species' oldest and quirkiest behavior. If you want to understand and harness the psychological power of rituals to live and think better, this is the book for you."

—Laurie Santos, Chandrika and Ranjan Tandon
Professor of Psychology at Yale University
and host of *The Happiness Lab* podcast

"Illuminating and inspiring . . . *The Ritual Effect* gives readers new insights into the everyday actions that shape our lives."

—BJ Fogg, *New York Times* bestselling author of *Tiny Habits:*
The Small Changes That Change Everything

THE
RITUAL
EFFECT

From Habit to Ritual,
Harness the Surprising Power
of Everyday Actions

MICHAEL NORTON

SCRIBNER

New York   London   Toronto   Sydney   New Delhi

Scribner
An Imprint of Simon & Schuster, LLC
1230 Avenue of the Americas
New York, NY 10020

Copyright © 2024 by Michael Norton

All rights reserved, including the right to reproduce this book or portions thereof
in any form whatsoever. For information, address Scribner Subsidiary Rights
Department, 1230 Avenue of the Americas, New York, NY 10020.

First Scribner hardcover edition April 2024

SCRIBNER and design are registered trademarks of The Gale Group, Inc.,
used under license by Simon & Schuster, LLC, the publisher of this work.

Simon & Schuster: Celebrating 100 Years of Publishing in 2024

For information about special discounts for bulk purchases,
please contact Simon & Schuster Special Sales at 1-866-506-1949
or business@simonandschuster.com.

The Simon & Schuster Speakers Bureau can bring authors to your
live event. For more information or to book an event, contact the
Simon & Schuster Speakers Bureau at 1-866-248-3049 or visit
our website at www.simonspeakers.com.

Interior design by Laura Levatino

Manufactured in the United States of America

10 9 8 7 6 5 4 3 2 1

Library of Congress Cataloging-in-Publication Data has been applied for.

ISBN 978-1-9821-5302-1
ISBN 978-1-9821-5304-5 (ebook)

For Mel

CONTENTS

Part 1: What Rituals Do

Part 2: Rituals for Ourselves

Part 3: Rituals and Relationships

Part 4: Rituals at Work and in the World

THE
RITUAL
EFFECT

Part I

What Rituals Do

Preface

Reenchanted

Before the sun rises, Flannery O'Connor begins her day with morning prayers and a thermos of coffee she shares with her mother. At 7:00 a.m., O'Connor attends daily Catholic mass. At the same time, Maya Angelou arrives not far from her house at a motel room, where she has asked to have all the art removed from the walls. Sometime midmorning, Victor Hugo strips naked and instructs his valet to hide Hugo's clothes until he has met his daily writing goals. At exactly 3:30 p.m. (*so* exactly the whole town can set its clock by him), Immanuel Kant steps outside his door with his Spanish walking stick in hand for his afternoon walk. In the evening, Agatha Christie slips into a bathtub and eats an apple. And at the long day's end, Charles Dickens pulls out the compass he always keeps with him to confirm that his bed is facing north, blows out the candle, and falls asleep.

The paragraph you just read—a composite day in the life of six world-famous writers—may look like a portrait of creative madness or, at the very least, eccentricity. But these famous authors are performing deeply meaningful actions, which they repeat over and over. Even though these actions might seem totally random to you, they felt deeply right to—and *worked* for—these writers. All of them were engaged in some form of ritualistic behavior.

You might be thinking that eccentric behavior is part of the job for creative people such as poets, novelists, and philosophers. But I could just as easily have picked any other category of high performers. Keith Richards has to have a piece of shepherd's pie—always the first slice—right before he steps onstage with the Rolling Stones. Chris Martin wouldn't leave his dressing room to go out with his band, Coldplay, until he had methodically picked up his toothbrush and toothpaste and given his teeth a quick but precise shine. Marie Curie—tragically—could only fall asleep if she had her tiny bottle of radium next to her bed. Barack Obama could only get through polling day by playing a carefully arranged game of basketball with certain friends.

Now, guess who the sources of these two preperformance rituals are:

I crack my knuckles and tap my fingers against certain areas of my body. Once these are completed, I take an inventory of my body from head to toe.

I close my eyes and imagine being with my dog. I list four things I see, list three things I smell, list two things I hear, and list one thing I feel.

Serena Williams? Tom Brady? Excellent guesses—and we'll get to know some of Serena's and Tom's rituals later. But these are simply the preperformance rituals reported by two regular folks who completed surveys my colleagues and I conducted in our more than ten years of investigating the science of rituals.

My colleagues and I at Harvard and around the world—psychologists, economists, neuroscientists, and anthropologists—have had the privilege of investigating a genuinely astonishing array of individual and collective rituals with the goal of better understanding what rituals are; how they work; and how they help us rise to the challenges and realize the opportunities of everyday life. For more than a decade, we've surveyed tens of thousands of people all over the world, conducted experiments in our labs, and even used brain scans to explore the neural underpinnings of rituals.

This is a book about what we discovered. In realms personal and professional, private and public, and in encounters that cut across cultures and identities, rituals are emotional catalysts that energize, inspire, and elevate us. Our research will lay bare this logic of ritual by successively stripping away different elements of specific rituals to isolate and explore their impact. Among the questions we'll take up are: What exactly are the differences between a ritual, a habit, and a compulsion? How do rituals emerge? And how do we ensure that our rituals work for us rather than against?

We will also explore why placing your socks in your drawer sideways, *just so*, like so many toppled snails, can spark joy; how families can turn dinners from drudgery to delightful; why brands such as Starbucks can benefit from encouraging their customers, "Take Comfort in Your Rituals"; the real reason open-plan offices don't work; why traditional rain dances and those annoying and seemingly pointless team-building exercises managers make their employees perform really *can* work; and why rituals' ability to generate a greater variety of emotions—a phenomenon I describe as *emodiversity*—is important for our psychological well-being in measurable ways.

For those of you who insist you don't have rituals, you'll come to see how they play key roles in the way you conduct business, relate to other people, mark milestones, and experience your daily life—down to what you eat and drink, and even how you brush your teeth.

Rituals often operate below our radar and enable us to savor the experiences of everyday life. We'll see how rituals help us start the day off right and bring it to a peaceful close; how they foster strong relationships, in life and work; how they operate in war and peace; and how they offer us a transformation from automated to more animated ways of living.

I want to take you on a scientific journey to discover the rituals that make up the fabric of daily life. By the end of this book, I hope that you will feel empowered and equipped to create and adopt your own rituals as you try to get over, get through, and get better at the many challenges all of us encounter, and also to do more of the things that make life worth living.

The many ways in which ritual enhances and enchants our lives—what I have come to call the *ritual effect*—is the story of this book.

Chapter 1

What *Are* Rituals?

Maeby: *Do you guys know where I can get one of*
those gold necklaces with a "T" on it?

Michael: *That's a cross.*

Maeby: *Across from where?*

—*Arrested Development*

On Sundays when I was growing up, my Irish Catholic parents
and I engaged in a full-throated battle as I valiantly tried—and
failed—to explain why I shouldn't have to go to St. Theresa's for mass.
It wasn't what was said during the service that bothered me so much
("do unto others" always seemed like solid advice). It was the script:
walk in, sit, stand, sign of the cross, sit, stand, walk, candles, eat, drink,
kneel, sit, stand, shake hands, sit, stand, sing, walk out. The people in
the pews around me, including some of the people I love and respect
most in the world, found deep meaning in this sequence. But I felt like
an automaton, literally going through the motions.

Those particular religious rituals didn't work for me, but other
rituals absolutely did. My preferred rituals, like most people's, were
selective. I didn't love holy days but I loved holidays, especially the
end-of-year run from Halloween to Thanksgiving to Christmas capped
by New Year's Eve. I'm sure you're thinking shrewdly: candles, candy,

7

doting relatives, relaxed bedtimes, presents. Of course eight-year-old you liked those rituals more. And there's no discounting that candy and toys cast a certain spell.

But I also know that what I loved most—and what has stayed with me—is the particular way my family enacted the holidays. This included the scratchy sounds of Johnny Mathis's *Merry Christmas* album emanating from my father's record player (used just once a year for this purpose) and that we had three kinds of stuffing at Thanksgiving (even though I disliked all three). There were plenty of nonholiday rituals, too. For example, we sat at the same places at the dinner table for decades (I sat across from my mom, between my dad and one of my sisters). All hell broke loose if anyone ever dared to switch places. When my mother had had enough of any of us five kids, she would give us to the count of three to knock it off; but when she starting counting—"Once, twice . . ."—one of us would jump in to sing, "Three times a lady." At the time, this made her even angrier. But decades later, she danced with my brother to this same song at his wedding. Now that she is gone, hearing that song brings her briefly back to me. These idiosyncratic behaviors somehow came to matter. As they were ritualized over time, they were among the things that made my family *my family*. They were us.

Welcome to a More Secular Age

Years later, it's easy to see that my resistance to traditional religious rituals and church attendance yet my enthusiastic embrace of many secular rituals—in particular, my family's idiosyncratic versions of them—tracks the broader cultural trends that define what the philosopher Charles Taylor has called our "secular age."

In the United States, in 2022, for example, roughly three in ten adults now identify as having "no religion"—whereas in the 1990s close to 90 percent identified as Christian—and some estimates project that the number of Americans who identify as "religiously unaffiliated" will approach those who identify as Christian by the year 2070. A 2022 Gallup poll showed Americans' trust in institutions such as the Supreme Court and organized religion to be at an all-time low. These numbers bear witness to a simple truth: the twentieth and twenty-first centuries have seen a widespread loss of faith in both the traditional authorities who once told us how to pattern our lives and the institutions that once held us to those patterns.

More than a century ago, the German lawyer and economist Max Weber developed a bold narrative that anticipated these trends. In 1897, after immersing himself in less than scintillating scholarship on topics such as the agrarian patterns of ancient Rome, Weber suffered a nervous breakdown and took to his bed. There, under the care of his wife, Marianne (who also was his second cousin), he started documenting what he described as the "disenchantment" of the modern world. He argued that technological systems and bureaucracy were the new organizing principles of society. Whereas once customs, religious obligations, and rituals dictated how we ordered our days and lives, society was now, Weber argued, under the reign of rationalized procedures and processes. Science and technology—and the institutions governed by them—would replace doctrines of faith, superstitions, and other forms of magical thinking. In what many consider to be his (unfinished) magnum opus, *Economy and Society*, Weber warned that a "polar night of icy darkness" was descending. Humankind, in his estimation, was entering a world stripped of light and warmth, meaning and magic. The result? A disenchanted world bereft of ritual.

The Great Reenchantment

In some ways, Weber was prophetic. The established, traditional rituals that he had in mind have declined in the past century. Yet our world is far from coldly rational or disenchanted. Belief in God remains pervasive among people around the world, including Americans—some 81 percent in 2022. Although one in six people worldwide report being religiously unaffiliated, many still engage in religious rituals. In China, for example, 44 percent of unaffiliated adults say they have worshipped at a graveside or tomb in the past year. Even belief in other supernatural beings, such as aliens, is on the rise.

When you start to consider ritual outside the realm of organized religion, it soon becomes clear that the late twentieth and early twenty-first century has produced countless secular or loosely spiritual rituals. Among the proliferation of new group affiliations that have quickly become ritualized are a wide variety of pilgrimages to the deserts of America—starting with Burning Man and now including the Coachella music festival and the Bombay Beach Biennale, an art commune held in the environmental wasteland of California's Salton Sea. Yoga and fitness groups have created initiation rites such as Orangetheory's "Hell Week"—replete with signature high fives for ensuring social cohesion—and SoulCycle's candlelit rooms with sermon-like coaching and "soulful moments" throughout class. During the years of the COVID lockdown, Peloton became a leader in the world of fitness for answering the collective need to gather and move in synchrony with other humans. The at-home workout provided a virtual space for people of all shapes and sizes to gather and breathe within a simulacrum of a sweaty studio. All over the United States, one commonly sees people wearing internet-famous T-shirts that read GYM IS MY CHURCH.

Rituals are also providing more meaningful ways for people to step away from technology's drive toward optimization and captured attention. Rituals delineate a sacred space to keep people connected to the present moment, while the practice of "I Am Here" days invites participants to meet up for time together without any digital devices. Journalist Anand Giridharadas, an originator of I Am Here days along with his wife, author Priya Parker, described these gatherings as a special time for "reveling in friendship and conversation of a kind that Facebook doesn't do; being thickly in one place, not thinly everywhere." This same desire for connection can also be seen in the group of teenagers gathering every Sunday at the same spot in Brooklyn's Prospect Park. They place logs in a circle and set aside their flip phones to discuss analog books and share sketch pads. These are the members of the Luddite Club, and they have designed rituals to support and enhance one another's efforts to move away from all social media platforms and live a pre-iPhone existence, if only for a few hours.

Consider, too, the rise of the Seattle Atheist Church, where atheists gather on Sundays to experience everything good about church—community, reflection, singing—just minus the God part. When the service is over, members of the church sit in a circle and pass around a "talking rabbit." Anyone who has feelings and thoughts to share holds this totem while speaking to the group. Using such rituals, the church's official mission is to offer the benefits of a religious community without the "cognitive dissonance" that belief in supernatural beings entails.

In all these examples rituals are alive, well, and flourishing. It's just that they've assumed forms that fly in the face of traditional ideas about what rituals are—and for that reason, they are often dismissed as New Agey or millennial or indulgent or just plain odd. Also, clearly the word *ritual* retains an aura, an air of the sacred or magical, that the wellness industry has monetized to great effect. One can now hire "ritual mavens"—corporate ritual consultants—and engage with a myriad of online apps and platforms offering daily meditations, gratitude practices, affirmations, and bullet journaling—just to name a few. What do these new developments tell us about the place of rituals in the twenty-first century?

The Story of a Ritual Skeptic

I am often as dubious of these new secular rituals as I had been about the many traditional ones I had growing up. At first, I wasn't especially curious about them, either. Despite these examples of secular rituals emerging in the culture, the idea of studying rituals was the furthest thing from my mind in the early days of my career as a behavioral scientist. I liked designing tightly controlled laboratory experiments, where I could strip down phenomena to their bare essentials, isolate key variables, and assess the effects of those variables on some outcome measure. My focus was on topics such as quantifying the precise effect of spending our money in different ways (for example, on ourselves versus others) on our happiness, varying the type of information conveyed by political "spin doctors" to assess the impact on our perceptions of politicians, and demonstrating which specific brain regions undergird the ubiquitous tendency for our minds to wander.

The challenges of measuring ritual's effects in a laboratory struck me (and many of my fellow colleagues in the behavioral sciences) as daunting, at best. The kinds of practices that came to mind when I thought of "rituals" were richly detailed, highly elaborate, tailored to specific cultures, often with centuries of embedded meaning, and therefore felt impossible to reduce to the same scientific method. How do you strip away culture and history from practices such as these? Would anything be left to study?

Even in my earliest explorations of how rituals work and why, I still identified as a ritual skeptic. What does it mean to be a ritual skeptic? Perhaps you already know. Many of us have friends or family members who scaffold their days—their whole lives maybe—with rituals. Like Flannery O'Connor, they might start their day at a precise time, in a specific way, and carry on like this all day until, like Charles Dickens, they end their day in another precise, specific way. But not me. I woke up at different times, ate at different times, took breaks at different times, went to bed at different times—there was nothing at all ritualistic in how I went about my life. Or so I thought.

Until the day something happened. I shouldn't say something— someone. My daughter. After she arrived, I instantly and unthinkingly transformed into a shamanic madman. Going to bed—a goal that had once involved a handful of dull but functional actions such as flossing and plugging my phone in—became over time a roughly seventeen-step ritual enacted with one goal: to get my child to go to sleep. There were key players: me, my wife, piggy, brown bunny, and (especially) gray bunny. There were key songs: a song my wife used to sing at Camp Wewa, the Buddy Holly song "Everyday" (known to my daughter as the "roller-coaster song"), the James Taylor song "Sweet Baby James" (the "cowboy song"). There were sacred texts: *Goodnight Moon; The Very Hungry Caterpillar; Oh, the Thinks You Can Think!* There were key actions: carrying her up to bed slowly so she could say good night to the stairs and ask them if they needed anything before bed, then repeating a quiet *shhh* until she fell asleep. (I was so convinced that my way of saying *shhh* was the most soothing in the world that I recorded it and looped it so that we always had ten minutes of me ready to go.)

I believed that I was performing these steps month after month, each and every night, because my daughter needed them. As with any ritual, I rigidly adhered to the precise order of actions and repeated them. Anything less and I was convinced she would be up all night. And, as with most rituals, my actions had some randomness—why two bunnies but only one pig? Why not *Oh, the Places You'll Go!*? Why the stairs and not the kitchen appliances? We didn't know but still we rarely strayed from each of the steps. The stakes were too high. The overriding feeling was that if we tried to vary it or—in desperation to get to sleep—to streamline it, the entire endeavor might fall flat. An abbreviation or variation might not conjure up the necessary drowsy comfort—and then we would have to start again.

Over time, I began to look at this nightly performance with a more analytical eye. What was I doing? The ritual was not just for my daughter; it was for me, too. I had been enacting this series of rigidly precise steps with the belief that they could and would *do* something. After night upon night of enacting the ritual, we had come to believe in its power to transition us from evening into night and to summon sleep. Somehow, without ever consciously deciding to do so, I had shifted from a solid ritual skeptic to a true ritual believer.

The moment I recognized this shift I started to wonder: Were all of the people I passed by on the street on an average day also relying on made-up rituals? And were they working? If so, why and how? Beyond ritualized group identities to fitness groups such as Peloton and Orangetheory, far from people seeking out collective effervescence at Burning Man, were other self-professed skeptics like me actually living everyday lives rich with the unacknowledged power of ritual?

My daughter's bedtime requirements confronted me with the startling possibility that almost everything I had believed about rituals was at best misinformed and at worst dead wrong. Yes—rituals are certainly religious traditions and ceremonies that get passed down from one generation to the next. But they are also idiosyncratic behaviors that can emerge spontaneously. I was living proof that seemingly any set of behaviors can become a ritual. The catalyst of all rituals is the need; tradition and ancestry are not required.

The new parent in me had reached for ritual instinctively to soothe to sleep the youngest human in my life—but to soothe my own anxiety, too. I'd started a few investigations into rituals, but now the scientist in me needed better answers about what was happening underneath the hood. If people can come up with their own rituals, on the spot, and yet still have their experiences and emotions shaped by them, what exactly are rituals and how do they work? These questions cracked a curiosity in me wide open; I was now determined to find out.

Where Rituals Come From

Aside from my childhood experience of religious ritual, much of what I knew about rituals came from research in anthropology and other de-scriptive fields in the social sciences. The idea behind anthropology's ethnographic methods has been to set forth and observe what the humans are doing, then try to figure out why they are doing it. Much of this now canonical body of scholarship was produced by Western scholars studying non-Western cultures, and most of it focused on one vein of rituals—time-tested rites received as tradition. These are the rigid, com-munal practices that most readily spring to mind upon hearing the word *ritual*. They are what I refer to as *legacy rituals*.

None of this body of research, although certainly fascinating, brought me any closer to understanding my experience with my daughter's bedtime. No ancestors passed knowledge of stuffies down to me; Buddy Holly is not mentioned in any ancient texts. Ritual, I was coming to understand, could be an individually designed experience.

Once I shifted my tacit assumptions about rituals—to include not only inviolable traditional rites but practices constructed spontaneously by individuals—I started recognizing them all around me. Just as I had done in trying to create calm at my daughter's bedtime, individuals and groups often grab for the props, pageantry, and stage-craft available to them in the moment. Sometimes they adapt aspects of a legacy ritual they inherited, other times they come up with a new ritual, and often they do both at the same time.

In the conventional understanding of rituals, such things don't just happen out of the blue. The ritual is the ritual: you sit up, stand, and kneel when you are told to sit up, stand, and kneel. You eat the food you are told to eat because that is what your people have always done and that is what they will do ad infinitum. In my experience with my daughter, I saw glimmers of a completely different way to think about rituals. People across time have been innovating their rituals to meet the moment with whatever resources and materials they have on hand. Maybe the legacy ritual passed down from generation to gen-eration didn't work for everyone, like the rituals I practiced as a child in church. Or, in some cases, maybe what was needed just didn't exist yet, sometimes because the world had presented the humans with an entirely new problem—such as a twenty-first-century pandemic.

This approach to the science of rituals—the idea that an indi-vidual might at some point say, "I'm doing this differently"—put me squarely in the domain of behavioral economics, or the science of how individuals go about making decisions. My PhD was in social psychology, and I did my postdoctoral work in behavioral econom-ics at the Sloan School of Management at MIT. When I first arrived there, fresh from defending my dissertation, I discovered an intel-lectual Shangri-la, a world filled with curious and generous people who were asking all sorts of unexpected, quirky questions about how people make decisions. From within this spirit of intellectual free-dom I was first exposed to a possible way forward for measuring the effects of rituals.

The prevailing assumption about rituals had been that they were inextricably linked with groups and culture and that made them impossible to study with the empirical methods of science. You can't just randomly assign some lab participants to one culture and others to a different culture. ("Okay, everyone in this group is now Ghanaian, and everyone in that group is now Brazilian.") By approaching rituals at the level of individual decision-making, however, I was suddenly free to examine ritual's utility using behavioral economics' yardstick of "Foolish or wise?" If your goal is to feel differently, is this ritual a foolish or wise use of your time? What if your goal is to feel more connected with your loved ones, or to achieve awe and transcendence? Do rituals make good sense given what you are trying to achieve? Using this straightforward approach—simply asking people about their goals and then measuring rituals' success in helping them to achieve those goals—I started to see a way forward, a trail of bread crumbs leading me toward a different way to measure the effects of rituals.

As I immersed myself in the logic of behavioral economics, I encountered another key influence on my thinking. When I first arrived at MIT, I was given office space in MIT's Media Lab. This lab was, and continues to be, a storied maker space for technologists, artists, dreamers, and inventors. It's a place where making something—whether it is a piece of technology, a human experience, or a system—takes precedence over studying it or writing a paper on it. The spirit of the lab has always been about designing in real space and with real materials: an ethos of "demo or die." For the first time in my academic career, I started thinking about social science not only as an effort to understand humans in their natural environments, but as a process of actively designing and changing those environments. This—I was starting to see—might be an alternative way of thinking about rituals. In the twenty-first century, people are designing ritualized experiences from whatever is on offer—Johnny Mathis and Dr. Seuss, apples and shepherd's pie, for example—within their environments.

However, not until I landed in my current position as a professor at Harvard Business School did I begin to seriously consider investigating the effects of ritual. While I was contemplating possible new conceptions for our experience of rituals, I discovered the work of contemporary University of California–Berkeley sociologist Ann Swidler. In her book *Talk of Love,* comprising eighty-eight interviews with men and women married, single, and divorced in Northern California in the 1980s, Swidler analyzed how people created impromptu rituals to express love and commitment—drawing from sources as varied as organized religion, New Age ideologies, the lyrics of pop songs, and Hollywood movie tropes.

This more informal, improvisational approach to rituals—utilizing ritual's uniquely efficient ability to generate different emotional states—felt of a piece with the tinkerer and maker spirit of the Media Lab. More than anything else, it felt true to my experience of the way rituals can simply emerge, seemingly ex nihilo. My efforts to craft rituals felt like bricolage—I used what was available (stuffed animals and stairs). Swidler's groundbreaking theory of how humans make use of the world around them gave me a framework for better understanding how rituals could somehow include ancient traditions but also brand-new behaviors. She called it "culture in action."

Culture in Action—
Adding to Your Ritual Repertoire

In Swidler's analysis, rituals—even the most timeworn and traditional—are among the array of resources available in a person's "cultural tool kit." People cobble together responses and actions from their cultural repertoire, picking and choosing in any number of ways. Take, for example, the ritual of a formal wedding with a tuxedo, a white dress replete with tulle, and traditional vows. For some of Swidler's respondents, acting out these steps of a formal ritual of marriage felt just right. It inspired the emotions—love, commitment, joy—appropriate for the moment. Yet for others who participated in a formal wedding, that traditional ritual was uncomfortable—fake or pretentious or both. It detracted from their ability to experience the full range of feelings the occasion deserved. Swidler's point was that these varied responses are an accurate reflection of how culture works in action. Instead of forfeiting our individual agency in dutiful obedience to the greater collective of a monolithic "culture," we navigate our cultural tool kits dynamically and tactically from inside, going through the same motions sometimes with heartfelt fervor and at other times with boredom, ambivalence, or even outright irony and rebellion, like the musician Kurt Cobain, who insisted on wearing plaid pajamas to his wedding on a Hawaiian beach.

The culture in action framework revealed a way forward for my investigation of ritual. Unlike ethnographers and anthropologists of the past, I was less interested in cataloging established rituals centered on large, communal, and often religious events. I wanted to know how people use and experience rituals in their day-to-day lives. If so many of our most treasured rituals are personal—individual and idiosyncratic—what then is the hallmark of a ritual? How do we distinguish a ritual from all the other routines and tasks we perform throughout the day? And are rituals foolish or wise? Can they really improve our lives?

I learned that the best way to answer what ritual is is by investigating what ritual is not: a ritual is not a habit.

Habit versus Ritual—
One Automates, the Other Animates

One of my earliest insights into the difference between ritual and habit occurred at the dentist. In a conversation with me about his theory of brushing habits—I did my best to respond by mumbling answers through his fingers—my dentist told me that one quick look inside someone's mouth was enough for him to discern that person's brushing patterns. Many people start with gusto, so those first teeth have less plaque, but then they lose steam—so, more plaque. As I began reconstructing my own brushing—*Am I one of those people who starts strong and then flags? Do I start on the left or the right? On my front teeth or back?*—I also began to consider a host of other everyday practices, from dressing to dishwashing; commuting to computing, including this one, which I have now posed to audiences around the world:

QUESTION: When you get up in the morning (or get ready
for bed), do you:

A: Brush your teeth and then take a shower?
B: Take a shower and then brush your teeth?

I pose this question in all my speaking engagements in front of a large audience. From Germany to Brazil to Norway, Singapore to Spain to Canada, from Cambridge, Massachusetts, to Cambridge, England, and even in a room full of behavioral economists (including two Nobel Prize recipients, Daniel Kahneman and Richard Thaler), I'm always amazed to find that the split is almost always close to fifty-fifty. There seems to be zero consensus on how to sequence these two important activities "right." (Note that a small percentage of people report brushing while in the shower, but it's clear that these minty-footed people are deeply troubled.)

Then I ask my audience to imagine completing those two tasks in reverse order. If you're a shower-then-brush person, imagine starting with brushing. If you're a brush-then-shower person, imagine starting with a shower.

QUESTION: How does that reversal make you feel?

    A: I didn't care.
    B: I felt weird but I have no idea why.

If you answered (a), then completing these tasks is closer to a morning routine. You need to shower and you need to brush but the order in which you complete these two tasks doesn't matter to you. They are things you do regularly for the specific purpose of *getting them done*. But if you answered (b), if you had even the slightest twinge that the reverse order was wrong, even though you can't begin to explain why, then this sequence of actions has become, for you, closer to a ritual. Your morning routine is more than an automated habit that will reward you with cleanliness and good health. It is a ritual that has emotional and psychological resonance in addition to practical rewards. It matters to you not only that you do these tasks (brush your teeth and shower), but how you do them—specifically, in this case, in which order.

So what makes a ritual a ritual and not a habit?

The Essence of Habit Is the "What"

Habit is the *what*. It's something we do: brush our teeth, go to the gym, consume leafy dark green vegetables, face email, pay bills, go to sleep at a sensible hour (or not). When we succeed in replacing a bad habit with a good one, we want that good habit to become automatic. We effortlessly, even mindlessly, perform routines that take us from point A to point B. We avoid filling our workday lulls with double-chocolate-chip cookies, minimize social media use and instead exercise for thirty minutes first thing every morning, and tidy up—and, as a result, we meet important goals (lose weight, focus, fend off domestic chaos).

The Essence of Ritual Is the "How"

A ritual is not just the action but the particular way we enact it—the *how*. It matters to us not simply that we complete the action but the specific way that we complete it. Rituals are also deeply and inherently emotional. Unlike most habits, rituals provoke feelings, both good and bad. For example, when people perform their morning ritual correctly, they report feeling as if they "started the morning off right" and are "ready to tackle the day." When those otherwise inconspicuous morning rituals are disrupted—say, you're out of your favorite toothpaste or cereal and have to use your partner's brand or a guest has claimed the shower first, hogging your hot water, people report feeling "off" all day. Brain-imaging research by my colleagues and me shows that our rituals feel so right to us that observing other people perform rituals differently from the way we do activates regions of the brain associated with punishment.

In teasing out the differences between ritual and habit, there is no distinct set of behaviors that belongs solely to rituals and another distinct set that belongs to habits. Instead, it's the emotion and meaning we bring to the behaviors. Two people could be doing the exact same thing, something as ordinary as making coffee. For one person, it's about the end goal—getting caffeinated by the quickest means available. The what. For the other, it's about the how. Coarse grind, never medium or fine. Or French press, always and only. For one, it's an automated habit. For the other, it's a meaningful ritual.

The science of behavior change can help shed light on the difference between the what of habit and the how of ritual. In the 1930s, the self-styled "radical behaviorist" psychologist B. F. Skinner first identified the three-stage sequence of "stimulus, response, and reward" as crucial in a system of shaping behavior he called *operant conditioning*. We all learn through positive and negative reinforcement from our environment. When we get a reward that satisfies us—we go for a run, say, and we experience a rush of endorphins afterward—our behavior is positively reinforced. We then repeat that behavior in anticipation of receiving the reward again. When we continue to get rewarded yet again in the form of more running highs, we come to crave the experience.

In *The Power of Habit*, Charles Duhigg identified this craving as the driving force behind the habit loop. Good habits are frustratingly hard to maintain until we get in the habit loop, at which point they become automated—meaning, effortless and mindless. Think of habits as well-worn solutions to the challenges and temptations we encounter every day: our friends' texts are interfering with our ability to focus on work, the smell of a fresh croissant is tempting us to consider a second breakfast, or a hard day is making the siren song of binge-watching TV at night irresistible. If our habits are aligned with the rewards of fitness, productivity, and wellness, we no longer need to pay attention to any of these environmental cues. Like a trusty algorithm—*if this, then that*—our brain reroutes us into familiar action. If the phone pings during work hours, then we put it on silent. If the smell of fresh bread wafting from the local bakery is making us hungry, then we hurry over to the other side of the street, away from that mouthwatering scent. Habits such as these are immensely helpful. In the field of behavioral economics, the interventions now famously known as *nudges* shape our behavior through a similar feat of engineering. Nudges scaffold good habits by designing "choice environments" to ensure our behavior aligns with our long-term goals—automatic withdrawals into your 401(k) plan, for example, or designing smaller plates and bowls to reduce how much we eat.

Much is gained by this hard-won automation. We don't have the time to agonize over every decision that confronts us in an average day. But I've increasingly found myself thinking about what might be lost as well. Is an algorithmic response of "if this, then that" the best way of finding happiness or meaning or love? Is it always a mistake to fail to execute on your good habits, or is the experience of savoring a decadent dessert simply a different kind of success? As useful as habits may be for optimizing certain aspects of our lives, they have inherent limitations that position us firmly in the mechanistic realm of cues, routines, and rewards. The title of Tom Ellison's satirical take on wellness in *McSweeney's* says it all: "I've Optimized My Health to Make My Life as Long and Unpleasant as Possible." Our fixation on optimal efficiency keeps us from seeing how the idiosyncratic behaviors that make up so many rituals can be an important part of what makes life worth living. It's akin to switching from black and white to Technicolor. Good habits automate us, helping us get things done. Rituals animate us, enhancing and enchanting our lives with something more.

Rituals as Emotion Generators

The intrinsically emotional nature of rituals gives them their animating power. Psychologists Ethan Kross and Aaron Weidman suggest that emotions are tools we use for specific needs and tasks: feeling sad might lead us to put on a favorite sitcom rerun to summon up happiness. Feeling lonely might make us seek out a hug to summon connection. But there are limits to our ability to use emotions as tools: we can't always just summon them at will. When we're sad or depressed, we can't just command ourselves to be happy. When we're stressed, it rarely works to admonish ourselves to calm down. We often need to act, to do something (to go see a movie or step outside for a walk or put on our favorite music) to change or amplify how we're feeling. Which is where rituals come in. Think of them as *emotion generators*. Once a particular set of movements becomes linked to a particular emotion, that set of actions, that ritual, is then available to summon the relevant emotion—not unlike a catalyst in the kitchen such as a sourdough bread starter.

A day filled with good habits can make us feel productive and proud. But habit is limited in its ability to deliver on life's most expansive range of emotional experiences. That range matters—more than I would ever have imagined. In research led by my colleague Jordi Quoidbach, we showed that the diversity of our emotional experiences—what we termed *emodiversity*—is associated with measurable benefits in our well-being. Emodiversity is akin to *biodiversity*, the term used to describe how the health of a physical ecosystem depends on the relative abundance and variety of species it features; an ecosystem that has too many hunters and not enough prey, for example, is not sustainable because it cannot dynamically manage its equilibrium.

Imagine that I asked you to list all the emotions you experienced in a day, both positive (such as joy or pride) and negative (such as anger or disgust), and that I also asked you to tell me how happy you were overall on that day. Our results show that the diversity of our different shades of emotions—contentment, amusement, elation, awe, and gratitude, but also sadness, fear, and anxiety—adds up to richer emotional lives and links to our overall well-being. It seems obvious that it is better to have three moments of joy in a day versus two moments of joy and one moment of anxiety. And it's true that positive emotions such as joy and contentment are indicators of the good life. But a set of studies of more than thirty-seven thousand people led us to a different and less intuitive insight. Drawing from the same research methods used to quantify the biodiversity of ecosystems, we showed that the variety and relative abundance of emotions we experience—not just the predominance of positive emotions—predicts our well-being.

Our findings on the benefits of emodiversity stand in stark contrast to many of contemporary culture's assumptions about the role of habit in organizing our lives. Yes, habits can be leveraged to bring us closer to our stated goals—more muscle, no more late-night binge-watching, less plaque—but they may be less helpful when it comes to channeling a range of feelings. What our emodiversity research reveals is that we may not be giving nearly enough focus to all the different aspects—the range—of our emotional repertoire. A painting analogy illustrates the point. Using only primary colors (red, blue, yellow) can produce brilliant artwork—Picasso famously did a lot with blue. But humans can also perceive countless different, subtle shades, using the full spectrum of color. Habits are the reds, yellows, and blues; rituals bring us the vibrant red-orange of coquelicot, or the deep darkness of Vantablack, which absorbs close to 100 percent of visible light.

Researchers who study emotion have increasingly accepted that our emotional range extends beyond the seven basic emotions—anger, surprise, disgust, enjoyment, fear, sadness, and, most recently, contempt—that Paul Ekman, a leading expert in the field, identified in the 1960s. But there is no consensus about the total number. Today some emotion researchers believe there are twenty-seven or twenty-eight emotions. Others identify as many as one hundred fifty.

Whether they are an invitation to have a good cry, a chance to channel anger, or a connection to awe and wonder, I see rituals as one of humanity's most efficient tools for summoning the widest possible range of our emotional repertoire. Ritual offers the possibility of transforming activities as ordinary as morning hygiene, household chores, or daily exercise from automated to animated experiences—conjuring up delight or wonder or peace.

But could the tools of behavioral science be used to test how rituals function in our everyday lives? Operating within the frame of behavioral economics, and imbued with the maker spirit of the Media Lab, I decided it was time to dive in. I began to design ways to measure the role of ritual in the world and to document its effects—both in the lab and outside it.

The first step was to determine how to assess the effects of ritual, to measure ritual's influence on the subjective experience of our lives. In my academic career, I have utilized a number of different methods, but I've found that one of the best ways to study subjective experiences is the simplest: just ask people. I first started to do this when I was conducting my earlier research on happiness. I asked people, "How happy are you . . . ?"—with the money they spent, with the origami frog they folded, and even with their lives overall.

Rituals and DIY Rituals

Following the same logic as above, my scientific investigations of different rituals often start by simply asking people whether they have any, and, if so, how they feel about them. Over the years, my research team and I have surveyed thousands of Americans across the country, young and old, religious and not. We've asked people if they rely on rituals in particular domains or times of life, from spending time with romantic partners to celebrating holidays with their families, from dealing with coworkers to trying to leave work stress behind at the end of the day.

Many of the rituals that people report are legacy rituals from cultural, familial, or religious traditions. These inherited rituals have the weight of ancestry or religion behind them. These practices reach through time and space to connect the individual with the collective: by performing these acts, "one" can be fused with "all," all who sang these same songs, held hands in these same ways, lit these same candles, and walked in this exact same pattern of steps. Legacy rituals have a powerful hold on our imagination because so many of them—whether it's dancing in the streets of Delhi on Diwali, celebrating the Day of the Dead with an offering of incense and sweet cakes and cookies, or eating matzo in the ceremonial Passover seder—create social cohesion through a dense layering of sensory experiences scaffolded by special clothes, lights, music, dance, and food.

But what we see time and time again is that people weren't always practicing inviolable, timeworn legacy rituals—they were crafting their own, in full or at least in part. The same way my wife and I had simply improvised my daughter's rigorous bedtime ritual as we went along. I refer to these idiosyncratic and novel practices as DIY rituals.

There were intimate-relationship rituals that bound couples together: *When we kiss, we do it in 3s. Not sure why this started, but after 22 years, it feels really weird if it is not in 3s.* Mourning rituals that were as unique as they were poignant: *I washed a loved one's car once a week, just as they had done while alive.* Rituals to prepare for performance: *I take several deep breaths, and I "shake" my body to remove any negative energy.* Rituals to close out the day: *When showering after work, I must imagine the entire hospital turning into liquid and circling down the drain.*

Our surveys on the ritual lives of everyday Americans confirmed just how pervasive rituals are, and also how idiosyncratic and emotionally rich they can be. Contrary to prevailing assumptions, my own included, rituals aren't just or even primarily sets of instructions or scripts we passively receive. They are practices that we adapt and create, picking and choosing from the vast repertoire of resources that make up our cultural tool kits.

Deciding Who You Are— Establishing Your Ritual Signature

In addition to their role as emotion generators, many of these DIY rituals accrue meaning by connecting us with the active process social scientists call *identity work*. These rituals are personal; creating them inspires a sense of ownership, of having imbued them with and used them to express a sense of self that is unique. Our specific ways of doing things, even the smallest, most mundane things—our *how*—is what I've termed our *ritual signature*. I might have a habit of going for a run every day, but my shoe-tying rituals make me embrace my identity as a runner. My partner and I might have a habit of eating dinner at the same time, but using a set of plates we made together in a pottery class makes us a couple. My parents and siblings might have a habit of celebrating every Christmas together, but that ritual of Johnny

Mathis on the record player is what makes us a family. In short, the how of ritual—our unique ritual signature—is part of the why of life.

As my research developed, I discovered just how important these links to our identities and our sense of ownership over our rituals really are.

Chapter 2

You Get Out of It
What You Put into It

Nothing will work unless you do.

—Maya Angelou

On a shelf in my office sits a small stone sculpture I made during a studio art class. I enrolled in the course fueled with a hum of determination. After my first night in the studio, however, and in every class that followed, I realized with alarm that, unlike me, many of the other students had talent. Every night we were in class, I would look around the room in envy as gifted sculptors from all walks of university life settled in their chairs and, with a seemingly breezy confidence, created elegant and recognizable renderings of the human form from their slabs of stone. My small stone sculpture, on the other hand, did not resemble anything from the human body or, really, anything at all.

Yet in the many times I have moved since graduate school, I always make a point to carefully wrap my stone sculpture with bubble wrap and pack it in a box to join me in my next life. I understand that it doesn't belong in a museum. If I saw the same sculpture on someone else's desk, I would ask if the person's child made it. Which is to say, it's not great art. Most people would never think to dignify it with the word *art*. But still, that stone creation is mine.

The value I place on this piece of personal handicraft can be accounted for in part by a phenomenon Nobel Prize–winning behavioral scientists Daniel Kahneman and Richard Thaler identified as the *endowment effect*. In a series of experiments in which they randomly gave people such items as mugs, chocolate, and baseball tickets, the scientists proved that merely owning something causes us to value that item more than we would if it weren't already ours. People are willing to pay more to keep the mug they already own than to buy an identical one they don't. No one needs an extra mug, but once we are endowed with it—once we own it—we are loath to part with it, much the same way I can't quite bring myself to part with my unprepossessing artwork.

But my attachment to my sculpture reflects another psychological phenomenon that the endowment effect doesn't fully capture. I invested effort in making it. Even though the result was undeniably not stellar, I worked hard for weeks in that studio sculpture class. Once I began turning a cool analytical eye on this labor of love, I found myself wondering whether my investment of effort was responsible for my emotional investment. This question lurked vaguely in the back of my mind but didn't come fully into focus until I read about the mid-twentieth-century world of industrial food and high-speed cookery—and, more specifically, about eggs and a freshly baked cake.

Becoming Invested in the Cake You Bake

In 1956, Street & Smith, the publisher of the cooking and lifestyle magazine *Living*, showcased the new era of modern convenience by taking readers back in time and reminding them how a cake was baked in the nineteenth century. The magazine detailed an exhausting process that required help from all the people on hand as well as two days of labor—pounding sugar, stoning raisins, and boiling milk were only a few of the dozens of tasks to complete before the baking ingredients could even be brought together in the bowl. In the article's concluding remarks, *Living*'s editors reminded readers how much they had to be grateful for in the cutting-edge kitchens of 1956: "One opens a box of cake mix, adds the liquid, plugs in the mixer, adjusts the oven to the proper temperature and then reads a book."

But by the time this reassuring promise of increased leisure was published, sales of cake mixes were stagnating. When the mixes were first introduced after World War II, women couldn't snap them up fast enough. In 1947, around $79 million of cake mixes were sold in supermarkets around the country. By 1953, that number had almost doubled, to more than $150 million. Cake mixes, it seemed, were poised to be a household staple, well stocked in every kitchen cupboard in America.

Until suddenly, only a few years later in the mid-1950s, sales stalled for no apparent reason. The young housewives who were now home with children to raise and a working husband to feed seemed to be the perfect market for easy-mix products. But these novice home cooks showed little interest.

Betty Crocker, a subsidiary of General Mills, and one of the largest companies in the cake mix market, was concerned about the drop in sales. The company hired a Viennese psychologist, Ernest Dichter, in the hope that he could provide insight into why convenient shortcuts to baking perfection were falling flat with younger women. Dichter, once an acolyte of Sigmund Freud, arrived from the helm of his own consumer research organization, the Institute for Motivational Research. Using psychoanalytic techniques he learned under Freud, Dichter touted his way of studying the subconscious thoughts and subliminal desires of consumers. This new approach to market research used what he called "focus groups."

Dichter discovered in his focus groups with young women for Betty Crocker that cake mixes were too easy. Because they involved so little effort, the women didn't feel as invested in their baking. "Yes, I'm using a cake mix," one woman somewhat sheepishly told Dichter. "It saves me a lot of trouble, but I really shouldn't." In another focus group, Dichter's colleague noted that one of the women made a Freudian slip when describing her cooking habits: "Especially when I'm in a hurry, I like foods that are time-consuming." Her slip of the tongue was highly revealing. On hearing the word *time-consuming* more and more women in the focus group confessed that they felt guilty trying to save time by using the mixes. Time in the kitchen— and more specifically, time spent baking a homemade cake—was a love language for young women in mid-twentieth-century America. One 1953 Gallup poll ranked cake the second "real test of a woman's ability to cook," behind apple pie.

After weeks spent analyzing the dreams and desires of these mid-century women, Dichter delivered his recommendations to the executive team at Betty Crocker: give the homemaker more work to do. Without more effort, he told them, she will never feel sufficiently invested in the product that comes out of the oven. Based on Dichter's advice, the Betty Crocker team reformulated their complete mixes by leaving out the dried eggs. Now bakers would be required to not only add liquid but to crack an egg into the bowl before getting out the electric mixer. Consumer experts cite this as the moment Betty Crocker cake mixes took off—a turning point in the history of packaged food. This small bit of extra effort, just one more step, allowed women to feel more invested in making a cake.

The reality is not quite as simple: Betty Crocker with its just-crack-one-egg mix and Pillsbury, with its complete mix, shared the bulk of the cake mix market between them throughout the rest of the 1950s and 1960s. But even if the just-crack-one-egg innovation was not the sole saving grace or was not appreciated by all consumers, Dichter's research captured an enduring truth about homemakers' experience in the kitchen. He understood that they wanted to invest something of themselves in their work. That added effort—of even cracking a single egg—transformed preparing a convenience food into a labor of love.

This idea was so compelling that we conducted research to prove it. My colleague Ximena Garcia-Rada noticed extreme online rancor directed at parents of new babies who were using the SNOO—a contraption that rocks your baby to sleep so you don't have to. One person wrote, "If you need that device, you shouldn't have kids," and another, "You can stop being a shitty parent and take care of your kids." In a series of studies, we showed that it's not just angry commenters who have negative feelings about products designed to make caregiving easier. Caregivers themselves feel that they are failing to show their love when they choose ease over effort. The only way we found to increase parents' willingness to get some help was to change the slogan from "With SNOO, get ZZZs with ease" to one that acknowledged parental investment: "You give the XOXOs, SNOO gives the ZZZs."

The IKEA Effect—Produce Something Yourself and You'll Value It More

The Betty Crocker and SNOO stories show people's preference for effort over ease. I wanted to see if this desire to take on effort was foolish, or sometimes wise. Even if we save some time, are we sacrificing something else important when we do? My colleagues and I started by experimenting with the most mundane, standardized, impersonal, least lovable product imaginable: a plain black IKEA storage box that had originally been designed to hold compact discs (which were already obsolete at the time of the study).

We enlisted two groups—fifty-two participants—for our experiment at a Southeastern university in the United States. Each participant, compensated $5, was assigned to one of two groups. The first group—the nonbuilders—were given a fully assembled plain black box to inspect. The second group—the builders—were given an unassembled box along with the assembly instructions and were told to assemble it.

Once the boxes had been inspected and assembled, we asked both groups how much they would pay for their identical containers. Those who had merely inspected the completed box were willing to pay just $0.48 for it. But those who had assembled the exact same box were willing to pay $0.78—a 63 percent increase. In several more studies, involving not just the IKEA box but also DIY origami frogs and cranes and LEGO sets, we found that participants consistently placed more value on objects that they had a hand in making.

The IKEA effect explains why I still treasure my homemade sculpture and why so many of us still can't part with that chipped mug we made in a pottery class way back when. We own these objects not only in the sense that they belong to us—they are our possessions. We own them also in the sense that we have invested something of ourselves in making them—and we identify with and value them more as a result.

More than a decade after the studies that identified the IKEA effect were published, it is a well-established psychological phenomenon. It has even found its way into pop culture. I was astonished to hear that the IKEA effect was featured on the television game show *Jeopardy!* as an answer to Final Jeopardy clue number 205641: "The 'effect' named for this company founded in 1943 refers to increased value of a product to a consumer whose own labor is needed."

A team of developmental psychologists have even conducted a follow-up study to see if children begin to show an IKEA effect at any particular age. Sixty-four children between the ages of three and six were given two different toy monsters, both made out of foam, to play with. The children helped to make the first toy monster from a set of instructions but had only briefly held the second toy monster. Would the children demonstrate the IKEA effect? The researchers found that five- and six-year-old children did rate their homemade toy monsters more highly, but three- and four-year-old children did not. What these results suggest is that slightly older children exhibit the IKEA effect because they have matured into a more cohesive sense of identity, increasing the value of their own little foam monsters by linking them to that sense of identity.

The Power of DIY

When we began asking people about the rituals in their lives, we found that DIY rituals were often especially important to them. They were displaying the same psychological phenomenon we had identified as the IKEA effect. Legacy rituals are ready-made—much like those pre-assembled IKEA boxes, we had no hand in their making. They were also, in a sense, preassembled. But our idiosyncratic, personal rituals? They are bespoke. We make them ourselves, not always fully from scratch but from whatever materials are ready to hand. Such as this couple, who crafted a personalized and meaningful ritual out of a series of seasonal home-brewing kits:

Every time the season changes, my husband and I brew our own beer. We pick out the beer in a kit and choose the beer selection by going on what sounds best for the time of year (light beers for summer, maybe a dark-flavored beer around Christmastime). This gets us excited to bring in the new season or holiday and gives us something to drink while we enjoy it as well. We also have different tasks for actually brewing where each of us does something specific in the process each time.

Whether it is a cake, an utterly forgettable CD storage box, or home-brewed beer, labor leads to more love. Over time, all of us have developed our own ways of performing life's most ordinary moments— and those acts of ownership are what define our ritual signature. They are one of the important ways we invest something of ourselves in the world around us and, in so doing, enrich and deepen our experience.

Consider just a few of the examples that people have shared with me over the years:

It started back when we were first married and we ended a winter meal by sharing one of the last Fuji apples left in the bowl. We decided to add a square of dark chocolate to our impromptu dessert because the package was left over in the refrigerator. The sweet and the bitter, the dark and the light. She said it felt poetic and that made us laugh. We did it again the next night because—why not? And then we started to plan for it: we made sure to buy the apples—only Fuji—and the same square of chocolate always wrapped in that same gold foil. Over time—many nights, then seasons, and eventually years—this one little act of eating apples and dark chocolate after dinner is just "us." It's just what we do.

When New York City shut down in March 2020, all of us volunteers got together and agreed to stay open and serve at the food pantry throughout the entire COVID-19 pandemic. We were scared—so little was known about the virus in those early months in the spring of 2020—but the alternative was worse. What would happen to all of the guests depending on us for food? When we all gathered together over the third week of March and prepared to open the doors to the hungry people lined up outside, most of us started to cry. That's when it started: we stood in that circle together and just started hugging. Then, without ever discussing it, we did this same communal hug every time we got together to serve. Today, three years later, we still stand in that circle and give each other a big communal hug every time we're about to open our doors to serve our guests. Now it feels like a promise of a new beginning, but it's also about the heaviness, the loss. Because it's a hug, it's about how vulnerable we all were in our bodies—still are. Every Tuesday at 1:55 p.m., that's where you'll find us. It's one hug just to feel all of it: everything that all of us have gone through—not just here but all over the world.

People's reports that their newer, homemade rituals can hold as much meaning—and sometimes more—as the legacy rituals that come with chanting, candles, music, awe-inspiring architecture, stained-glass windows, and ancient texts was a revelation that opened up entirely new questions and new ways of investigating the role of rituals in our lives. Why seasonal home-brew kits? Apples and dark chocolate? Every Tuesday at 1:55 p.m. a communal hug? Knowing that even made-up rituals could have an emotional impact, we began to design controlled experiments using completely novel rituals that did not have any cultural or religious significance. This methodology allowed us to bring people into our laboratory, ask them to enact one of our rituals (or not), and start to assess whether our rituals actually shape our experiences and, in turn, our lives.

Chapter 3

The Ritual Effect

And those who were seen dancing were thought to be insane by those who could not hear the music.

—Friedrich Nietzsche

Rafael Nadal is widely considered to be one of the world's most skilled tennis players. The thirty-seven-year-old Spaniard has dominated on clay courts for so long—as of this writing he holds the longest single-surface win streak in the Open Era—many fans argue he is the greatest of all time.

Nadal is also known for something else: his eye-catching, unique ritual signature. The signature's most notorious element is his wedgie pick—*GQ* magazine anointed him "the most famous underwear adjuster in history." But that is only one part of a much-longer sequence of actions including a shirt tug, hair tuck, and face wipe. In one particularly grueling match, he completed this pattern of behaviors 146 times. Before his matches even begin, however, Nadal needs to eat his energy gel. First, he rips off the top, folds the side over, and finally gives it four distinct squeezes. Instead of his pursuing a goal—"I need to eat this gel for my match"—his actions seem random. Why four squeezes? Why not three or five? Why not a hair tuck, then a shirt tug and not vice versa? Why pick the wedgie every single time?

Nadal explains that these actions have psychological benefits: "It's something I don't need to do, but when I do it, it means I'm focused." Some debate whether Nadal's eccentric behaviors are superstitions or compulsions—or both. But to begin to explain how and why Nadal might have arrived at such specific behaviors, it's worth looking back seventy-five years to a discovery American psychologist B. F. Skinner—the theorist behind habit formation's "stimulus, response, and reward"—made in one of his lesser-known experiments. In that research, Skinner designed and built boxes outfitted with levers and switches that when pecked or pulled (by pigeons or rats) would release food.

In what eventually came to be known as Skinner boxes, Skinner created environments that conditioned the behavior of his lab animals by rewarding them for each step toward a desired goal. He taught his pigeons to press levers and pull cords, each time reinforcing their behavior with treats. Turn by turn, he also rewarded his pigeons for moving in a circle and even, eventually, for accomplishing astonishing feats such as playing games including table tennis. Skinner became the father of an approach to learning that emphasized the role of reinforcement; he called it *operant conditioning*. If an action leads to a bad outcome, we do it less. If it leads to a good outcome, it's reinforced and we do it more. When a pigeon pecks on a lever and a bounty of food pellets arrives, the pigeon's behavior is reinforced and it continues pecking on the lever.

In the year 1948, however, Skinner flipped the script. He took a group of pigeons that had been well-fed and brought them to a stable state of hunger—which meant reducing their mass to 75 percent of their normal weight. For a few minutes every day, each pigeon was placed in a Skinner box containing a food hopper that would feed the pigeon at random intervals no matter what the pigeon did. Actions such as pecking down on levers that used to result in a food reward no longer had any effect on the outcomes. You might think that, given this total lack of control, the pigeons would give up and sit back and enjoy the free lunch when it arrived. But that's not what happened. Skinner shared some of the idiosyncratic techniques the pigeons developed to summon their meals:

One bird was conditioned to turn counter-clockwise about the cage, making two or three turns between reinforcements. Another repeatedly thrust its head into one of the upper corners of the cage. A third developed a "tossing" response, as if placing its head beneath an invisible bar and lifting it repeatedly. Two birds developed a pendulum motion of the head and body, in which the head was extended forward and swung from right to left with a sharp movement followed by a somewhat slower return.

Most of the time, the pigeons' movements did not correspond with a timely portion of food. The hopper delivered when it delivered. Occasionally, and randomly, however, these movements coincided with a food reward. That yield might coincide with a pigeon's third counter-clockwise turn, for example. If so, that pigeon—positively reinforced— would repeat that action, assuming that doing so would conjure up more meals. "The experiment might be said to demonstrate a sort of superstition," Skinner observed. "The bird behaves as if there were a causal relation between its behavior and the presentation of food, although such a relation is lacking." (There is a sense here of the pot calling the kettle black: Skinner, on the lookout for ways to increase his productivity, slept in his office in a bright yellow plastic tank, going to bed from 10:00 p.m. to 1:00 a.m., rising and working for one hour, then returning to bed from 2:00 a.m. to 5:00 a.m.)

What did Skinner's lesser-known pigeon study reveal? In my view, Skinner had stumbled upon the foundations of rituals and how they emerge in real time. Stuck in a confusing and uncertain environment they couldn't control, Skinner's pigeons improvised, enacting random behaviors, repeating them, and relying on them as if they could cause their meals to appear. They had developed their own ritual signatures.

Ritual as a Response to Uncertainty and Stress

Pigeons are far from alone in relying on ritualistic behavior to manage anxiety, stress, and lack of control. For many decades now, researchers across the social sciences have emphasized the link between uncertainty and forms of magical thinking such as ritual. In his mid-century classic, *Magic, Science and Religion and Other Essays*, one of the twentieth century's most famous chroniclers of ritual, the anthropologist Bronislaw Malinowski, noted that those who fish in choppy waters have more rituals than those who fish in calm lagoons. Before venturing on a fraught journey across the dangerous open waters of Milne Bay Province by homemade canoe, the Trobriander fishermen in Papua New Guinea engaged in Kula—elaborate ceremonial exchanges of shells and beads. Given the uncertainty of the journeys from island to island, Kula was one of the many rituals that emerged to manage it.

The relationship between uncertainty and risk, and ritual, has been extensively documented. For example, communities in regions with unpredictable droughts develop rituals for summoning rain: some Southwestern Native Americans wore symbolic materials such as goat hair and turquoise to perform their rain dances. In Thailand, people turned to the Cat Parade, a long-standing tradition of placing a single gray or black female cat in a basket and parading it through a village so that people in each home could splash water on it.

In baseball, the vast majority of rituals are tied to batting, where the success rate is a low 30 percent even if you're world-class. In the case of fielding, however, where the success rate is about 98 percent, rituals are much rarer. Sports fans, too, are more likely to make sure to have their "lucky products"—their favorite hats, special socks, or the famed rally monkey—on hand when they're the least certain of a win. If you feel confident that you or your people will hit a home run or catch a fish or that rain is imminent, you are less likely to look to ritual to help make it happen.

For the hungry pigeons, the ritual signature emerged because, in the face of uncertainty, they were trying to figure out how to summon more food. Consider again some of the random repetitive behaviors of the pigeons: turning counterclockwise in the cage, thrusting a head into one of its upper corners, pendulum motions of the body. At first glance, it might seem hard to imagine humans (other than Nadal) engaging in such wildly random behaviors. Yet, many of our most time-tested legacy rituals comprise similar behaviors. Imagine humans tapping their forehead with their fingers, then moving those same fingers to the center of their chest, then moving them again to the left, then to the right. Why are they doing that? What does it mean? For many people, those taps seem just as randomly sequenced as the movements of Skinner's pigeons. But for members of certain faiths, these mechanical motions are sacred—they signify the sign of the cross.

The Ritual Stance

Harvard psychologist Dan Wegner—widely regarded as one of the most original minds in late twentieth-century psychological research—was fascinated by what he described as "the relationship between what people are doing and what people *think* they're doing." Wegner's key insight was that any action can be identified by its mechanical parts, the literal movements, or by the higher-level aspirations that inform it. If you belong to certain Christian religions, you see the sign of the cross as a way of honoring your faith. You make that sign—the demonstration of faith—by tapping four spots on your body. Wegner's research shows that, when possible, we prefer the higher-level identification. If you ask someone what they're doing, they're more likely to say "Making the sign of the cross" than "Tapping myself four times," even if the latter is technically just as true.

This quirk of human psychology begins to explain why so many rituals involve such seemingly random actions. Why did Agatha Christie eat an apple in the bath, for example, and what made the Thai villagers put a gray or black female cat in a basket? It's no accident that the mechanical actions underlying so many rituals are strange.

For the most part, we don't engage in actions that are purposeless—we move our legs to walk somewhere or we wave our hands to greet hello. We close the window because of a cold draft, and we turn out the lights because we're going to sleep. This means that when we see someone engage in actions without any apparent purpose, we search for a reason. If strangers are walking around in circles on the sidewalk, head down, we infer that they must be searching for something they dropped—such as keys or money. If people gesture expansively and converse with the air, we conclude that they must be on a call with their earbuds in. One study showed that when children watch an adult remove a toy from a jar by (uselessly) tapping it with a feather before unscrewing the lid, they infer that the feather tap must be important. When it's their turn to retrieve the toy, the children repeat this feather tap.

Social scientists Rohan Kapitány and Mark Nielsen dubbed this tendency the *ritual stance*: the more pointless and unnecessary a behavior seems, the more likely we are to search for an explanation. When that search fails to provide a simple explanation, we are prone to infer a more complex one—that those random actions must have some deeper meaning. The actions have what researchers call *causal opacity*, and precisely because we are unable to glean their purpose or predict their outcome, we encode them as special.

To see what I mean, imagine that your friend Anna has lost power and is rummaging around in her pitch-black kitchen to light candles. Given the circumstances, Anna's behavior makes perfect sense: she has to find a source of light because none of the lamps is working. But what if Anna is rummaging around in the kitchen again, looking for candles and matches, when the kitchen is already fully lit? In that case, because Anna's candles aren't necessary to provide light, we intuitively conclude that they must be serving some other, ritualistic purpose—such as for topping a birthday cake or preparing for a seder or honoring a loved one's memory.

Even our most functional activities—stretching before a competitive race, say—can become ritualized. Routine actions become ritualized when we need to do them in specific ways. *How* we complete these actions matters to us over and above our doing so. This might mean that you need to perform them at a precise time or in a precise sequence. It could also mean that you need to wear a specific piece of clothing while you do them, such as Justice Ruth Bader Ginsburg with her lace bib collars; or to sit in a certain spot, such as my family at dinnertime when I was growing up; or to face a precisely predetermined direction, such as Charles Dickens at bedtime. In all of these examples, the particulars that go above and beyond what is needed—actions that have no relationship to direct cause and effect in the outside world—

transform ordinary activities that might have started as merely functional into something that matters to us deeply, something that may even make the ordinary feel extraordinary.

The ritual stance also helps to explain why once practical choices can linger on as ritual even when they've lost their original purpose. In some cultures, for example, the groom is not permitted to see the bride's face before the wedding; the bride wears a veil to ensure that no peeking is possible. But in many cultures in which brides and grooms have not only seen each other but in some cases lived together, the veil still makes an appearance at the wedding. Although the original logic for the veil does not apply, we carry on nonetheless, coming to imbue that practice with meaning—the veil offers a sense of mystery, and the reveal a sense of emerging into a new, coupled self. The less explicable the action is, the riper it is for a ritual interpretation.

Rituals depend on our ability—and our willingness—to make the leap from the merely mechanical to the deeply meaningful. When we invest the mundane with deeper meaning, we give ourselves a way of using what we have at our disposal—hands, candles, veils, apples, cats, baskets—to channel emotions.

Of course, batting rituals and rain dances don't guarantee success, no matter how much effort and expectation we invest in them. Skinner noticed in his famous pigeons this tendency to indulge in magical thinking by pinning our hopes on our rituals:

A few accidental connections between a ritual and favorable consequences suffice to set up and maintain the behavior in spite of many unreinforced instances. The bowler who has released a ball down the alley but continues to behave as if she were controlling it by twisting and turning her arm and shoulder is another case in point. These behaviors have, of course, no real effect upon one's luck or upon a ball halfway down an alley, just as in the present case the food would appear as often if the pigeon did nothing—or, more strictly speaking, did something else.

Like pigeons, people can engage in any kind of ritual they want, but turning counterclockwise or choosing the right color cat is not going to cause the food to arrive or the rain to fall. So why do we—all of us, in our distinctive ways—persist? If we can't magically summon a killer home run when up at bat, or a strike when bowling, why do we so consistently often go to such elaborate and effortful lengths to do so?

Skinner provides us with part of the answer: at least some of the time, the ritual is followed by the outcome we want, so our behavior is reinforced—sometimes the food shoots into the hopper, sometimes the canoes arrive safely back onshore after a storm, and sometimes the most devoted fans experience a big win when they wear their lucky jersey to the stadium. But that only happens some of the time. Why is it that rituals are constantly emerging and then being repeated in our lives, even though they frequently fail to produce the desired result?

Can Performing a Ritual Actually Change Us?

It's absurd to think that the right ritual could prepare me to walk onstage with Keith Richards or that a well-performed rain dance will somehow summon clouds, isn't it? Skinner certainly thought so when summarizing his pigeons' efforts: "These behaviors, of course, have no real effect."

We can all agree that rain rituals don't actually bring rain. But drought, like many other forms of scarcity (of food, money, housing, respect), also provokes social tensions—fear, anger, frustration, greed (with so little water left, I can't afford to share). Rain rituals might not bring rain, but they do bring the larger group together and serve as an affirmation—reminding us that together we have gotten through this experience before. The work of rain rituals is psychological and social. By our enacting synchronized, structured, patterned behaviors, rituals connect the people who practice them with one another by invoking both a shared past and shared hopes for the future.

Even if rituals don't always affect our outer world, they do affect our inner worlds. And it is to this aspect of the ritual effect we will turn to next.

Part 2

Rituals for Ourselves

Chapter 4

How to Perform

Why You Should Never Say "Calm Down"
Before Going Onstage

See the man with the stage fright
Just standin' up there to give it all his might.

—The Band

Five minutes to showtime. You're backstage, the lights are low. Soon the curtains will part and the spotlight will shine. You can hear the hum of the crowd, rising and falling like the swell of the ocean. The theater is filled to capacity, ready to sweep you up—or crash down against you. They've come this evening to see you, and only you. At center stage stands a solitary grand piano, polished to a perfect shine. In four minutes, you will walk out, and the crowd will erupt, only to recede again to a pin-drop silence. You will sit at the bench, put your hands on the keys. The audience has come to hear you perform three sonatas at the upper limit of human ability. They want to hear you at your very best, because that's what it will take. Three minutes now, and a cold sweat covers your back. You have practiced for this, but usually alone, in your own space, at your own speed. Now you wonder, "Did I practice enough?" Two minutes left. The house lights go out. You're sure you can hear the audience shifting to the edge of their seats. One minute before the curtain opens and you're left to face the endless sea of faces. Sixty seconds to quell the pounding in your chest and swallow the surge of panic rising in your throat.

How the hell are you supposed to stay calm?

For Sviatoslav Richter, widely regarded as one of the greatest pianists in the world, the answer was simple: remember your lobster. Before every concert, the virtuoso placed a pink plastic lobster in a satin-lined box and carried it with him until the very moment he stepped onstage, ensuring that the lobster was close enough to affect his performance. "Should he take the lobster onstage?" Errol Morris wrote in his profile of Richter. "Perhaps not. People might ask questions. But there is one thing he knows with certainty. He can't play without it." Despite Richter's immense talent, he felt that he was nothing without his pink plastic lobster. Whenever it came time to perform, he didn't dare stray from his ritual. His charmed crustacean was as important as his finely tuned piano.

What We Can Learn from the Rituals of High Performers

Performance rituals are among the most high-profile and colorful examples of ritualistic behavior, and many stars at the peak of their abilities are known to rely on them. Tennis champion Serena Williams bounces the ball five times before her first serve and two times before her second. Portuguese soccer player Cristiano Ronaldo will only take his first step out on the field with his right foot. And do you remember the baseball player Nomar Garciaparra? First, he steps into the box, then out of the box. Then he tightens his batting gloves, adjusts the wristband on his left forearm, and tightens the batting gloves some more. Now it's time to touch both batting gloves, then the wristband, right thigh, back, left shoulder, helmet, belt, helmet again. Step back into the box, tap toes against the ground.

Amazingly, Nomah (as he was known to the locals) isn't an outlier. In one study of baseball players, researchers classified and counted the number of movements per at bat for each player in thirty-three categories, such as touching the body or clothing, refastening batting gloves, and tapping the plate with the bat. The average number of movements was an astonishing 83, ranging from 51 to 109. Players knew they moved around, but they underestimated their number of movements by a factor of four—and were surprised when watching videos of themselves to see many behaviors that they had never noticed themselves doing. But they didn't stop doing them. Watching them just made them more aware of how they count on these behaviors to "get them in the groove."

The range of odd performance rituals is no less rich or colorful or creative in other fields. Ballerina Suzanne Farrell pinned a small toy mouse inside her leotard, then crossed herself and pinched herself twice before going onstage—her performances postritual were so impressive, she was later awarded the Presidential Medal of Freedom for her contributions to the arts. The writer Joan Didion, finalist for the Pulitzer Prize for *The Year of Magical Thinking*, put her working drafts in a bag in the freezer when she was feeling stuck. Computing pioneer (and U.S. Navy rear admiral) Grace Hopper approached her creation of an innovative programming language (later named COBOL) with precision logic. But when it finally came time to test her code, she and her team would pull out a prayer rug, face east, and pray that the code would actually work. What started out as a tongue-in-cheek exercise in superstition had evolved into an indispensable work ritual—a magical moment in striking juxtaposition to the rigors of pure math.

But why all the fuss, especially from those who seem to be already at the top of their game? Errol Morris captured it perfectly in his profile of Richter: "Being able to do something means thinking, believing that you are able to do it. It's not enough to have the skill to play the piano. Something *more* is needed." Skill is the baseline. But to apply that skill—in the right place, at the right time, in just the right way—is another matter.

Rituals Help Us Find the *More* We Are Seeking

The point of preperformance rituals is to give us that elusive *more*—to help us overcome our anxiety and perform to our potential. It isn't just the world's famous peak performers who need more. We know about their needs and rituals because they're famous. We mere mortals also rely on performance rituals to calm and ready ourselves in countless areas of daily life: when we need to lead a meeting, nail a job interview, make our case before the town council, or otherwise step into the spotlight. In class, I ask my high-achieving Harvard students if they have rituals they perform before tests, sporting events, or other stressful occasions. They hesitate to share at first, but as soon as one person speaks up—"I always have to use the same toothpaste and have the same tea, and then I make sure to have three pencils"—the floodgates open. Every student in the class seems to have a ritual—and every one of those rituals is different.

Nor is it only high-stakes, pressurized moments that spur ritual responses. The prompt is often more mundane. For some of us, the prospect of small talk—at a cocktail party, on a train, in the doctor's office—feels as daunting as a solo at Carnegie Hall. For others, the idea of standing in front of a few colleagues and delivering a pitch is enough to elicit beads of sweat. In one study, researchers asked participants to try their hand at public speaking while enlisting motion-capture technology to show how the stress of the experience generated ritualistic behaviors. As people's heart rate ticked up, they spontaneously moved their hands in more specific and repetitive patterns.

Exploring these rituals made me realize that I had been practicing my own performance ritual for years now, another way in which my ritual skepticism gave way to belief. In my preteaching ritual I pace back and forth in my office thirty minutes before the start of my class, running the flow of the course through my mind, then taking my teaching plan, written on yellow paper (always), and placing it in the black leather binder my father gave me twenty-five years ago—the binder I carry with me to every single class I have ever taught at Harvard Business School.

Extraordinary and ordinary performers all over the world swear by their highly personalized performance rituals. They freely admit that they would be lost without these idiosyncratic rites—even though most of them also know that the rites sound silly and they haven't even a remotely logical explanation for why they believe their particular actions work. So, what's going on? Are they right? Do these variously weird behaviors help anyone—superstars or the rest of us—when it comes time to perform? Or do some of them get in the way, impeding our performance instead of improving it?

Cool, Calm, and Collected

One of the main reasons why rituals abound not only in game-day performance but in response to our everyday stresses is that many of our

other go-to strategies to stay calm and improve our performance fall
short. Or worse, they backfire. Have you ever tried telling yourself to
calm down—perhaps half panicked, staring yourself down in the mirror? Or have you ever experienced the aftermath of telling your irate
significant other to calm down?

How did that work out?

It might seem as if a straightforward reminder to remain calm
should work—or at least have some positive effect. We are surrounded
by motivational mantras and platitudes aimed at keeping us placid.
Perhaps the most famous example is Britain's World War II–era slogan "Keep calm and carry on." But the British government seemingly
realized once the Blitz began that already-panicked citizens might find
the slogan patronizing or ineffective, so it pulped 2.5 million copies of
the poster. (Its afterlife as a global meme only began in 2000 when
a secondhand bookseller found a vintage copy of the poster and ran
with it, as it appealed to twenty-first-century audiences as a now subtly
ironic reminder of a bygone stoic era.) The Brits' decision to abandon
their catchphrase is vindicated by a wave of recent research. In addition
to his fascinating work on how we identify our actions, psychologist
Dan Wegner also conducted research on our inability to control our
thoughts. Wegner invited people to *not* think of a white bear, a seemingly simple task, but when we try not to, all our mind can see is white
bear after white bear. If we can't suppress randomly cued thoughts of
white bears, why would we think we could suppress performance anxiety? An experience such as anxiety is considered a state as well as a
trait—we can be anxious at the thought of performing and we can also
be an anxious person in general. In neither case will the admonition to
calm down be helpful.

When we tell ourselves to calm down, we are not just trying to
suppress our thoughts. We are also trying to suppress *arousal*, a term
researchers use to describe both a psychological state of high energy

and tension as well as a physiological one, including the activation of the limbic and sympathetic nervous systems. Imagine telling yourself to just "calm down"—white bear white bear white bear—while simultaneously experiencing an arousal cocktail of stressful energy. Studies by my colleague at Harvard Business School Alison Wood Brooks show that telling ourselves to calm down in this way fails to work and can sometimes stress us out even more: "Not only am I still anxious about the performance, but now I'm also anxious that I am failing at the task of calming down . . . and then anxious about being anxious about that." You can imagine how well this doom feedback loop works.

Some performers believe that it's a matter of timing. They just need to wait until they "get in the zone" to achieve optimal performance. But there is little evidence that this strategy works, either. One study found that people who are allowed to throw darts only when they feel zoned in do no better than people told to throw darts at random times. Even prepping strategies that are logically related to the task at hand often fail to help. Does stretching before an athletic performance calm us down as well as warm us up? The evidence is decidedly mixed. And while antianxiety medications such as Xanax are often effective, they can have side effects that slow down our processing speed—not helpful when we need to be able to think and react quickly.

We all know these preperformance jitters don't always have negative effects. The Yerkes-Dodson law provides a framework for understanding the relationship between arousal and performance, asserting that a healthy dose of tension and stress improves our performance in a high-stakes interview, exam, or athletic competition. It can prompt us to practice or prepare more, setting us up to perform at our best when the rush of energy boosts our motivation and stamina. But there is a tipping point. When these jitters, or arousal, become too intense, they foil us, undermining and impeding our ability to perform to our potential.

My colleague Alison Wood Brooks is not just a fellow researcher with me at Harvard; she is also a good friend. With the addition of another HBS colleague, Ryan Buell, we formed the imaginatively named Harvard Faculty Band. (We're now called the Lights—you can hear us at www.thelights.band.) Playing publicly in a band gives all three of us direct access to performance anxiety. Alison is the least nervous performer I have ever played music with: she lives out her research by reframing all those butterflies and jitters as excitement. Ryan's anxiety onstage tends to manifest in the form of audience patter. I, on the other hand, tend to reframe my performance anxiety as inconvenience: "Why does being in a band mean we have to stand up in front of people and play music?" Luckily the band tolerates me.

Moving On and Managing Loss

In 2001, after a tough loss to the division rival Miami Dolphins, the New England Patriots team members arrived at their practice field to find a large hole in the ground. Coach Bill Belichick was standing next to the hole, with a shovel and the ball from the losing game. He threw the ball into the hole, covered it with dirt, turned to the team, and said, "That game's over. We're burying it and moving on." The team entombed the unlucky game ball. As the team backed away from the burial site, quarterback Tom Brady stomped on the dirt, muttering under his breath, "It's over." And it was. Over the remainder of the season, the Patriots turned an abysmal 1-3 start into the team's first Super Bowl championship.

Rituals aren't a guarantee, just as the best preparation isn't always enough to save us from failure. But when our best-laid plans do go awry and our most rigorously rehearsed performances fall flat, rituals can do different work, helping us cope with feelings of disappointment and defeat. If intense stress before a game spurs ritual behavior, intense disappointment after a losing performance seems to spur still more, as rituals step in to help us manage the negative emotions that arise from falling short.

Research backs up Belichick's and Brady's decision to bury that ball. In 2017, Nick Hobson, Devin Bonk, and Mickey Inzlicht, psychologists at the University of Toronto, enlisted forty-eight people in a one-week study to measure how they handled failure. Some people were assigned to complete this ritual once a day for a week: "Bring your fists together at your chest, slowly raise them above your head, and as you do, draw in a large inhale through your nose. Return your fists to your chest while drawing out an exhale through your mouth. Repeat this three times." All the participants were then assigned a series of difficult cognitive tasks over the course of the study—including an ingeniously frustrating task designed by the psychologist John Ridley Stroop in the 1930s and now widely (and appropriately) known as the Stroop Color and Word Test.

Imagine you see a list of words, presented one at a time, and your only task is to name the color of the font. It's easy at first: you see *dog* written in blue, and you answer, "Blue." Stroop wanted to make it harder, though: on the next trial, you read the word *red* written in green. Reading is such an automatic process, many people can't help but blurt out, "Red," though the type is green. While they tackled the tasks, participants were hooked up to an EEG machine via electrodes placed on their scalps, which assessed error-related negativity (ERN), an electroencephalographic waveform sensitive to differences between our expectations ("I am going to do well at this task") and our occasional failures to meet those expectations. Consider these failures as the neurological equivalent of the feeling "I messed up."

Those who enacted the breathing rituals throughout exhibited a muted response to failure compared to those who hadn't enacted any rituals. The results of the experiment suggest that rituals dampened our negative response to errors—that familiar feeling of messing up. Rituals seem to regulate the brain's response to failure, helping us to bounce back more quickly after setbacks.

The Dangers of Ritual

In *Ball Four*, his bestselling baseball tell-all published in 1970, the maverick pitcher Jim Bouton commented on how the feeling of ownership that athletic expertise affords can easily tip into the opposite—obsession, or a feeling of being owned by the very game we struggled to master. "You spend a good piece of your life gripping a baseball and in the end, it turns out that it was the other way around all the time." For all the benefits performance rituals bring, they can carry costs, too. If we depend on our rituals too much, we can end up beholden to and lost without them.

Consider the case of another Major League Baseball player, longtime Red Sox third baseman Wade Boggs. Boggs had a spate of rituals all tied to the number seventeen. At 5:17 before each game, he began batting practice, and at 7:17 he ran his wind sprints. Boggs's ritual was so well-known that Bobby Cox, then manager of the Blue Jays, asked the scoreboard operator to skip from 7:16 right to 7:18 at a game in Toronto just to throw Boggs off.

Baltimore Orioles pitcher Jim Palmer was just as beholden to his rituals. Jim "Pancake" Palmer was having a breakout season in 1966 with a win streak of eight games, each one preceded by his signature breakfast of good-luck pancakes. But when the Orioles had flight trouble en route to a game against the Kansas City Royals and Palmer was forced to skip his pancake breakfast, he worried that the upcoming game was in jeopardy. After losing, he told reporters, "I don't know whether missing my pancake breakfast had any bearing on the game. But I don't want to find out." When our rituals are interrupted, the experience can elicit acute anxiety. For Palmer, his inability to perform his morning ritual didn't just mean that he felt "off" all day—his game was off, too.

Then there's the problem of the overly elaborate ritual, the one that becomes so intricate that it interferes instead of prepares. Recall that baseball players engage in an average of eighty-three movements when batting, but some players exceed one hundred. Royce Lewis, a once highly touted prospect in the Minnesota Twins organization, may have been too close to the higher end. As his career stalled, one evaluator offered the following assessment: "His mannerisms—Nomar [Garciaparra]-level batting glove tinkering, deep, heavy, deliberate breaths between pitches, constant uniform adjustment—are manic, and they seem to pull focus away from the task at hand rather than grounding him in a ritualistic way, and the game often seems too fast for him." Taken to the extreme, preperformance rituals get in our way. If we can't stop engaging in the ritual, then we can't redirect our focus and move on to the actual performance. We're stuck in the dugout, or backstage—while the world carries on without us. (I should note that one of my students at Harvard told me that she deliberately makes her pregame rituals too difficult to enact perfectly—that way, if she doesn't perform well, she can blame the flawed ritual, instead of herself.)

———————

No ritual has the power to create rock stars or savants out of us. We still have to contend with the realities of aptitude and proficiency and the discipline of daily practice. But rituals can give us a way to manage our nerves and dial up skills we've worked so hard to achieve. As Errol Morris might say, our preperformance rituals offer us that elusive *something more*—allowing us to step into the spotlight and shine.

Chapter 5

How to Savor

Getting the Most Out of
Our Cabernet and Cleaning

THE PURIFICATION: A cold-water bath to chill the chalice and sustain the head of the pour.

THE SACRIFICE: The first drops are sacrificed, a small price to ensure the freshest taste.

THE LIQUID ALCHEMY: The chalice is held at forty-five degrees for the perfect combination of foam and liquid.

THE CROWN: The chalice is gracefully straightened, forming a perfect head and sealing in the freshness.

THE REMOVAL: A smooth and fluid exit, while closing the nozzle.

THE SKIMMING: A skimmer trims the head at a forty-five-degree angle, removing the large, loose bubbles.

THE JUDGEMENT: Three centimeters of foam, no more and no less.

THE CLEANSING: A final dip in cold water for a brilliant chalice and stunning presentation.

THE BESTOWAL: A moment to assure and admire a perfectly served Stella Artois.

If you're not a beer drinker, you might read a few of these steps before realizing that they're not for a religious ceremony—but, rather, a pouring ceremony. (Beer drinkers have an easier time.) The Ritual, as it's called, is a half-winking marketing campaign launched by the Belgian brewer Stella Artois in the 1990s. If this elaborate nine-step throwback to the Middle Ages has you rolling your eyes, I get it. It's meant to be over-the-top—but it does help the mega-brewer Anheuser-Busch InBev get away with pricing Stella Artois above many of its competitors.

Gimmick or not, imagine how you might feel preparing your favorite drink in this highly ritualized manner. Doesn't the ceremonial nature of it all—the elaborate discipline in performing this precise series of distinct steps—add a certain something to the experience? Something akin to the mystique of the shaken-not-stirred that defines a perfectly made martini? In both cases, the *how*—the precise way in which these otherwise ordinary actions are performed—elevates them. Now imagine preparing a beer the way I do instead: by twisting off the screw cap. Can you feel the difference? When we pair a glass or morsel or a special moment with the right ritual, our experience can change—transforming even the beer we buy in a twelve-pack on aisle nine into an elixir to savor.

Rituals provide us with many opportunities to incorporate more savoring into our everyday lives. Take one of the simplest and most common rituals of savoring—a small bite to eat or drink that happens at the same time each day. You will find some version of it in almost every culture in the world. If you live in Scandinavia, that means you are stopping to savor at a *fika*, or a break for coffee, tea, and sweets around 10:00 a.m. In most Scandinavian workplaces, this isn't even a choice. No one is interested in whether you, personally, are hungry for a *fika*. *Fika* is simply what one does. It's not about hunger or productivity or optimization. *Fika*—both a noun and a verb—is about taking a moment to eat together and to enjoy the company of others.

If you are in India at 6:00 p.m., chances are good you are making your own chai, a black tea, perhaps sweetened with honey or sugar or spiced with star anise, fennel, or cloves. Some choose a bit of ginger, just to bring out the flavors. Others prefer to add more milk to get just the right thickness. Teatime is its own time—in the liminal space between what you have done with your day and whom you will become once you're back home.

Or say you're in Italy grabbing your early-morning coffee *al banco*. The espresso comes fast and cheap and it's a straight shot. Slam it down fast with a lemon on the side. The joy is in the rush here—no lingering, just a ritualized performance of speed. It's just one strong sip but— don't worry—there could be as many as seven or eight later in the day.

In the 1970s, American schools would serve their young students a midmorning snack of graham crackers and a carton of milk. The carton opening was too tight to dunk those mildly sweet squares, but students often found a way to break through and submerge their crackers until they became dangerously and deliciously soggy. The line between graham crackers and milk and a new blend of graham cracker milk was often murky.

If you are French or have spent any significant time in France, you already know about the ritual pleasures of midmorning *pain au chocolat*. Just stop at your local patisserie on the way to work and buy one of their buttery, flaky croissants with the *chocolat* already inside. Taste, breathe, sigh. Savor the feeling that life is right now, at this moment, very good.

In each of these examples, the drinks and food are the props that set the scene for our experience of staying present in the moment.

Now think about whether savoring rituals are a part of your day. When I asked people in the past, I heard about variations on traditional rituals—tea, coffee, a cocktail after work—as well as entirely new ones that had been made up from whole cloth.

When it's midmorning and I need to stand up and stretch, I usually do my own little tea ritual. I've been collecting tea from all over the world for years now, so I have a vast collection. It started as a kit I received called Teas from Around the World, but now I mix and match with my own purchases every time I see a tea I want to try. Around ten or eleven a.m., I get up and walk over to a globe I keep in my office. I spin it around and I let my finger land on a continent or a country. The location on the globe determines my tea for the day—whether Earl Grey, a golden chai, a maté lemon, say, or a jasmine green tea. Whatever I am drinking, I always take a few minutes just to enjoy what makes each cup so special and distinct. Every tea is different—it just takes a few minutes to really appreciate how and why.

The bakery down the street brings out their loaves of bread every day at two p.m. It's the perfect moment to stand up, go for a walk, and enjoy the smell of the bread baking from down the block. When I arrive, the loaves are still warm so I take mine home, place it on a beautiful piece of china from my grandmother, and cover it with a thick square of my favorite

French butter. I never use that butter for anything else, so one stick lasts for weeks. Just watching the butter melt a bit against the warmth of the bread fills my happiness cup for the day.

In the middle of the day, I love to get up from my office desk and go outside for a walk. I look for coins on the street because that is something my father used to always do. When I see one—whether a quarter or a dime—I pick it up and use it to buy myself a gumball from the toy store down the block. It's a fun little treat that reminds me of my dad and the feeling of being a kid—the joy of waiting for that colorful round piece of sugar to come rolling out of the gumball machine door. I can hear my dad's laugh every time I pop one in my mouth. The flavor only lasts a few minutes, but it always lifts my spirits and it makes me smile.

There are endless ways to enhance and even enchant your day. If you have consumption rituals that punctuate your daily life, I encourage you to think about what you can do to make them even more resonant. If you can't think of any, I encourage you to take this opportunity to add in a moment of pause and pleasure. Savoring rituals like the ones above can be small but powerful generators of everyday joy, an easily accessible and often inexpensive means of transforming the ordinary into something more.

Consuming Concepts

My favorite pizzeria in the world is Regina's in the North End of Boston, and my favorite pizza is their sausage and onion. Yes, of all the pizza I have tried all over the world, the very best pizza is made just a few miles from where I grew up. I've also never even tried a sausage-and-onion pizza from any other pizza place. I'm not even sure I like onions all that much. So why is the pizza at Regina's my favorite? Regina's is also my parents' favorite. I associate it not only with my own childhood, but also with the stories I heard about my parents as children. When they were growing up in the 1950s, they used to hang out there back when Italian food was considered exotic by their Irish Catholic clan. Regina's is, for me, a family tradition, one that connects me to a past that predates me and that I carry forward. When one of my best friends, Scott, and I were in our twenties, we had a habit—or so I thought of it at the time—of meeting up at Regina's and ordering sausage-and-onion pizza as we tried to figure out what we were doing with our lives. It revealed itself to be much more than habit. For me, it was a legacy ritual with deep local roots. (Regina's is now my daughter's favorite, too.)

The emotional satisfaction I derive from a simple slice at Regina's is an example of what I have termed *conceptual consumption*. I'm eating the piece of pizza—a mix of nutrients such as whole grains and calcium—but that act stretches back in time and allows me to experience so much more: emotions and aspirations, memories and nostalgia. As the anthropologist Claude Fischler has observed, "Man feeds not only on proteins, fats, carbohydrates, but also on symbols, myths, fantasies." Certain foods, consumed in certain ways, nourish us in ways that go far beyond our physical need to fuel up. Consumption can also be a profoundly meaningful way of tapping into the repertoire of resources that make up our cultural tool kit—sometimes by using those resources in time-honored ways, other times by using them to improvise something utterly new. There can be no deep-fried Snickers bar until the world has provided us with both the candy and the technology to fry it.

All of which raises the question: What does consumption of proteins, fats, and carbohydrates look like when devoid of the symbols, myths, and fantasies that rituals channel? I suspect it might look (and taste) a little like Soylent.

In 2013, Rob Rhinehart, a recent graduate in electrical engineering from Georgia Tech, resented the demands of eating. He was living with roommates in San Francisco and trying to get a start-up off the ground. Eating meals was a nuisance—expensive and time-consuming. He looked for a work-around to avoid the endless drudgery of finding fuel. Wouldn't it be easier and more rational, he thought, to just figure out the chemical nutrients necessary to sustain his body and consume that—whatever *that* might be—by mouth? He identified thirty-five chemical ingredients, including potassium gluconate, calcium carbonate, and monosodium phosphate, and threw all of them into a blender each night. He continued tweaking the formula until it had just the right consistency—the texture of strained pancake batter—while also addressing the drink's alarming tendency to cause flatulence. He eventually ended up naming it Soylent—ironically referring back to the cannibalistic science fiction film *Soylent Green*—"It's people."

Today Rhinehart's meal-replacement company offers people all the benefits of nutrition in one serving. The point of Soylent is to enable maximum efficiency by eliminating the savoring. When you sit down to consume the viscous meal, you simply open up the bottle and pour. There is no sensory explosion or moment to pause and consider connection and belonging. There is no smell to transport you back to your grandmother's posole simmering on the stove for hours before magically landing in front of your young eyes with that bright pink radish on the top. No texture or sound—no flake, no crunch, no crackle—to remind you of the way your Danish family served cardamom buns, plush and fragrant, on dark winter afternoons during visits home. And as a liquid, which doesn't require effortful chewing, Soylent will never distract you by calling to mind your favorite food from childhood, such as your next-door neighbor's famous snickerdoodles.

In Soylent, all opportunities to savor—memories of the past, antic-ipation of pleasures to come, and the quietly optimistic enjoyment of a small good thing—have been stripped away. When you choose Soylent, the company promises, consumption is effortless and food nothing more than necessary fuel. Hunger is solved by complete automation without any labor-intensive emotional distractions. Rational, maybe, as a time-saving measure. But at what cost?

A Drink with Legs

Now compare Soylent to its spiritual opposite, a drink whose sole pur-pose is to elicit savoring. People who regularly consume wine are part of such a rich culture that drinking it can become essential to who they are. Oenophiles consider their experience of what's in the glass in the con-text of varying agricultural practices—the surfeit of sun or lack of rain in such places as Napa Valley or Tuscany or the south of France; what the soil was like in a given year; and whether the grapes were picked a day late or a day early. Oenophiles may have visited the vineyards and know the owners' family histories—or met the people who work there.

In the movie *Sideways*, which both satirizes and celebrates this world of wine, Paul Giamatti plays Miles, a prickly wine lover and failed novelist who is down on his luck. In a seduction scene with Maya, played by Virginia Madsen, the two characters dance around each other—talking about themselves by talking about their immer-sion in the world of wine. Miles begins by describing his love for pinot noir:

It's a hard grape to grow. As you know. It's thin-skinned, tem-peramental, ripens early. It's not a survivor like cabernet that can grow anywhere and thrive even when neglected. Pinot needs constant care and attention and in fact can only grow in specific little tucked-away corners of the world. And only the most patient and nurturing growers can do it really, can tap into pinot's most fragile, delicate qualities.

Maya then responds with great intimacy and vulnerability, all of which she expresses through her own immersion in the world of wine:

I love how wine continues to evolve, how every time I open a bottle it's going to taste different than if I had opened it on any other day. Because a bottle of wine is actually alive—it's constantly evolving and gaining complexity. That is, until it peaks—like your '61—and begins its steady, inevitable decline. And it tastes so fucking good.

This is the seduction of savoring. Wine gives us a sensory repertoire through which to share experiences and connect on a deep level with others. It's no surprise that Maya and Miles have coupled up by the end of the film. It's a love story but also a story of shared savoring.

Immersing Yourself in the Glass

Wine culture presented me with many opportunities to observe and consider rituals in daily consumption—everything from the suspense and anticipation of opening the bottle to the decanting of the wine to the aerating techniques of swirling the wine in the glass. It seemed evident that some of wine culture is about wine, the *what*, and some is about ritual, the *how*—the special ways we pour, swirl, and imbibe it.

But what exactly are these rituals of consumption doing for us? Whom better to learn from than people whose entire lives are dedicated to savoring: *sommeliers*. Kathryn LaTour, who has the enviable title of Professor of Wine Education and Management at Cornell, and my Harvard Business School colleague John Deighton interviewed ten master sommeliers in San Francisco, Las Vegas, and New York about their tasting processes. These interviews are a trove of firsthand accounts that offer insight not just into the ritual elements of wine tasting, but the experience and ethos of expert tasters. "I guess what I try to do," one sommelier, James, explained, "is to be inside the glass even though I'm imposing myself on the glass. I try to be immersed in the glass and then come out of it. . . . Maybe [that's] a metaphor for being inside a giant pool of the wine."

Throughout these interviews with the world's greatest tasters, the theme of immersion—a feeling of being deeply, intensely in an experience—came up time and again as a crucial aspect of savoring consumption. Luckily for the job security of master sommeliers, just watching someone exert effort on our behalf can enhance our experience. Simply seeing the chef who is making our food, as one study showed, can increase our enjoyment of the final product.

The vision of a master chef gave me a unique perspective on how all of us experience savoring emotionally. Before the restaurant shuttered its doors in 2011, I was lucky enough to dine at legendary chef Ferran Adrià's restaurant El Bulli in the town of Roses, Spain. With three Michelin stars, El Bulli was hailed as "the most imaginative generator of haute cuisine on the planet." As Clotilde Dusoulier, a Parisian food writer, wrote on her blog, "It took us six hours to go through the entire meal—from 8 PM to 2 AM—but we were in such a state of elation that it was hard to tell if it had been two minutes or two days since we first sat down."

Would my meal elicit elation? Would I suddenly encounter the possibility of transcendence through elevated dining—the great prix fixe in the sky? All these thoughts of cosmic connection came crashing down the moment the server brought out my amuse-bouche—a lone strawberry, lightly grilled, on a plate. How could it possibly measure up to my investment of effort and sense of longing? My amuse-bouche couldn't possibly be part of the same foodie nirvana Dusoulier rhapsodized over on her blog.

Half-heartedly biting into the strawberry, I was suddenly hit with three distinct tastes: the char of a grill, gin and tonic, and the strawberry itself. I was transported immediately to a summer barbecue, eating a slightly burnt hamburger, washing it down with a cocktail, and ending with a fruit dessert. Dusoulier was right: in a single moment, I experienced a lifetime. This collapsing of time and memory point to Adrià's vision of turning eating into an experience that "supersedes eating." As a master of savoring, he created a bite of strawberry that was somehow the ur-strawberry, fully immersing me and catapulting me into a web of associations and memories. This lone strawberry earned its place in my mind alongside Proust's iconic madeleine as an example of food's ability to conjure up nostalgia, longing, appreciation, and wonder all at once.

The immersive experience of Adrià's strawberry met—and exceeded—my expectations. But savoring needn't require a long trek through the mountains to Roses. Consumption rituals are emotion generators that offer the potential for more joy and pleasure, elation and nostalgia, anywhere.

Eat Dessert First

In 1997, Sue Ellen Cooper, an artist based in Fullerton, California, spotted a red fedora in a store. Cooper, in her midfifties, was experiencing the newfound freedom and ease of making her way in the world without looking for approval from anyone else. "Why not?" she thought, as she tried the floppy red hat on her head. She bought it and started wearing it around because it reminded her of a line in a Jenny Joseph poem she loved—a riff on one of T. S. Eliot's most famous lines. In "The Love Song of J. Alfred Prufrock," the narrator gloomily laments aging: "I grow old . . . I grow old . . ." In her poem, Joseph approaches the prospect of aging as a bold new beginning: "When I am an old woman I shall wear purple / With a red hat which doesn't go, and doesn't suit me."

Around this time—while enjoying her red fedora—Cooper was looking for a gift for a friend who was turning fifty-five. She wanted it to be offbeat, not the usual Hallmark card or bouquet of flowers, but also meaningful. "We should all be like the woman in Jenny Joseph's poem," Cooper thought. "Why don't more of us take time to enjoy life and do things because we want to—isn't it time to make fun and friendship two of our greatest priorities?" She bought another red fedora for her friend, then another for another friend, then more, as more women around her started taking note of the floppy red hats. It was partly a joke, but it was also a ritual in the making, a ritual that said, "Life is short, let's enjoy it while we're still here." Before long, Cooper invited all of her red-hat friends out to tea—insisting that they wear their floppy hats and purple dresses. April 25, 1998, was the first official meeting of the Red Hat Society, but membership—once only for women over fifty but now open to all women—has been growing ever since. Fifteen chapters alone are within twenty miles of my office at Harvard, including the JP Red Hatters in Jamaica Plain and the Red Hat Rowdies in Billerica. It's by no means a local phenomenon, with chapters in thirty different countries with a total membership of more than thirty-five thousand.

Cooper ultimately told the *Deseret News* that she considers the Red Hat Society a "play group" for adults. "I have worked for my kids' school, my church, raised money for the local children's center, and of course we love to do those things," she explained. "But someone has got to give these women permission to take a whole day or a weekend and just goof off." She dubbed herself the Exalted Queen Mother of the Red Hat Society and encourages norm-bending forms of indulgent fun.

One of the Red Hatters' core practices, enacted at every gathering, is to "eat dessert first." It's a reminder to savor life's joys, *now*. One sixty-eight-year-old Red Hatter, Catherine, expressed her enthusiasm for savoring life in the moment by indulging: "A drink in one hand, a chocolate bar in the other, and slide into heaven saying, 'Woo-hoo! What a ride!' Oh, I figure I'm gonna die, when I'm gonna die, and I'm gonna live, until I die."

Opportunities to follow the lead of Red Hat Society members are everywhere. Cooper encouraged all of the women in her community to make fun, playfulness, and indulgence the organizing principles of their society. But rituals of savoring can bring people together in other unconventional ways as well. In the years following COVID's lockdown and social isolation, even one of contemporary culture's most common feasting rituals is getting a complete overhaul.

Eating with Strangers

In 2021, in the thick of the pandemic, Anita Michaud moved to Brooklyn Heights, a brownstone-filled neighborhood in New York City. She arrived from Ann Arbor, where her entire family shared a multigenerational history as restaurateurs, chefs, and masters of hospitality. Her grandfather started a Chinese restaurant in Plymouth, Michigan, and then her mother, following in her father's footsteps, opened her own restaurant with Michaud's father—this one a French bistro.

After a childhood spent in the world of food and fine dining, Michaud had hospitality on her mind when she arrived in New York. What she discovered, however, was not the city that never sleeps. Instead, it was a city shattered by lockdown and looking to find its social footing. In 2022, although people were ready to socialize again, a mood of trepidation hung over many social gatherings. For people such as Michaud, young transplants still new to the city, the question was, How do you possibly find IRL friends after two years of Zoom happy hours? Instead of starting with people already in her network, Michaud took a bolder and bigger chance. She identified six strangers—friends of friends and people she found on Bumble BFF, a friendship app—and invited them to a meal in her home. She didn't call her party Dinner with Strangers, however. Instead, she sent out her invites and welcomed people she had never met to join her for an intimate evening around her dining table. It's a "Dinner with Friends," her invite stated. A promise or a pipe dream?

As documented in the *New York Times*, one by one, women arrived for dinner—total strangers—and learned, once again, how to have a conversation with new people in the same room. What does it look like to make friends again? The question was on everyone's mind after the worst of the pandemic. Researchers estimate that people's social networks decreased in size an average of 16 percent during COVID's lockdowns and in the following year of social distancing.

When the strangers at Michaud's dinner party erupted into laughter or split off into side conversations, she knew they had all found a bit of chemistry. Before the night was over, she connected everyone on a group chat and added it to her growing collections of text streams, each from a different cohort of guests at one of her dinner parties. She now has a waiting list of more than eight hundred people to attend one of her "stranger" events—primarily young women, all with a simple intention: today I might make a friend.

Comfort on a Cold Day

Even a simple soup, when dashed with a dose of ritual, can create that sense of community. Countless cultures have some version of a hot broth for a day of healing—either of body or soul. Some Jewish families have throw downs about how to make a chicken noodle soup *just right*. Thai families might turn to their favorite coconut soup, while Korean households are more likely to reach for a *samgyetang*, a stew made with ginseng and chicken. If you are an Italian *nonna*, you probably have a special recipe for *stracciatella* up your sleeve, and if you grew up in Vietnam, there's a good chance someone served you pho on a cold, wet day.

The comfort of such soups and broths comes from their nutritional and medicinal qualities but also from nurturing evoked by each bite. Valerie Zweig, the founder of Prescription Chicken and Chix Soup Co, a homemade chicken soup delivery company, explained to *Oprah Daily* what people are really seeking when they try to order up the healing broth of their childhood:

People don't order chicken soup just because they're hungry. There's usually something else going on. Maybe they're tired, or feeling the need for some TLC. Maybe they're heartbroken or homesick. Maybe they're seriously under the weather. The soup needs to make the problem better, whatever it is.

The savoring people experience while consuming a healing broth is one of care: they can taste the tenderness. They are experiencing the cold compress, the tucked blanket, the cooing and shushing sounds of a parent tending to their needs. Soups and broths—regardless of their simplicity—contain profound flavor. People are consuming caretaking and love. Whether we are opening with optimism the door to a dinner party of strangers, or sinking into the familiar comforts of a childhood meal, the taste of food and drink often delivers the emotional experiences we seek. Consumption rituals can prompt us to savor even our smallest and most ordinary pleasures.

Yet while most of us associate savoring with consumption, the word *savoring* has a broader definition in the scientific literature, as a form of heightened attention and appreciation that extends to all aspects of our everyday lives—one we can both sustain and augment. Behavioral scientists have identified four of the most successful strategies for achieving this broader definition of savoring: try to be present for our positive moments and appreciate them; communicate and celebrate savoring with others; express our savoring through nonverbal behaviors such as smiling; and, finally, richly remember details about past positive experiences while also anticipating the details of those still to come—the process I described in my response to Adrià's magical strawberry. Researchers have dubbed this *positive mental time travel*, or *positive MTT*.

Positive Mental Time Travel

In my role at Harvard Business School, I mentor doctoral students through a group we affectionately refer to as our NerdLab. One day, my student Ting Zhang asked me an unexpected but intriguing question, Why do people make time capsules? Ting suspected that the experience of rediscovering the past might transform the familiar into something delightfully novel. Burying mundane, everyday stuff in the ground (today's newspaper is common) only to dig it up later is a prime—if offbeat—example of how we can use rituals not just to remember but to rediscover, savoring the present moment as well as the past and the future at once. Rituals can deliver the opposite of déjà vu: an experience of jamais vu, or "never seen." We decided to document and understand that experience of rediscovery—to figure out what turns the humdrum facts of ordinary life into something more.

We asked 135 college students in the Boston area to create time capsules at the end of the school year, filled with evidence of their recent lives—the last social event they attended, three songs they recently listened to, an excerpt from a final paper for a class, an inside joke. Right after they had created their time capsules, we asked these students how interested and curious they thought they would be about their contents when they viewed them again, in three months. They were not enthused: they described the items as mundane, borderline garbage, all too familiar. Why would it be interesting to encounter them again?

But after the three months had passed, their perspective had significantly changed. Our participants reported that they were now excited to see the contents of their time capsules—and they later told us how delighted they were when they got to see them again. Despite feeling that they would remember the contents all too well, they had forgotten much of what they had stored away, and rediscovering those contents produced outright joy.

From the perspective of a behavioral scientist investigating rituals, one of the most striking findings of our research is that the benefits of rediscovery apply most robustly to ordinary events, not extraordinary ones—that is, the kinds of events and moments we barely notice while they are happening. They mostly fly under our radar, too small or familiar to capture our inevitably limited attention. In another study, we assigned 152 people in romantic relationships to write descriptions of two different days in their lives: February 7, and February 14. We followed up three months later, had them reread their descriptions, and asked them how much they enjoyed reading them. You might think that reminiscing about the romantic evening you spent on Valentine's Day would be more thrilling than calling to mind a mundane February 7. But since people tended to remember their Valentine's Day fairly well, they didn't have much to rediscover. Instead, they were more delighted to revisit that random day that they were more likely to have forgotten about.

As one parent in another one of our studies put it, "Rereading this event of doing mundane stuff with my daughter has certainly brightened my day. I'm glad I chose that event to write about because of the incredible joy it gives me at this moment." While feelings of nostalgia can sometimes be bittersweet—tinged with sadness for days gone by—there is evidence that nostalgic thinking can increase our feelings of happiness, and even our sense of meaning in life. The seemingly odd ritual of burying our present offers us a unique opportunity to take us back to our past.

Savoring by Stripping Away

In Sweden, a ritual called the *döstädning* has recently emerged—the Swedish word *dö*, "death," combined with *städning*, "cleaning." It's loosely translated as "death clean," but this ritual does not directly precede or follow a death. Instead, it is an invitation to reflect on all the things in one's home—do they benefit you and your loved ones now? What about your future self? Will that self use or cherish them? If not, it's probably time to say goodbye to them. In Iran, spring brings Nowruz, a ritual of renewal that metaphorically goes beyond just reflecting on the house; *khoneh takooni* means "shaking the house."

In 2017, Margareta Magnusson published a bestselling book, *The Gentle Art of Swedish Death Cleaning*, advising readers on how to best approach this ultimate cleaning ritual. She described *döstädning* as an opportunity for rediscovery, an intentional process of elimination that elicits a joyful clarity: "It is a delight to go through things and remember their worth." The cleaning is less about sweeping and mopping—although that can certainly be a part of it—and more about acknowledging that none of this "stuff" is going to join us on the journey to the next life. We can savor not only consumption, but also subtraction. Less, as the modernist starchitect Mies van der Rohe famously observed, is often more.

In the past, spring cleaning was a practical necessity: in the 1800s in the United States, spring marked the time to scrub off the winter's worth of soot from burning wood, coal, and whale oil. For many people today, by contrast, spring cleaning signifies purifying their space and celebrating what's next, a reset for a new season of life. In 2022, 78 percent of Americans participated in a spring-cleaning ritual—up from 69 percent in 2021. Rajiv Surendra, an actor and calligrapher living in New York City, is of those enthusiastic seasonal cleaners. Surendra believes in getting down on his hands and knees "Cinderella-style" to do all of his cleaning. "For the week that I'm cleaning," he told the *New York Times*, "I feel like I'm not living, like I pressed the pause button." Part of his ritual is to "make a point of touching every item" in his apartment at least once.

Surendra's ritual of purification is not dissimilar from that of the iconic lifestyle guru Marie Kondo. Kondo tells her many fans and followers, "When tidying, the key is to pick up each object one at a time, and ask yourself quietly, 'Does this spark joy?' Pay attention to how your body responds. Joy is personal, so everyone will experience it differently." She describes that joy as "a little thrill, as if the cells in your body are slowly rising." And if no cells are rising? In the trash. These cleaning rituals exemplify the power of less. Kondo's many followers can attest to the effects: the "spark-joy method" helps them to be more intentional about what they keep, and to savor these items.

———————

Rituals of consumption and rediscovery scaffold and enhance our daily lives. Marketers, too, have discovered their allure and are selling us countless rituals with their products attached. Stella Artois is hardly alone. The list of companies hopping on the ritual bandwagon is long and growing longer. Today you can buy ritual-branded vitamins, bath products, coffee, take-out dinners, and tequila. In 2017, Oreo launched the Oreo Dunk Challenge, including Shaquille O'Neal's first-ever hands-free dunk, with the stated goal to "integrate *OREO* cookie dunking into culture." The beverage ujji describes consumption as "a liquid ritual." At Nebraska football games, hamburgers are grilled in the shape of the state, and true Cornhuskers fans squeeze their condiments down the Platte River. While these rituals can work—ujji's customer Anastasia from Philadelphia gushed, "Thank you for making magic in a cup"—the science suggests that instead of passively accepting (or buying) rituals that companies design and market to us, we can be active agents, investing effort and attention in crafting our own. Consumption rituals remind us to savor, drawing more joy out of each moment of our lives, each memory, every sip and any bite.

Chapter 6

How to Stay on Track

The Joy of Self-Control

I want to do right but not right now.

—Gillian Welch

Have you ever started your day with a breakfast like this? Organic low-fat vanilla yogurt, raspberries, blackberries, pecans, and sprouted-whole-grain cereal. If so, kudos. A healthy start showing great discipline.

And maybe lunch was equally impressive. Organic power greens, say, with fat-free lime basil dressing?

But what about the rest of the day? Has your impressive start ever ended in this kind of bad finish: mint chocolate chip ice cream sandwich, Goldfish crackers, beer, and white wine? We often seek to exert self-control, in this case by adopting a healthier diet, but will win some battles—and lose some. Ice cream sandwiches paired with beer and wine were definitely not part of the plan.

Food is only one example of how we struggle to exercise self-control. Resisting temptation is a constant undercurrent in our daily lives, and temptation takes many forms.

The psychologists Kathleen Vohs, Wilhelm Hofmann, Roy Baumeister, and Georg Förster recruited 205 people from in and around Würzburg, Germany, for a weeklong study of temptation in everyday life. Seven times per day, people's smartphones pinged to ask if they were "currently experiencing a desire"—such as a craving, an urge, or a longing to do certain things. Nearly half of the times people were pinged, they reported feeling torn between doing what they should be doing and what they wanted to be doing—what was for centuries described, harshly, as "weakness of the will." More than half of all reported conflicts involved procrastination—resisting time-wasting temptations in order to get stuff done. Another common source of struggle was health and fitness—trying to work out, eat healthily, and cut down on drinking. Desire for coffee peaked in the morning and desire for alcohol in the evening, while the desire to nap was a constant temptation. Abstinence goals included both not spending money and not cheating on partners.

All were then asked a follow-up question about their particular temptation: Did you manage to resist it? Their success rates were underwhelming—some 42 percent of the time, their efforts at self-control failed. Those urges became even harder to resist the more urges they'd already resisted that day. We all have our limits.

By automating our decision-making, habit formation can take us some of the way toward better self-control, but it's not foolproof. We might have good habits at home—no snacks in the house—but those habits may not be portable. For example, we may also have a habit of snacking with particular activities, such as going to the movies. Psychologists David Neal, Wendy Wood, Mengju Wu, and David Kurlander intercepted people as they were about to enter a cinema and gave them each a box of free popcorn. While half of the people were given fresh popcorn, the other half were given popcorn that was seven days old and stale. The good news is that people who were not in the habit of eating popcorn at movies ate less of the stale than the fresh popcorn. But those who were in the habit of eating popcorn at movies appeared not to notice the difference—they mindlessly consumed just as much of the stale popcorn as the fresh popcorn.

Rituals, however, operate differently from habits. They offer a different path to self-regulate.

The Original Life-Changing Magic

Many of us feel deadlocked in an internal, never-ending battle—as the better angels of our nature seek to resist our worst impulses, and our demons urge us to take the path of least resistance by giving in. Either we're trying to be good but struggling with it, or we've already failed and are wallowing in guilt. Given our evergreen struggle to exert greater self-control, it's not surprising that religions the world over have devised rituals to help us. Religions from Buddhism to Christianity to Hinduism to Islam to Judaism—to name just a few—incorporate elements of abnegation, asking us to flex our self-discipline to prove our devotion. During certain times of the day or certain days of the week or certain months of the year, we must give up something we love. (People make occasional efforts to game the system; for example, a mom wrote, "Once again my child has vowed to give up broccoli, a food he has never actually tasted, for Lent.")

Political theorist Michael Walzer suggests that John Calvin, the leading figure in the sixteenth-century Protestant Reformation and the founder of Calvinism, designed many of the denomination's austere rituals—such as a ban on musical instruments in church services—not only as a rejection of what he perceived as the excessive ornateness of the Roman Catholic mass, but also to encourage people to practice austerity after services ended, in their daily lives.

Does religion help us to listen to our better angels? In one obvious way it almost certainly does. Being observant often means being observed. Belonging to a public congregation can offer social and emotional support to bolster us, and also social shame if we fail. But psychologists Zeve Marcus and Michael McCullough suggest that there is more to it than the fear of social stigma. They emphasize instead religions' emphasis on effortful rituals—the discipline of attending services, prayer, meditation, and fasting—to help people improve their capacity to regulate and control their behavior, that is, their self-discipline in general.

Religion has certainly been implicated in some of humanity's most astonishing feats of self-control. Starting in the eleventh century, for instance, monks of the Shingon school of Buddhism in Japan embraced the following ritual:

For the first one thousand days, engage in strict exercise and subsist on water, seeds, and nuts.

For the next one thousand days, drink tea made from toxic sap typically used as lacquer.

Then be buried alive sitting in the lotus position, in a stone tomb, breathing through a tube and ringing a bell once daily. When the bell stops, seal the tomb.

When the tombs were opened after waiting an additional thousand days, monks who had self-mummified while dying—*sokushin-butsu*—were displayed and venerated at their temples.

As extreme as their ritual is, these monks are not outliers nor are such practices limited to the previous millennia. The monks at the monastery of Simonopetra, in Greece, founded in the thirteenth century, have a ceremony in which they remain standing without food or drink for a full twenty-four hours. As Simon Critchley described it in the *New York Times*:

The scent of myrrh hung heavy in the air from the swinging incense burner that functioned like a percussive accompaniment for the chanting. . . . The physical discipline of the monks was hard to comprehend. They stood for hours on end without moving, twitching, fidgeting or biting their nails. No one drank anything or looked thirsty. Toward the end . . . around midnight, I noticed one or two stifled yawns, but nothing much.

In both examples, ritual is intricately tied to otherworldly acts of self-control. Research suggests that religious rituals can help people marshal their resources toward specific goals—the religiously observant are less likely to go to jail, less likely to use drugs, and more likely to further their education.

But all of these examples are missing a critical control group: people who tried similar feats of self-control, but *without* a religious, ritual component. A crucial question remains: Is it religious rituals in particular that help people exert greater self-control, or could people have pulled off similar feats with rituals less steeped in tradition— or rituals with no history at all?

Testing the Marshmallow Test

Most people are familiar with the psychologist Walter Mischel's "marshmallow test": give young children a marshmallow and tell them that if they wait fifteen minutes without eating it, they will get two marshmallows instead of one. The task perfectly encapsulates the idea of delayed gratification, our ability to resist our desires in the service of a greater, later good. (The religious analogy is living a virtuous life on earth to be rewarded with an afterlife in heaven.) Children who take part in the experiment suffer, squirm, and struggle to hold out. Can anything be done to help them delay immediate gratification and double their allotted treat size?

In an experiment with 210 children (mostly seven- and eight-year-olds) from Slovakia and Vanuatu, anthropologist Veronika Rybanska and her colleagues set out to boost children's ability to delay gratification. Over a period of three months, students were pulled out of their regular classes for a series of games. In one such game, called Drum Beats, the children were taught to respond to different drum cues with different movements:

Children were instructed to walk quickly to fast drumming, walk slowly to slow drumming, and freeze when the drumming stopped. Teachers also asked children to respond to opposite cues (walking slowly to fast drum beats and quickly to slow drum beats) and associated different actions with specific drum cues (e.g., hopping to fast drum beats and crawling to slow drum beats).

Each of the games was designed to require children to practice self-regulation. In the case of Drum Beats, for example, responding to opposing cues—switching from walking quickly to fast drumbeats to walking slowly to fast drumbeats—takes effort and self-discipline.

After three months, all the children were given a version of the marshmallow test—they could either receive one piece of candy now or three pieces of candy later. The exercises did make a difference. Children who had practiced for three months were able to delay gratification significantly longer than children who didn't get to play the games.

But Rybanska's study had an additional layer of complexity. The researchers had divided children who engaged in the games into two subsets. Teachers gave the children in the first subset a clear rationale for why they had to participate in these games—namely, that if they practiced and improved at hopping fast to the beat, they'd be better dancers. The teachers didn't give any rationale at all to the second subset of children. For months on end, the teachers just told the children to start walking and hopping in unison. The result? The children who were not given any rationale seem to have come up with their own reason: the actions must have some deeper meaning. (Remember Skinner's pigeons that came to see their random pecking and head bobbing as meaningful?) This meant that the children in the first subset were trained to see the games as mere practice, while children in the second subset were trained to see the games as something more ritualistic. The data for children in this second subset revealed that they held out for more candy for longer than any other group.

This is the tool-kit nature of rituals. Yes, we turn to them to help us savor when we most want to savor. But we also turn to them for help when we've decided the savoring has gone on long enough.

Trapped in the Loop

The monks of the Shingon school of Buddhism performed the same actions for thousands of days. Rituals and repetition can be powerful tools for honing our self-control, but ritualistic behavior can, over time, start to control us instead. The humorist David Sedaris famously struggled with obsessive-compulsive disorder (OCD) and developed a range of repetitive rituals in his childhood. Sedaris detailed his experience in the essay "A Plague of Tics," which captures the experience of living with OCD in an eye-opening (yet also hilarious) confrontation with his grade-school teacher.

"You're up and down like a flea," his teacher says. "I turn my back for two minutes and there you are with your tongue pressed against that light switch. Maybe they do that where you come from, but here in my classroom, we don't leave our seats and lick things whenever we please. That is Miss Chestnut's light switch, and she likes to keep it dry. Would you like me to come over to your house and put my tongue on your light switches? Well, would you?" I tried to picture her in action, but my shoe was calling. TAKE ME OFF, it whispered. TAP MY HEEL AGAINST YOUR FOREHEAD THREE TIMES. DO IT NOW, QUICK, NO ONE WILL NOTICE.

OCD is defined by ritualistic compulsions and the "need for order or symmetry." The psychologists Richard Moulding and Michael Kyrios write that OCD "is characterized by the individual striving to control their thoughts and by using rituals to control the world." That is, people with OCD have a low sense of control but an elevated desire for it. Rituals help to restore that sense of control, but not fully—leading to ever more ritual. Kate Fitzgerald at the University of Michigan says that it's as if "their foot is on the brake telling them to stop, but the brake isn't attached to the part of the wheel that can actually stop them." This is why a core symptom of OCD is engaging in controlled, repetitive behaviors—such as double-checking locks and appliances, repeatedly confirming the safety of loved ones, and other actions such as counting and tapping.

The anthropologist Alan Fiske suggests that the antecedents of OCD run deep in human psychology. He argues that OCD-related behaviors have a functional similarity to that of the rituals performed by early hunter-gatherer societies. These early civilizations had an urgent need to check for contamination—to purify food and drinking water—as well as to keep a vigilant watch for the dangers of animals and enemies. He argues that OCD is a pathological expression of the rituals our ancestors performed regularly to stay healthy and safe.

People who experience OCD find it tremendously challenging—sometimes impossible—to stop performing their rituals. The ritual has become an end in itself. Sedaris says as much about one of his childhood behaviors: rocking back and forth. "There was nothing else I would rather do. The point was not to rock oneself to sleep: This was not a step toward some greater goal. It was the goal itself."

It is also impossible to talk about ritual and self-control without acknowledging the role that rituals play in eating disorders such as anorexia nervosa. Many people with anorexia develop rituals of non-consumption, or abstinence. For example, in research by Deborah Glasofer and Joanna Steinglass, one woman going by the pseudonym Jane reported that she had developed a ritual of eating a "150-calorie lunch: nonfat yogurt and a handful of berries . . . using a child-size spoon to 'make the yogurt last' and sipping water between each bite."

The ritual worked from Jane's perspective. In her adolescence, it made her lose weight and feel accomplished, at first. But over the years, Jane lost control, becoming dangerously thin and ill. As Glasofer and Steinglass write, "Her routines occur almost automatically without regard for the outcome." These repeated rituals of nonconsumption can become associated with a temporary burst of pleasure and control, which makes it challenging for people suffering from anorexia to move away from them.

Some therapeutic options seek to subvert destructive rituals by using other rituals to interrupt them. For example, among the most common treatments for compulsive behaviors is "habit reversal" training. The idea is to identify the root behavior that is causing problems and replace it with something else. If the bad habit is nail biting, for instance, people would be trained to notice when their hands begin to move toward their mouth, and to do something else instead—clench their fists, put them down by their side, and count to three. This is called a "competing response" in the literature. It's also, you might recognize, a basic ritual—a repeatable set of movements that helps us to pause and reclaim control of what we're doing.

Many strategies for beating vicious cycles such as drug addiction or overeating are based on developing rituals as countervailing or competing responses. Mark Seaman is a recovering addict who works at Earth Rhythms in West Reading, Pennsylvania. He leads a recovery program called Drumming Out Drugs, which aims to replace the pull of addiction with a community built around music. Seaman knows all too well that addicts often feel isolated, and that making connections is crucial to breaking the cycle. Seaman has set up his program so that drumming offers a new ritual and a new form of connection to replace the behaviors tied to addiction. "Drums penetrate people at a deeper level," Seaman says. "Drumming produces a sense of connectedness and community, integrating body, mind, and spirit."

When Seaman begins a meeting, he asks people to pick up a drum and show the rest of the group how they are feeling by playing. The initial cacophony slowly becomes more coordinated, and the group begins to create music together. Each session ends by incorporating percussion into a form of meditation. It's a new take on the group therapy of programs such as Alcoholics Anonymous, and a new ritual designed to bring people together regularly and limit their opportunities for relapse.

Chapter 7

How to Become

Rites (and Wrongs) of Passage

Everybody knows
It hurts to grow up.

—Ben Folds

The Japanese phrase *wabi-sabi* is difficult to translate—*wabi* roughly means "the elegant beauty of humble simplicity" and *sabi*, "the passing of time and subsequent deterioration." The phrase captures an entire ethos: both the realization that all things break and decay in time and a larger appreciation of how this can create new beauty.

Throughout our lives, we are changing—we grow, we learn, we age, we mature. We also *make* deliberate changes to our lives all the time. Some are easy. We switch from being a vanilla ice cream person to ordering chocolate ice cream without too much drama. But for the big transitions—when we become a parent or come out to our parents; when we start a new career path or start on the path to recovery—it's not so simple. For these transitions, changes that cut to the core of our identities, we don't get to just abandon the old and start entirely new. Instead, we pull some elements of who we were along with us, even as we pursue a bold new vision for ourselves. As in *wabi-sabi*, the beauty comes from breaking who we were, gathering the shards, and forging them into a new self, one that's more meaningful and truer for all that struggle and effort.

Rites of Passage

At the turn of the twentieth century, as part of his research on the history of French folklore, Arnold van Gennep coined the term *rites of passage* (in his book titled, appropriately, *Les rites de passage*) to describe these transformational moments in our lives. He observed that people across very different societies and cultures rely on a common practice when they seek to remake themselves: they use rituals to guide them to their destination. Van Gennep noted three distinct transitional phases: rites of separation, when we leave our previous identity; rites of the margin (*marge*), when we're in the throes of change; and rites of incorporation, when we enter fully into our new identity. The second phase—the liminal rites—is the most nebulous, yet in many ways the most important. It's here where a rite of passage moves us from being to becoming, from the margins back to the center, from the murky middle to solid ground, from who we were to who we will be.

The elegant simplicity of van Gennep's framework becomes apparent when you survey the frequency, range, and complexity of rites of passage across all cultures and realize that, despite the extraordinary variety in the form of rites of passage, they are unfailingly used to help move people from one self to another.

For the Amish, adulthood is marked by the end of Rumspringa—

literally, "running around"—which began at age sixteen. This is the liminal phase when teens are momentarily excused from some of the strictures of Amish life and can try things such as driving vehicles not drawn by horses, or even consuming alcohol and drugs. Rumspringa ends when the teenagers decide either to be baptized or to leave the community forever. In Brazil's Sateré-Mawé tribe, thirteen-year-old boys undergo a bullet ant initiation. Eighty bullet ants—the insects whose sting ranks highest on the sting-pain index—are woven into special gloves, with stingers pointed inward. To transition into adulthood, each boy must wear the gloves for five to ten minutes, not just once, but twenty different times. In Judaism, adulthood is marked by bar and bat mitzvahs, in which participants recite from the Torah, at age twelve or thirteen, in front of their family and community. Bar and bat mitzvahs take place at the age when, according to Jewish tradition, children are ready to cross a milestone into a more independent relationship with their faith. They can now hold themselves accountable to their community and grow in faith toward a more mature version of their Jewish identity.

In Norway, high school students participate in the *russefeiring* during their final spring semester. In this rite of passage, students wear hats with strings, and for each accomplishment officially sanctioned by their local "*russ* committee," attach a "*russ* knot." Challenges include spending a night in a tree (attach a stick from the tree to their hat), crawling through a supermarket while barking and biting customers' legs (attach a dog biscuit), and asking random people in a mall if the students can borrow a condom (attach the condom). Mixed in with this list of uncomfortable and embarrassing behaviors is a seemingly simple one: go for a swim before May 1. It doesn't sound like a behavior that challenges the ability to withstand pain until you remember what country it is that celebrates the *russefeiring*.

Although the content of these rituals from various cultures is strikingly different, the same elements emerge again and again. The element of physicality is omnipresent—we're reciting and climbing and crawling our way to adulthood. Those physical feats often double as tests of bravery (whether it's enduring bullet ants or asking a stranger for a condom) and independence (reciting a dense passage from a sacred text before a crowd; spending unsupervised time away from home . . . in a tree). The two elements reinforce each other to make a child feel ready to take the next step, move into the next phase of life, and then go out there and do it.

But rites of passage are present in transitions far beyond the change from childhood to adulthood. The ancient Sanskrit word *samskara* connotes preparing, putting together, and making perfect. In Hinduism, *samskara* also refers to rites of passage that cover every transition in our lives, from the moment our parents contemplate conceiving us to well after our lives end. There is Garbhadhana (intent to have a child); Pumsavana (nurturing the fetus); Simantonnayana (parting hair); Jatakarman (childbirth); Namakarana (naming the baby)—and on and on, through the baby's first outing, the baby's first solid food, the baby's first haircut, the baby's earlobe piercing. And these only get us through early childhood; the *Gautama Dharmasutra* (dated to 600–200 BCE) lists forty rights of passage in total.

We rely on rites of passage at each major transition in our lives. When graduating from college, we don a cap and gown and collect our diploma. When we get married, we dress up, walk the aisle, and deliver our vows. When we retire, we might be toasted or roasted or sent on an all-expenses-paid cruise around the world. Whoever we were before, we are now someone else: an adult, a graduate, a spouse, a retiree. These ritualistic ceremonies mark the occasion, signifying that this series of actions provides a bridge from our past to our future, helping us to see ourselves anew.

The "I" in Ritual

Think back to how you felt at a time when you were shifting from one identity to another: leaving home for the first time; becoming a "husband" or "wife" or "parent"; changing from one job to another in a different field.

What springs most immediately to mind for me is an academic meeting when it seemed as though all were present, yet somehow the meeting wasn't starting. The minutes just kept dragging on, making me increasingly uneasy—what was happening, or, maybe better, not happening? Until I realized that I was the oldest person in the room, and that everyone else was waiting on me to kick things off. Suddenly I was expected to be the wise elder; my newcomer upstart phase had run its course.

My cluelessness was due partly to the fact that no ritual had (yet) occurred to confer this status on me—I hadn't yet been granted tenure, when the entire faculty votes to let you join the club (at Harvard Business School, you even get an honorary Harvard degree). When you're tenured and the other folks aren't, it's clear who starts the meeting. I was caught in what the Scottish anthropologist Victor Turner called the "betwixt and between" period, the liminal space between two identities at work—a junior peon and a senior guru—and I didn't know how to act. Rituals play a crucial, and uniquely significant, role in these in-between moments in our lives—moving us from one identity to the next. In that particular instance, without a ritual to orient me, I felt lost.

When I received tenure, my actual job didn't change that much: I taught the same number of classes, published the same number of academic papers, procrastinated by watching the Red Sox for the same amount of time. But I began to see myself, my identity, differently. I was now a standard-bearer for the institution, someone others looked to as having knowledge and expertise. It had gone from being a school I worked at, to *my* school—to part of my identity.

Such moments show the tight coupling of rituals and "identity work." Consider how this type of work plays a role in an iconic transition of identity and becoming. Cadets in Russia's cosmonaut program have to survive years of intense, often grueling, training necessary to withstand the physical and psychological strain of space travel. When they are finally ready to make the transition from space cadets to real astronauts at Russia's Baikonur Cosmodrome in Kazakhstan, they follow a ritual with three steps before they blast off for outer space. The night before launch, they watch the 1969 Russian movie *White Sun of the Desert*. The day of the launch, they drink champagne and sign their hotel room doors. Finally, on the drive to the launchpad, all members of the crew leave the bus and pee on the left back wheel.

Some of this prelaunch initiation rite pays homage to the pioneering Russian cosmonaut Yuri Gagarin, who was the first to christen the back left bus tire. Like other preperformance rituals, this ritual is also designed to deliver the psychological benefit of calm. More than anything else, the ritual illustrates the importance of identity in moving from one phase of life to another. Signing a door is a literal way of leaving our mark, and peeing on someone else's property is another. Animals enthusiastically mark their territory this way, too. For the cosmonauts, these marks confirm the transition from trainee to full professional and signal their readiness for departure.

The rituals that are most effective in helping us transition from one identity to the next are often those that give us a marker, a set of legible actions we can feel ownership over. We can see this dynamic in the endowment effect and our research on the IKEA effect discussed in chapter 2. I love the mug because it's mine, and if I made that mug myself, my sense of identification and ownership only increases. As with mugs, so too with rituals: The rites of passage that we create ourselves provide us with immense value. They give us ownership, agency, and a way of making our mark on the world around us. Our ritual signatures are one of the ways we express our identities, our values, ourselves.

A New You

The power of rituals to help us mark who we are, and whom we want to become, explains why we call on them at key turning points throughout our lives—when we become adults, life partners, parents, widows. But there are also gaps. Many important turning points fall outside the purview of the "traditional" rites of passage. Here our ability to craft entirely novel rituals becomes most important.

In the early 1990s, sociologists Nissan Rubin, Carmella Shmilovitz, and Meira Weiss interviewed thirty-six obese women who had decided to undergo the then relatively novel gastric bypass surgery, in which surgeons reduce the stomach to the size of an egg in an effort to engineer weight loss. How did these women respond to this potentially identity-changing surgery? Some women referred to their "last meal"—a deliberate and darkly humorous reference to people awaiting execution. Some women threw out all of their clothes to start fresh; other women kept their old clothes as a reminder of who they had been. These last two approaches may seem contradictory, yet both mark a symbolic boundary between old and new, past and present. Drawing that boundary with these "personal definitional rites" helped the women to embrace their new selves.

Gender-transition rituals perform similar work. As a person of faith, Elin Stillingen felt it deeply important that her name change be recognized by the Norwegian church when she legally changed it, along with her gender, in 2020. She held a name-changing ceremony, led by Pastor Stein Ovesen, at the nearly one-thousand-year-old Hoff Church in Lena, Norway—a striking example of mixing aspects of legacy rituals and novel rituals for an entirely new purpose. The following day, Stillingen wrote that her naming ceremony "was like coming home, and Jesus was there." Ceremonies such as this also underscore why deadnaming—when someone uses the birth name of a transgender person as a way of denying the person's identity—can be so profoundly hurtful. Deadnaming conveys that a transition that is deeply meaningful to the person means nothing to you.

Many people undergoing gender transition borrow from existing rituals in crafting their own. For example, Rebecca from Newton, Massachusetts, asked her rabbi to perform a traditional funeral for her male self on the first anniversary of her life as a woman. Rabbi Medwin instead suggested that Rebecca affirm her womanhood with the practice of mikvah, a bath typically used as a purification ritual. During the ceremony, "Rebecca dipped below the surface of the water three times, envisioned herself as a Jewish woman, and let go of her male self."

Across cultures and across time, people report feeling different, changed, and transformed after undergoing rites of passage. Sometimes the initiation is a combination of preexisting and novel rituals, and other times, it is a traditional ritual performed at an untraditional time. Consider the practice of holding a second bar mitzvah. Mark Koller from Mount Kisco, New York, was a captive in a Ukrainian labor camp on the day of his bar mitzvah: April 23, 1943. He felt for decades that he'd missed out. So, in his eighties, after a life spent journeying from a labor camp to Israel to the United States, he arranged a second bar mitzvah—which he celebrated at age eighty-three. His rabbi wholeheartedly supported this decision with help from the Torah: an average life span is around seventy years so an additional thirteen years warrants a second celebration. The reading given to Koller by his rabbi was Ezekiel's vision of lifeless skeletons returning to life—which, Koller said, "felt like *bashert*"—the Hebrew word for "destiny." The whole day, he told the Jewish publication *Forward*, "was a dream come true. It made me feel like I was meant to stay here and have this experience. It was a symbol that I made it. It's called a second bar mitzvah, but for me it was the first."

Much simpler rituals can elicit similarly powerful feelings of growth, independence, and maturity. Initiations into using makeup are a common element in coming-of-age rites across cultures. In an ethnographic study of the makeup habits of teenaged girls in France, the identity work performed by cosmetics is striking. "When I was younger, when my mother refused to let me put on makeup," a seventeen-year-old told the ethnographer, "I put makeup on to annoy her and to show her that I am no longer a child." Another seventeen-year-old, Emeline, summarized the effect of wearing makeup: "I feel like a woman." More than amplifying beauty, the lipstick, mascara, eyeliner, and other assorted products make it possible to cross the uncertain threshold from girl to woman. Sociologist Sara Lawrence-Lightfoot, in her study of endings and exits, notes, "The ability to exit . . . is the ability to see yourself, to give yourself a break, to make yourself a new life."

Much like Max Weber lamenting the loss of ritual and tradition at the turn of the twentieth century, our current cultural commentators have suggested that young people lack meaningful rites of passage to guide them from childhood into adulthood. Suzanne Garfinkle-Crowell, a psychiatrist to young adults in New York City, wrote in an op-ed in the *New York Times* observing that teenagers suffer for many reasons, one of which is "being fragile and in formation—a human construction site." Without rituals, do all these human construction sites remain structurally unsound well into adulthood? Some psychologists are investigating this possibility by studying the increasing phenomenon of "extended adolescence"—children who remain emotionally and financially dependent on their parents long into their twenties. These adolescents are caught in the betwixt and between—stranded between two worlds. Perhaps they have not found a meaningful ritual to mark a shift in identity. Or perhaps the ritual remains incomplete: there is no graduation ceremony for the child who stays in college for six or seven years; nor is there an identity shift to independent living for the young adults who still sleep in their childhood bedrooms.

This need for completion and closure is an important element of many of the rituals I have studied across cultures. It is the basis of an additional study in my investigation of the IKEA effect. In this study, we asked people to build boring IKEA boxes again, but with new constraints. We allowed some people to finish building the box. Others were made to stop halfway through. Those in the latter group weren't willing to pay as much for the box—even though they could have finished it right after purchasing it. Incompletion made the ugly box remain just a box, while completion, only a few more steps, transformed it into something more valuable: *my* box.

So it is with ritual, too, though the stakes are usually much higher. As ritual scholar Ronald Grimes puts it, "The primary work of a rite of passage is to ensure that we attend to such events fully, which is to say, spiritually, psychologically and socially. Unattended, a major life passage can become a yawning abyss, draining off psychic energy, engendering social confusion, and twisting the course of the life that follows it. Unattended passages become spiritual sinkholes around which hungry ghosts, those greedy personifications of unfinished business, hover."

In rites of passage, the failure to complete means that the passage hasn't happened—and so the destination hasn't been reached, either. When Barack Obama was sworn in as president in 2009, Chief Justice John Roberts accidentally switched the placement of a single word. The difference was between "I will execute the Office of President of the United States *faithfully*" (Roberts) and "I will *faithfully* execute the Office of President of the United States" (the Constitution). No big deal, right? The meaning is clearly the same, and even the words are the same. But something was off about the ceremony—and interrupted the transition. So, the following day, they went back and enacted the oath down to the letter. (In 2013, they decided to practice the day before.)

Arnold van Gennep—the scholar who coined the term *rites of passage*—is generally described as a "Dutch–German-French" ethnographer, an amalgam of identities that may point to why he was so interested in the space between identities—the liminal betwixt-and-between space he called the *marge*. He described publishing *Les rites de passage* as a rite of passage in itself, "a kind of inner illumination that suddenly dispelled a sort of darkness in which I had been floundering for almost ten years."

Ritual can be a light that leads us out of that moment (or decade) of darkness. Rites of passage transform us as people, helping us with a deeper, more permanent need—the need to become someone, or something, else. We mark for ourselves, and to the rest of the world, who we truly are.

Part 3

Rituals and Relationships

Chapter 8

How to Stay in Sync

Why Rituals Help Relationships Flourish

For as long as I can remember, I've woken up at six thirty every day to make Shelly coffee. Splash of milk, two sugars. I would make it and bring it to her in bed. She says that her day doesn't even start until she's got caffeine in her veins.

And then one day, I woke up, six thirty like always, and I made myself one. I just didn't feel like making Shelly one.

And the worst part is she didn't even notice.

We stopped noticing each other, Jack. We stopped trying to make each other happy. When we realized that, we knew it was over.

In this scene from the first season of the TV show *This Is Us*, Miguel is attempting to explain the dissolution of his marriage to a friend. He offers an evocative example of an otherwise-mundane act—making coffee—that had become his marriage's signature ritual. The ritual was so meaningful for the couple that its demise also signaled the demise of the entire marriage.

Miguel's story about the end of his morning coffee ritual is poignant precisely because it illustrates how both partners, in losing their dedication to their daily ritual, have also lost their dedication to each other.

What similar rituals do we share with our partners in everyday life? What are the surprising, silly, seemingly nonsensical actions we perform—over and over—to elicit feelings of affection, admiration, or attraction? In the many years I've been studying rituals, I've been listening to people recount their romantic rituals in casual conversation. These stories are the emotional contours of our everyday expressions of devotion, wonder, delight, and appreciation for one another:

On the first Sunday of every month, my husband and I do a sunrise hike. We choose a spot somewhere within a few hours of our house in San Francisco, and we set out when it's still dark. We've been doing this for seven years now, so we both know exactly what we need to bring: I get up and brew the coffee and pour it in our old camping thermos, he makes the peanut-butter-and-jelly sandwiches and puts the Fig Newtons in the plastic Ziplocs. We put everything in the same backpacks we used in college when we met as biology lab partners.

Every Saturday, we make it a point to get to the empanada food truck near our apartment as soon as they open for lunch. Sometimes I eat too much breakfast and she starts poking me because I won't be hungry for our favorite order. We always get the pork carnitas, and then we each get our own Orange Crush in the glass bottles. Once we tried to share a bottle and that was a disaster.

The first time we met, we were at a party in our friend's garage and a ladybug landed in his drink. I tried to get it out for him, and the drink spilled all over him and then we both started laughing. That was over twenty years ago, but it's how this whole ladybug thing started. Whenever we see a ladybug, we always text or call each other. Then he was traveling for work a few years ago and he saw this cheap plastic ladybug figurine in the airport store, so he brought it home and hid it in my toothbrush cup. We never talk about it—this weird little ladybug game. We just surprise each other with it every few weeks. I don't know how to explain it, but we both get so much out of it. It's probably the most romantic thing we do.

Sunrise hikes, Fig Newtons, pork empanadas, and plastic ladybugs: nothing about this disparate collection of actions and objects, all culled from the detritus of our everyday lives, would suggest an epic romance or the sizzle of seduction. Despite what the cultural clichés around us suggest—most of them mass-produced by commercial and corporate entities—rituals between romantic partners often have less to do with champagne, red roses, and violins and more to do with deeply personal gestures that catalyze and sustain an intimate and exclusive human connection. Just as Ann Swidler demonstrates in the interviews that inform her book *Talk of Love*, the culture of romance is a repertoire, and we, as players, get to decide the tenor, cadence, and rhythm that suits our connections best. For some couples, a cold Orange Crush in a glass bottle is the most seductive bubbly available. For others, a plastic ladybug is more romantic than lingerie.

If rituals can affect our outcomes as individuals, how do they feature in relationships and romance? Can these random sets of physical
actions that no other couple has ever performed before animate our
most important relationships with something more—more happiness,
more connection, more pleasure?

In a project led by my colleague Ximena Garcia-Rada, we set out
to answer these questions by investigating relationship rituals. Garcia-
Rada, an alumna of NerdLab who explored people's hatred of parents
who use the SNOO, brought a unique perspective. She asked couples
what they would do if only one of them was offered an upgrade to first
class on a flight. Would they take advantage of the upgrade and sit
apart or forgo luxury for togetherness? If you're asking yourself this
same question, note that staying seated together in 18a and 18b is a
pretty good indicator of how close you feel emotionally.

Across all our surveys, between 60 percent and 75 percent of people in relationships report having a relationship ritual. When we ask
people about rituals in their current relationship versus their past relationships, they are far more likely to report having a ritual with their
current partner. This may be selective memory ("I never shared anything important with that terrible person"), but it may also be evidence
that rituals are associated with relationship satisfaction, and relationship staying power, too.

Some couples in our surveys reported legacy rituals with long traditions, many of which were tied to religious practices. For example:
"We pray before I leave to work every day." "We go to church at least
every other week." Some of the rituals were highly practical, imbuing
mundane actions with a deeper and richer meaning: "We do house-
cleaning chores together and always at the same time" or "We make
sure we go to the grocery store together, every Sunday at nine a.m."
Many rituals centered on affection and intimacy: "We snuggle together
in bed, watch films together, then we make love"; and many were quite

bespoke, such as the utterly endearing "When my partner and I eat dinner, we always clink our silverware together."

Individuals often use rituals to enhance their savoring of food and drink, so it's no surprise that a substantial portion of relationship rituals involved date nights—food, drink, and the two partners finding some special time together, such as "We drink wine and have Chinese food every Friday night when the kids go to bed" or "Every Friday night we make popcorn and watch a movie together." Research by psychologists Kaitlin Woolley and Ayelet Fischbach shows that commensality—the simple act of sharing a plate when eating—leads people to feel closer. Conversely, when people are not able to eat the same meal—due to a food allergy, for example—it increases feelings of social isolation.

Cataloging relationship rituals was just the start. We designed our research to learn as much as we could about their logic—which aspects of relationships they influenced and how. We asked people to tell us not just about their particular relationship rituals, but about the quality of their relationship. For example, we presented them with a series of prompts assessing how much they agreed with such statements as "I feel satisfied with our relationship."

No single ritual can elevate us into relationship nirvana. But our surveys showed that people who reported having rituals also reported being 5 to 10 percent more satisfied with their relationships. Rituals, as discussed in Part One, function as emotion generators in our lives. That means that the right romantic ritual—appropriate for the particular people, time, and space—can be one catalyst for feelings of love.

One couple we surveyed had started taking "awe walks" together. On weekend mornings, they both rise right before sunrise and choose a place to walk in the neighborhood that brings them joy and wonder. "Lately our awe walks have focused on walking past a nest of baby birds we discovered about a half mile away. We go and check in on the nest and watch to see if the eggs are hatching. This slow and simple practice has given us an unexpected connection to the nature all around us. When the birds all hatch and fly off, we'll look for another small corner of the world. It's surprisingly romantic to directly observe the same thing as a couple."

We also found that couples with rituals expressed a greater sense of gratitude for their partner. These benefits held whether the couple had been together for a short or a long time. That is, rituals don't take years to develop. Happier couples seem to develop them both early and late in their relationship.

Another indicator of the emotional power of relationship rituals is how we feel when we're deprived of them. In a three-week study of forty-two couples who were temporarily separated—for example, when one partner needed to travel for work—researchers found that both parties felt the loss. Not being able to practice their little bedtime rituals together caused partners to have a harder time falling asleep and staying asleep. When the researchers examined saliva samples tracking cortisol—shown to be elevated when animals are isolated— the levels were elevated in the separated partners as well.

The Price of Enchantment

Arlie Russell Hochschild, a sociologist at UC Berkeley, has written extensively about class, capitalism, and the bonds that hold us together. Among the subjects that fascinate her are the boundaries between relationships that are genuine and caring and those that are cold and transactional. In one exercise, she presented students in her class on the sociology of family with the following personal ad:

I'm a mild-mannered millionaire businessman, intelligent, traveled, but shy, who is new to the area, and extremely inundated with invitations to parties, gatherings and social events. I'm looking to find a "personal assistant," of sorts. The job description would include, but not be limited to:

1. Being hostess to parties at my home ($40/hour)
2. Providing me with a soothing and sensual massage ($140/hour)
3. Coming to certain social events with me ($40/hour)
4. Traveling with me ($300 per day + all travel expenses)
5. Managing some of my home affairs (utilities, bill-paying, etc., $30/hour)

You must be between 22 and 32, in shape, good-looking, articulate, sensual, attentive, bright and able to keep confidences. I don't expect more than 3 to 4 events a month, and up to 10 hours a week on massage, chores and other miscellaneous items, at the most. You must be unmarried, unattached, or have a very understanding partner!

As one young woman in Hochschild's class commented, the ad essentially makes a mockery of love: "The beautiful intertwinement of loving, caring, spiritually connected partners . . . is reduced to mechanized, emotionless labor for hire."

My colleagues and I have seen similar consequences when relationships are reduced to transactions. Tami Kim (another alumna of NerdLab), Ting Zhang, and I asked people in romantic relationships questions about their partner's tendency to "track who paid for what when we go out for dinner or entertainment" and "notice when I'm late down to the last minute." People with petty partners were less happy. Why? Tracking dollars and cents is what we expect from banks, not from our loved ones. We saw, just as Hochschild did, that people wanted to see their relationships as something more than a series of transactions, an ongoing tally of debits and credits.

Instead, Hochschild writes, we want our relationships to feel *something more*. "For a couple to feel their relationship is enchanted, they must feel moved to imbue the world around them with a sense of magic. . . . In an enchanted relationship, not only the relationship but the whole world feels magical."

But what is this magic, and how do we generate it in a relationship?

In recent years, researchers have sought to quantify this sense of relationship magic. Psychologist Maya Rossignac-Milon and her colleagues have done so via a psychological concept they refer to as "shared reality." Shared reality does not imply sharing beliefs, as when we vote for the same candidate or belong to the same religious group or root for the same soccer team. It's perceiving the world in the same way as another person—finding the same joke funny, say, or processing events with the same thoughts and feelings. These researchers measure the phenomenon by asking couples a series of questions about their relationship. Think of your own partners (current and past) as you read these:

We frequently think of things at the exact same time.
Events feel more real when we experience them together.
We often anticipate what the other is about to say.
We often feel like we have created our own reality.

Couples who agree with these statements have a strong sense of shared reality and—unsurprisingly—a high level of relationship satisfaction.

Drew Magary, one of my favorite sports columnists, captures the concept of shared reality perfectly. He writes that all couples "have their own weird cinematic universe"—telling us that he and his wife "say 'congratumalations' instead of 'congratulations,' as a recurring gag. Why? I have no idea. You're your own culture as a duo, so you naturally develop your own rituals and vernacular. I think that's healthy."

Novelist Norman Rush put it another way: "A couple's private language can develop in peculiar ways that look ordinary to the couple, but very strange to any outsider."

Now ask yourself this: Have you ever felt that you and your partner had, in some sense, merged minds—such as when you exchange a shared glance across a room, and you each know just what the other is thinking? Your answer options are "yes," "no," or "I have no idea what you mean by that." (About 10 percent of people report having no idea.) Couples with a high sense of shared reality have these moments—when we feel that our partner understands us so fully that we lose our sense of self, even for a moment, and experience the magic of merging with another person.

Now consider this example from one of the art world's most magical—and decidedly unusual—romances.

In the winter of 1975, a young performance artist who still lived with her mother in Serbia received a letter in the mailbox inviting her to perform at a well-funded gallery space in the Netherlands. The invitation arrived along with a plane ticket to Amsterdam. When the artist disembarked from the plane at the Dutch airport, the gallery owner was waiting to meet her along with a German artist, Frank Uwe Laysiepen. From the moment the two artists encountered each other, they both felt a sensation of the uncanny, as if they were two parts of the same self now, at long last, reuniting. Not only were they both pale and sinewy and about the same height, they also both wore their dark and flowing hair tied in back with a chopstick. Like twins reunited in a Shakespearean comedy, both artists experienced a shiver of recognition: *You.*

Later that day, after they had spent the afternoon together touring Amsterdam, the Serbian artist revealed that her birthday was November 30. The German artist brought out his datebook and showed her that the page for November 30 had been torn out. This was his birthday, too, he told her. Every year, he tore the date of November 30 out of his datebook to honor his day. When she saw this ripped page in his calendar, the outside world ceased to exist.

I just stared at his little book. Because I hated my birthday so much, I would always rip that page out of my datebook. Now I took it out of my pocket diary and opened it. The same page was torn out. "Me too," I said.

These two young artists—the performance artists better known today as Ulay and Marina Abramović—sat in that restaurant in Amsterdam holding out their star-crossed datebooks to one another under a powerful trance. They were suddenly living in a universe consisting of only two people. As Abramović remembers it, they went back to Ulay's apartment and stayed in bed without leaving for the next ten days. In the decade that followed, they created all of their performance pieces together—whether connecting themselves with one single hair braid and sitting in submission to each other's egos for seventeen hours straight or holding an arrow pointed straight at Abramović's heart and balancing it perfectly between their two bodies such that even one movement or slip by either of them would have instantly killed her. Every work they created together was an attempt to explore—and sometimes explode—their cosmic connection and dependence on each other. Now that they had finally found each other, they intended to do the artful work of creating a third self—neither male nor female but whole, new, and united.

This kind of shared reality might seem as if it only exists in the lives of our most eccentric and dramatic artists, performers, and poets. Yet, though few of us can claim a life-threatening arrow held against our chest as a relationship ritual, most of us have experienced the decidedly more quotidian and often uncanny pleasures of a shared reality with a life partner.

What role do rituals play in these kinds of relationship experiences?

The Four Lessons of Relationship Rituals

LESSON I: Rituals Wake Up Our Experience of Commitment

Most of us think of weddings, marriage, and moving in together as the quintessential commitment rituals, but we perform smaller acts of commitment from the moment we first consider sharing a life with another person. Just as we are assessing—either overtly or in more subtle ways—our own capacity to commit to one person, we are also gathering evidence of our partner's level of commitment to us through this partner's repeated and often most ordinary actions: Does the partner pick us up at the airport or make a point of applying sunscreen to the middle of our back? Does the partner bring us our favorite doughnut—the one with chocolate sprinkles—when out for the partner's own morning treat?

There are also many more unconventional ways to carve out a meaningful life with another person. The iconic French intellectuals and existentialists Simone de Beauvoir and Jean-Paul Sartre created an utterly unique ritual, and only for them. After discovering each other in

1929 through mutual friends at the Sorbonne in Paris, the two became romantic partners, close readers of each other's work, and trusted confidants, engaged in a conversation that only ended with Sartre's death in 1980. It was impossible for one to think a thought without running it past the other, or at least imagining what the other might say. Yet, when it came to conventional marriage—a bourgeois contract of monogamy and, for Beauvoir, subservience—they both recoiled. Instead, they gathered in the Tuileries, a garden and palace alongside the Seine in Paris, and conducted their own private ceremony on a stone bench. They committed to signing a contract. They would be together for two years and then reassess whether they wanted to continue. Instead of "till death do us part," two of France's most vociferous advocates for existential freedom could only authentically commit to "till two years do us part." When the two years passed by in a haze of caffeine, cigarettes, and copious handwritten pages—letters, plays, philosophical treatises, novels—they continued with their philosophical pact committing to each other as their primary and essential relationship and allowing for any contingent relationships that emerged along the way.

Historians and biographers have created an entire branch of scholarship devoted to determining who was really running the show in this unconventional relationship. To judge from afar and wonder at the strangeness of it, however, is to lose sight of two people coming together and creating their own commitment ritual from scratch. As we have seen with the IKEA effect, the amount of time and effort—not to mention emotion—they invested in its performance year after year gives us further insight into their lifelong bond. Their commitment ritual was their labor of (decidedly unconventional) love.

Our survey results revealed similar labors of love, albeit in more quotidian and conventional forms. The words people used to describe their rituals communicated reliability and repetition—phrases such as "every Friday night"; "together every Sunday at nine a.m."; "every day"; "every morning."

Whether you are performing a ritual that explodes conventions or a simpler set of actions that demonstrates you care, these rituals accrue meaning in a way that a signed legal wedding document or a mortgage never can or will. You might invest in rituals such as Chinese food in bed every Friday night, going for a polar bear plunge on New Year's Day, leaving the shower running and hot for your partner every morning, or giving each other an album from your favorite jazz instrumentalists for every single birthday; it matters much less what you do and much more that both of you do it regularly together.

LESSON 2: Relationship Rituals Are Exclusive

Whether it is a snuggle every morning, a cup of coffee made just so, or Olivia Wilde's "special salad dressing"—originally whipped up for her ex, Jason Sudeikis, and then audaciously served to new beau, Harry Styles—relationship rituals are *exclusive*. People are often furious when they discover that a ritual they thought was unique to their relationship is being practiced in a new relationship. "She has a special salad dressing she makes for us," Sudeikis supposedly told his children's nanny in a fit of emotion, "and she's taken it to have it with *him* now."

Exclusivity in relationships is often considered nonnegotiable, but why is it that exclusivity in ritual is required as well? Research confirms that we are sensitive to relationship rituals we perceive as unique. In a study by Lalin Anik and Ryan Hauser examining gift-giving rituals, people indicated which of two mugs they would prefer to receive from their partner—Style A or Style B—and were told that Style A "is made from more durable ceramic and got slightly better reviews online." In general, and not surprisingly, people preferred Style A, except when they learned that their partner had already given Style A as a gift to someone else. In that case, they gave up quality and chose the mug that signaled relationship exclusivity: Style B.

This means that we want our partners to be committed not just to *a* relationship ritual, but *our* relationship ritual. Why is that? For the same reason we want our partners to be committed not just to *a* relationship but to *our* relationship. Rituals are one way that we make our mark on the world, together; our joint ritual signature.

LESSON 3: Rituals—Not Routines—Bring the Magic

Consider a tale of two weekends: In the first household, a married couple named Tim and Seth are setting out to do what they do every Saturday morning. Tim gets the bags for the farmers market down from the closet while Seth makes their tea and lets it steep. Tim feeds the dog and takes him out while Seth quickly unloads the dishwasher. At nine o'clock, they each take their favorite travel mugs filled with tea—milk for Tim and sugar for Seth—and set out to get food for dinner from the market down the street. Both of them look forward all week to this ritual. Saturday morning—walking to the market, looking at the fresh fruits and vegetables, talking to the butcher, discussing their dinner plans—is their favorite part of the week.

In another household in another part of the country, Dave and Angie wake up and set out to complete their Saturday tasks. Dave gets the grocery bags ready while Angie makes them both fresh coffee. Dave quickly runs the garbage out and Angie feeds the cats. Then it's nine o'clock and time to set out. They grab the bags and their coffee mugs filled to the brim for the ride. They both sigh before taking a big gulp— they need it. Trudging to the grocery store every Saturday morning is a dreary chore they both dislike. From the mindless repetition of the grocery list, to waiting in the long lines to check out, to the arduous loading and unloading of all the food from the bags. When the chore is finally finished, they both feel relieved and part ways to enjoy what's left of the day.

The difference between these two households has nothing to do with their actions: they both plan to spend time shopping for food for the week. For the first couple, it is the highlight of the week, and for the second, it is an errand that is annoying and even dreaded. The difference is that the first couple feels the action is symbolic of their love, while the second feels it is merely routine, a habit not a ritual.

Human beings are regulated by an emotional thermostat; regardless of circumstances, we tend to revert to our happiness homeostasis. After the initial highs of relational milestones—new love, a wedding or commitment ceremony, buying a home—our happiness stabilizes and we no longer feel so ecstatic. This phenomenon, referred to as *hedonic adaptation*, gives us some insight into why even the most compatible couples start to experience the relationship blues. Psychologists Kennon Sheldon and Sonja Lyubomirsky argue that, due to this hedonic adaptation, we stop noticing all the wonderful aspects of what was once fresh and captivating.

Here, intentionally distinguishing between routine and ritual can play a meaningful role. When we perform routines, we are getting things done: the *what*. If the house is dirty, then we need to clean it. Shared rituals have a deeper meaning attached to them: the *how*. Taking out the trash, eating food, or drinking coffee couldn't be more mundane, but how we engage in these activities together, the specific actions we take as a couple with a shared reality, can transform the mundane into symbols of our lasting love.

We set out to measure the difference by canvassing some four hundred people not only about their shared rituals, but also about their shared routines. We defined a routine as "an activity that you do together every so often, is repeated over time, and is something that you do because it is a habit or a task that needs to be completed." Our results for rituals may have simply indicated that couples who spend more time together were happier, regardless of what they were doing in that time. But when we asked about routines as well, we found that it wasn't that simple. The majority of our respondents reported having a relationship ritual (74 percent), and even more reported a relationship routine (81 percent). Relationship rituals were more likely to be things such as date nights, whereas routines centered on activities such as chores.

Just as we saw in our tale of two Saturdays, the rituals reported by some couples could easily have been routines for other couples—such as going to the grocery store or making coffee. What mattered was how the couples experienced the activities. When they saw these actions as symbolic of their love, the actions took on new importance, leading the ritual-prone couples to report greater levels of happiness and satisfaction.

We often seek out something unique and extraordinary when we're looking for romantic fulfillment, but it can actually be the ordinary daily rituals—and not the extraordinary ones—that matter in the long run. Ximena Garcia-Rada and Tami Kim conducted research showing that many couples believe that extraordinary experiences are better for the relationship than ordinary ones—they might plan a memorable wedding, for example, but have no daily, smaller-but-still-special rituals. For people in long-distance relationships, this means that when they do get a weekend together, they try to spend every minute doing something fascinating and unforgettable (think skydiving and impossible-to-get theater seats). But this focus solely on extraordinary adventures can come at the cost of the smaller activities that accrue meaning over time and give shape to our everyday lives. Even if they don't sound like the stuff of an epic romance, these experiences—such as shopping together and planning what you'll cook—can become ritualized, scaffolding and animating the "cinematic universe" that couples create together.

You don't necessarily need the excitement of helicopter rides or trips to the other side of the world. The most ordinary of rituals—a walk in the park or a glass of wine on the stoop—repeated weekly have the potential to enchant. The key to creating magic is to share the same spell book.

LESSON 4: You Say Ritual, I Say Routine

Just as one person's animating toothbrushing-and-showering ritual can be another's automated routine, not all couples agree that they even have a ritual—and that's cause for concern. We know that Miguel thought of making coffee for Shelly as a ritual, but she might only have seen this as a mere routine all along. Our final, most heartbreaking, insight about relationship rituals came when we realized that *consensus* was a critical factor.

In the final stage of our research, we asked each of the two people in more than one hundred romantic couples—people who were married, living together, and had been together for an average of twenty-eight years—to complete the same survey on their own, without talking to each other. This allowed us to compare each person's report to the partner's. We found that couples tended to agree with each other. If one member of a couple reported a ritual, the other tended to as well. But nearly 20 percent of couples diverged: one said that they had a ritual in common, and the other one said they did not. Date nights were a case in point. If one partner classified a date night as a ritual, the majority of the time the other partner would agree. But more than one-third of people whose partner claimed the couple had a date night ritual classified that same date night as a routine. That's a sad date to keep going on, again and again—one person seeing it as a ritual, symbolic of love, while the other is seeing it as habitual, mindlessly punching the clock.

We also asked these same hundred-plus romantic couples how sat-isfied they were with their relationship. Couples who agreed that they had a ritual were the happiest. But the couples who disagreed experi-enced no benefits at all from their one-sided ritual. Poignantly, they were no happier than the couples who agreed that their relationship had no rituals at all.

Rituals and Rough Spots

If relationship rituals offer couples emotional generators to affirm their shared reality and identity, rituals to end relationships—whether we call it breaking up, divorcing, or separating—provide opportunities for much-needed transitions. This is the betwixt and between we dis-cussed in our chapter on identity roles and shifts. Paul Simon, describ-ing the dissolution of his marriage to Carrie Fisher, sang, "You take two bodies and you twirl them into one . . . And they won't come undone." How can we craft new rituals to acknowledge that our reality—once shared—is now fragmented?

This is precisely where Ulay and Marina Abramović found them-selves in the spring of 1986, despite their cosmic connection and shared birthdays. They had just performed a show together at the Burnett Miller Gallery in Los Angeles. The show, for her, was symbolic of their love and their artistic vision. It represented what she describes in her memoir as "creating this third element we called *that self*—an energy not poisoned by ego, a melding of male and female that to me was the highest work of art." Ulay, on the other hand, felt their performance and the interactions with the spectators afterward were becoming rou-tine. The business and networking aspect of their art had become a habit he wasn't sure he wanted to cultivate. Whereas Abramović was

ready to embrace the life of a world-famous art star—with its requi-
site duties and attendant inconveniences—Ulay longed to live a more
itinerant and anarchist existence. Instead of attending celebrity parties
and art pavilions, he was eager to return to his nomadic life traveling
across Europe in a van.

"Oh, you know how to deal with people," he told Abramović while
she worked the room at the show's after-party. "I'm just going to have
a walk." During his lengthy absence, Abramović later found out that
Ulay was cheating on her with a beautiful young gallery assistant. It
was (another) tale as old as time.

How do two people who have spent more than a decade making
work about becoming inextricably linked find a way to call it off? The
artists did the most reasonable thing they could think of doing given
the circumstances: they devised their own unique ritual for breaking
up. They decided to take the better part of a year to walk the Great
Wall of China together—each starting from an opposite end of its
13,171 miles—and meet in the middle to say goodbye. The project—
initially called *The Lovers* and conceived of as a kind of wedding—had
turned, over years of waiting and broken trust, into a meditation on
their incompatibility and separation. On March 30, 1988, after close
to a decade of cutting through bureaucratic red tape, the artists were
finally granted permission to perform their walk. Abramović started
at the Bohai Sea, a part of the Yellow Sea, which sits between China
and Korea. Over months of trekking, she walked the more treacherous path through eastern China's elevations and along parts of the
path that had been destroyed to only shards of crumbling rock and
stone under Mao's Communist diktats. She and her guides had to
walk hours from the wall each night just to reach the villages where
they slept.

Ulay set out seven hundred miles to the west in the Gobi Desert.

While Abramović had the mountains to conquer, much of Ulay's journeys took him through hundreds of miles of desert dunes. Instructed
to lodge in the nearby villages and hostels, he characteristically broke
the rules and spent many of his nights sleeping under the stars on the
broken stones of the Great Wall. Both of them invested extreme effort
in putting their bodies in motion to prepare for the moment of meeting
again and severing all ties to each other.

After each walking for ninety days and covering around twelve and
a half miles a day, the artists reunited on a stone bridge in Shaanxi
Province. Ulay arrived first and sat down to wait. Abramović eventually approached toward the end of the day. They looked at each other
as they had once done so many years ago in that Amsterdam airport,
and they embraced. They then parted ways and did not speak again for
twenty-two years.

Colleen Leahy Johnson, an expert in the psychological impact of
divorce, uses the wonderful phrase "socially controlled civility" to describe how former couples can move past their acrimony by engaging
in patterned, symbolic ceremonies—that is, rituals—that help them
to keep their emotions in check. One divorcing couple chose to have
their dissolution ceremony in their church and created reverse vows:
"I return these rings which you gave me when we married, and in so
doing I release you from all marital responsibilities toward me. Will
you forgive me for any pain I have caused you?" The ceremony was
so moving that one attendee later had an epiphany: "Too often I see a
ritual as an ending to a process without realizing at the same time it is
a new beginning."

The philosopher and public intellectual Agnes Callard lives with
her ex-husband, Ben Callard, a fellow philosopher, as well as her former graduate student, now husband, Arnold Brooks, in one household. The three adults have shared domestic and caretaking duties

with their three children—two from her marriage with Callard and one from her current marriage with Brooks. Because she and her ex-husband are still close, the two of them celebrate their divorce every year with their own unique ritual. "Happy Divorciversary to us! This is a big one: #10," she wrote on her Twitter feed with a picture of her beaming next to Ben. They went out to dinner and savored the joys of growing old together—over a decade of successful divorcing is nothing to sneer at. "Remember kids, marriages come and go but divorce is forever so choose your exes wisely!," she quipped on social media.

The equanimity of the domestic situation of these three might be hard for many people to emulate, but luckily there's a ritual for less amicable former couples, too: the "annivorcery." An investment banker named Gina explained, "I've been divorced for three years, and each year I throw a big party to celebrate my separation. I make my ex look after the kids while I invite all my best single boyfriends and girl-friends."

The pomp and pageantry of love and commitment—whether that of a traditional wedding or a conventionally romantic night out with red roses and candles—looms large in our collective imagination. Yet our research revealed that the most meaningful rituals for couples are often idiosyncratic to them. These rituals make no sense to the outside eye but enable us to create a unique shared reality with just one other person. They are by and for a country comprising only two residents—a cowritten ritual signature.

Often after I give talks about my research on rituals, someone will come up to me and say something like "Your talk totally resonated with me because my [wife/husband/partner] has like a million rituals"—the implication being that this person has none. The person's partner often denies this and sometimes accuses the person of having all the rituals. Rather than focus on identifying which partner has more rituals, the best way to tend to relationships is to focus on identifying which rituals you share. If neither of you can come up with a ritual that you do together, try starting one. We all want to share a reality with the one we love.

Chapter 9

How to Survive the Holidays

Rituals for the Ups and Downs
of Kith and Kin

The following are three descriptions of three different cherished family rituals. Can you guess which holiday they are celebrating?

I grew up on a commune in British Columbia, so all of us celebrated together. The grown-ups took out their collection of sitars, and then some of them came out dressed in the costume of a snake made out of beautiful green and orange silk. There were several people forming the snake's slinking body, and one person crouched inside the snake's head making its tongue hiss. I was both excited but also scared by the snake. It danced around to the sitar music for what seemed like hours before it was our turn to each go up and take a present from the snake's mouth. I squeezed my eyes shut in fear, and then reached my hand into the snake's mouth. When I did, I pulled out a new baby doll sewn from old fabric and yarn. It was exactly what I had asked for.

As a Muslim American, it's my favorite holiday of the year. We always choose meat raised and harvested according to Muslim dietary guidelines. And, in my family, we invite everyone so it is always a chance to see aunts and uncles, cousins and their children. For us, the holiday is all about the verse, "Worship God, and be of those who give thanks" (Quran 39:66). I feel so blessed to have this sacred time for reflection and gratitude.

Our family is vegetarian so I use a beet and an egg decorated with flowers instead. For us, the evening and the readings are a chance to talk about social justice issues and what we, as a family, can do to address them. The kids are usually hungry after our vegetarian version of the traditional meal, so we always take them out to get a Playa Bowl at their favorite restaurant afterwards to fill up.

Would you have guessed that number one is Christmas (celebrated by a nontraditional Buddhist family), number two is Thanksgiving, and number three is Passover?

Holiday rituals are powerful emotional generators. How can we best use their power to conjure up the feelings of belongingness, cohesiveness, and trust that so many of us long for when we gather with family? What can we take—and leave—from our vast cultural tool kit to reinvent and reignite our relationships with kith and with kin? Today's more traditional family rituals are being repurposed and often completely reinvented to reflect our expanding definition of what makes a family and how we can commit to cherishing one. Rituals show us that sometimes a family is what you are given and that sometimes a family is what you choose.

Home for the Holidays

Holidays present a perfect opportunity for exploring the value of ritual. Though it's impossible to randomly assign people to different families for a few years and measure the effect, the scientist in me was determined to drill down on the consequences of these rituals as precisely as possible. Do happy families simply happen to have more rituals than unhappy families, or can rituals make a family happier? Tolstoy tells us that happy families are all alike; but each unhappy family is unhappy in its own way. What role might rituals play in generating these different emotions?

Övül Sezer from Cornell University and I teamed up to tackle these questions together. Sezer is both a behavioral scientist and a stand-up comedian. Like all funny people, Sezer draws on her family experiences as a key source of material, so I knew she would bring a compelling perspective to our project. As we surveyed families during different holidays while they enacted rituals with their kin, we had two questions in mind: Do rituals influence people's overall feelings about their family? Would rituals predict spikes in familial liking right away, on the day they were enacted?

Hundreds of Americans told us about how they spent major family holidays. Did they have any rituals, and if so, what were they? Did they enact rituals with their family or by themselves? How did they feel about their family as a whole, and how did they feel that day?

We started with Christmas, a widely celebrated holiday in the United States. More than 60 percent of the 140 people we surveyed reported celebrating Christmas and having at least one family ritual. Many of the rituals, 39 percent, were related to opening gifts, while 34 percent focused on the Christmas meal. These two categories thus accounted for nearly three-quarters of all Christmas rituals—whether it was ham and chicken wings and tons of desserts or alternating pro-tocols of age-based gift opening.

When we repeated the survey for New Year's, with a new sample of 152 people, we found fewer family rituals—only 37.5 percent of people reported one—and nearly 50 percent of rituals cited family dinner as the most central element with specific cocktails emerging as the ritual signature. Whether it was with Crown Royal with Canada Dry, Russian vodka with cranberry juice, or champagne served in Moscow-mule copper mugs, New Year's Eve celebrants were summoning up a spirit of conviviality through their rituals.

Despite the differences among the American holidays we stud-ied, the rituals we documented had predictable similarities. Food and drink were a constant, but the most important ingredient seemed to be the shared family signature: the *how* that was core to their identity. They were owning their experience of the holidays by enacting them in their particular way. Often it was as simple as "Our family always adds lemon zest to the cranberry sauce" or "I dye the eggs in the same porcelain bunny bowl my mother used as a child." But these simple actions mattered mightily and showed that we don't always need grand pageantry or bold statements to pronounce our familial bonds to the world and to ourselves. More often, everyday gestures and objects are central to each family culture.

We also asked people about the effect of these rituals. Did they gather with family to enact them, and if so, how did their rituals influ-ence how much they enjoyed that time with their family? From their responses we gleaned some key insights about the ritual effect in the midst of holiday highs and lows.

Holiday Rituals Are Logistics Management (Made Special)

At the most basic functional level of many of our family rituals, what is really happening? Logistics management. Holiday rituals coordinate us. With bigger groups, sometimes this can be as simple as "Kids sit there" or "We start eating at four forty-five p.m. EDT" or "Their side of the family always brings dessert." Rituals such as these also provide a helpful script for family members to avoid uncharted, dangerous familial waters.

In a 2020 study, Jeremy Frimer and Linda Skitka found that politically diverse Thanksgiving dinners were thirty-five to seventy minutes shorter than family meals where the group had uniform beliefs. Arranging family members so everyone remains civil is an art, and a mistake can have real costs. Columnist Michelle Slatalla notes how pure vitriol can be triggered by no more than two seats side by side at the table. "The seating arrangement is more challenging than the cooking," she lamented. Ritualized holiday actions can diffuse the tensions and keep everyone engaged in a comfortable activity. Simple but familiar actions such as chopping down the tree, baking the Christmas pies, carving the turkey, opening the wine, folding the napkins, and arranging the flowers offer up a welcome reprieve from conflict and provide everyone with a designated role to perform.

The emotions generated by these coordination rituals could be as simple as calmness or even relief. These low-arousal emotions leave us feeling less excited but also, quite likely, much more content. Psychotherapist Harriet Lerner, author of the bestselling book *The Dance of Anger*, argues that if anxiety is contagious—"intensity and reactivity only breed more of the same"—calm can be contagious, too. When many members of the family feel calm, chances are greater that this energy will spread to the rest of the group. Rituals that manage and coordinate even the most basic actions of sitting, standing, and eating can increase equilibrium in the midst of a large, chaotic, potentially combative group of people.

I'll Be Home for Ritual
(but Probably Not for Routine)

In the data from our surveys, one finding was clear: rituals can be the practices that call us home. People who reported that their family had at least one ritual that they enacted each year were more likely to make the trek back to be with their family on the appointed day. For Christmas, 96 percent of people—almost everyone—who told us that their family had a Christmas ritual spent that holiday with family, while around a third of those who reported no rituals chose to skip out on family time over the holiday. For New Year's, 90 percent of those with a family ritual got together with family, while more than half without a family ritual did not. In all the holidays we studied, members of families with rituals were also more likely to report that they enjoyed the day—more than families who gathered but without rituals. The benefits of ritual were evident even in families who told us they didn't like each other all that much. Holiday rituals made them feel just a little closer to those disliked family members—at least while they were enacting the ritual.

As with our research on relationships in romantic couples, we wanted to know whether families were enacting rituals that mattered to them or just going through the motions of a boring but familiar routine. Psychologist Barbara Fiese, director of the Family Resiliency Center at the University of Illinois at Urbana–Champaign, makes the distinction between family routines: "This is what needs to be done"—and family rituals: "This is who we are." For some families, the identity work is in an elevated approach to baking and cooking: "I come from a family of great cooks. I have to keep up the tradition and master Auntie's scallion pancake recipe. I can't let her down." While for others, the shared identity involves musical expression and singing: "In our family, it's not a holiday if we're not taking out the guitars and singing Dylan and playing late into the night around the firepit." Some families celebrate by sitting quietly and reading books together in the evening: "After dinner, we usually all sit together on the big sofas in the living room and we all snuggle up with our books. I like to put my feet in my mom's lap." And for some, it's about choosing a show to binge-watch together: "We start texting about which show we're going to watch together back in October. People get to throw out options, and the show with the most votes wins. Then we sit down on Christmas morning and just watch all day. No one is allowed to opt out or zone out on their phone. We have a rule: 'All eyeballs required.'"

The quality of connectedness—the link to a sense of a family identity—transforms these activities from routine into ritual. In her memoir and recipe collection *How to Celebrate Everything*, food writer Jenny Rosenstrach describes how even the simple walk with her kids to the school bus each morning contained potential for something more:

The school bus send-off transcended routine because it connected us to our community in a way that, I later realized, would be hard to replicate once there was no more bus to catch. Mostly, though, it connected us as a family. As harried as we felt, as chaotic as the workday ahead of us promised to be, we started off every morning together. From beginning to end, I'd estimate that the bus stop ritual lasted under eight minutes each day, but it was pretty much guaranteed that at least at one point during those eight minutes, a little hand would mindlessly reach up and latch on to mine. . . . That gesture alone put enough fuel in the happy tank to power an entire day at the office.

Rituals can't move mountains, but they can move us. If you are feeling far from your kith and kin—whether emotionally or logistically— the performance of a shared ritual with them has the potential to bring you back together.

Kinkeepers Keep It Together

Family rituals allow us to tell one another a story about our bonds: this is who we are and how our family will continue to be. Somewhat ironically, though, family cohesion is rarely a group endeavor. It is often the product of the work of just one or two people: the kinkeepers. Sociologist Carolyn Rosenthal at McMaster University describes these people as the ones who are the most responsible for keeping the family in touch with one another and for ensuring that the family rituals continue into the next generation. One fifty-two-year-old man noted how his family kinkeeper maintained everyone's connections: "She urges us to write to each other and she writes to all of us." A fifty-eight-year-old man described his kinkeeper's responsibility for organizing ritualized gatherings that kept the family together: "He has get-togethers for the family picnics and birthday parties."

The emotional labor of kinkeepers is essential to a family's identity work. Someone in the family needs to be the impresario, the carnival barker, the event planner, the master of ceremonies. Someone has to figure out the seating chart. Someone has to conjure up and plan the activities and events that create a shared sense of belonging and even fun. There is compelling evidence that kinkeepers are the glue that holds it all together. Families with kinkeepers are more likely to see extended-family members and more likely to gather for important celebrations. The siblings of kinkeepers also stay in closer contact with one another.

But kinkeeping is not a permanent position. In my experience, kinkeepers shift as roles within the family shift. When I was very young, Thanksgiving arrived to me fully formed, and my most fervent wish was to graduate from the kids table. When I was in my self-absorbed teens and twenties, I considered my willingness to travel home for Thanksgiving a deep sacrifice. But as I moved into my thirties and forties, and particularly when I became a father, it suddenly dawned on me that I was in charge of making sure the traditions and the lore got passed down. My desire to impart the richness of identity and legacy to my own daughter meant that I stepped into a kinkeeper role. The holiday wasn't arriving fully formed anymore. The curtain had been pulled back, and I realized that I'd better go out and learn how to carve that turkey.

As in most families, the rituals that emerged for my new family were crafted somewhat haphazardly from my wife's and my cultural tool kits. We adopted some holiday traditions from my family (multiple kinds of stuffing on Thanksgiving are a big deal), added some traditions from my wife's family (copious and precise hanging of lights at Christmas is key), and came up with some new ones all our own (putting candles in meat loaf and singing, "Happy meat loaf to you").

In one of our survey interviews reporting on holiday rituals, a mother shared the following:

Our son is a scientist. He used to concentrate on his theories. . . .
Now he seems to have become aware of a pattern in life and he

follows many of our ways again. He is close with his family and shares the family things like birthdays and holidays that he for a while thought unimportant. He is coming back to tradition.

This response resonated with me. Just as this particular mother's son "came back to tradition" after once feeling that it was incompatible with his identity as a scientist, I, too, stepped into the role of kinkeeper. For many of us, this happens because the arrival of a child shows us what we had and failed, until then, to value. But kinkeeping can also be thrust upon us after a painful loss. In a moving essay, writer Rembert Browne describes his first Thanksgiving after his mother's death: "My cousin Erin and I sat on my mother's couch—full, tired, shocked by a recent revelation. As I stared down 30 and she looked at her new baby, we both realized this would be our family to run one day. Looking at me, as we both looked out at our elders in the kitchen, she muttered: 'We need to learn how to make this food.'" Browne has the feeling that so many of us have experienced: How do we progress without forgetting the past? This is the question all kinkeepers seek to address.

Something Old and Something New: Legacy and DIY Rituals

In late 2018, the *Atlantic* magazine asked readers to send in their "Weird Holiday Traditions." Reader Nate Ransil responded:

My wife's grandfather said that Christmas was too good, and so there should be at least one thing you don't look forward to.

So he cooked a Christmas breakfast of eggs, bacon, toast, and orange juice, put it in a blender, and served it to his kids as a smoothie. My father-in-law heard this story about his father-in-law and thought it was hilarious, so he made it a tradition with my wife and her sisters. But instead of doing the same thing every year, certain family members come up with an idea with which to surprise everyone else. There is always a theme to it: It could be food from *The Grinch* (Who pudding, rare Who roast beast, triple-decker toadstool sandwiches with arsenic sauce, and of course banana with a greasy black peel) or Elf (spaghetti, crumbled Pop-Tarts, and maple syrup) or poop (cat box filled with Cocoa Krispies topped with plops of undercooked pumpkin-pie filling, refried beans served in diapers, etc.).

Nate's dispatch offers a highly entertaining example of how DIY rituals emerge and gain traction over time. Another family with a Scottish background insists on finding the right "first footer"—ensuring that the person who takes the first step into the house on New Year's morning is a tall, dark-haired, and brown-eyed man, carrying bread, whiskey, milk, and a lump of coal.

In these unique and novel combinations of action—idiosyncratic ritual signatures—families show themselves, and the world, who they are. As Nate puts it, "I bet nobody else in the world is eating the same thing we are right now."

Researchers have shown that 88 percent of people reported having a family ritual in their childhood, and 81 percent continued to enact that ritual with their own children. But 74 percent of people also layered a new ritual into the mix. These statistics show us not only the staying power of older family rituals, but also people's creativity and flexibility in adapting them into something new. Often these adaptations give rituals a patina of feeling both old and amazingly new—updated and enhanced to suit each generation's emotional needs.

One grandmother shared a ritual with a perfect blend of tradition and change. When she was a child, her family always baked pasties over the holidays, a traditional meat pie that her coal miner father and grandfather used to carry with them for sustenance during long workdays. She passed that ritual on to her daughter, who passed it on to her children. Over the generations, however, this heavy meat pie no longer felt appropriate for more modern sensibilities and diets. Instead of treating the meat pasties as an inviolable tradition, the youngest generation adapted and reconfigured the recipe. Today they sometimes use tofu and curry; other times they bake the pasties with sweet potatoes and spinach. One descendant married a man from Argentina, and their family's pasties have been transformed into empanadas. The crust always remains the same—a recipe written down on an old index card, photocopied several times, and now living on people's iPhones. Each of the generations makes the pasties with different fillings, shapes, and sizes, but the ritual remains intact, and the recipe for the crust maintains and honors the family culture.

The Family Table

Everyday family meals offer another opportunity for reinvention. In the United States, one in five family meals are now consumed in a car, and close to three-quarters are eaten outside the home. Fewer than 33 percent of American families eat together at an actual table more than two times a week.

An abundance of research over the past two decades has confirmed the power of reviving this ritual. In 2012, for example, a survey conducted by the National Center on Addiction and Substance

Abuse at Columbia University found that regular family dinners were linked to a decreased rate of substance abuse in teenagers and an increase in feelings of connectedness between adolescents and their parents. One study of ninety-three parents with a first-grader showed that the benefits of mealtime rituals are particularly pronounced for boosting relationships between fathers and daughters, family members who otherwise spend less time together. It's not a question of if for most families; it's more a question of how. Between sports schedules, after-school jobs, commutes, and school days and work meetings that run late, how can we make the family meal into a meaningful event?

Psychiatrist Anne Fishel has some ideas. Fishel directs the Family and Couples Therapy Program at Massachusetts General Hospital, where she saw a need for more guidance on making this meal happen. She started the Family Dinner Project to help families add a touch of a ritual back into their lives. The project is designed to transform family meals from habits to rituals; that is, from empty routines (this is what we do) to meaningful experiences that connect family and enrich the lives of children (this is who we are).

Fishel starts small. She recommends picking one meal, or even one snack time, when the family commits to being together—which often means poring through everyone's schedule to find that single thirty-minute window that works for all members. The key is to pick just one. Thinking that family dinners are all-important can be self-defeating if we focus on the impossibility of having dinner (or any meal) together every day. It's important to be realistic about the time you have.

It's also worth starting small on the food, too—while home-cooked, healthy meals are best for everyone, the stress of preparing an entire meal from scratch is another barrier to getting started. As in so many other areas of life, the great can be the enemy of the good. What Fishel has in mind is decidedly more playful and improvisational: think less

Sunday roast and more silly snack time when the family eats popcorn together on Tuesday evening. Whether it's "Surprise gift-wrapped snacks," "Panini madness (throw leftovers from the fridge on two slices of bread and pop them in the panini maker)," "Dinner on a stick (one parent we spoke with confirmed that everything tastes better on a stick)," or a "Carpet picnic (shake it up by bringing out the checkered tablecloth and picnic basket and serve simple sandwiches and snacks in a new context)," the family meal can come back to life when we throw convention aside.

In Fishel's vision, scripted, banal conversation topics such as "How was school today?" are banned. The Family Dinner Project turns that standard script on its head and transforms it into a Choose Your Own Adventure. Instead of conformity, Fishel encourages belonging by inviting members of the family to use conversational gambits that are designed to produce surprise, delight, and curiosity.

There are even questions specific to each age group, such as:

If you had superpowers, what would they be, and how would
    you use them to help people? (ages 2 to 7)
If you were principal of your school, would you change
    anything? What? (ages 8 to 13)
If you had one week, a car full of gas, a cooler full of food,
    and your two best friends, where would you go and what
    would you do? (ages 14 to . . . 100)

It's not that these particular questions are the magic key. It's that the family has committed to a time and space for one another, and that they're going off script and flying blind. Fishel is encouraging a family dinner where all members are invited to be themselves. Don't hold back in the name of pleasantries—conversational pablum that interferes with our most meaningful connections. Bring it all on.

——————

Family rituals gather us together, immersing us in the moment and bolstering our sense of identity as a family. But one of their most lasting benefits is the gift of memory. The settings for many of our memories of our families—the aunts and uncles, the cousins twice removed, and all the people we love who have left us—are often those moments when family was engaged together in ritual. At first, the rituals may feel like more effort, but the ones that work become labors of love. Their familiar structure paired with their ready adaptability gives us a shared repertoire—and a memory bank—we can draw from for the rest of our lives. Much more than occasions to see family, they're occasions to *be* family.

Chapter 10

How to Mourn

Coping with Loss

It's not something you get over
But it's something you get through.

—Willie Nelson

I n 1863, in New York City, the retailer Lord & Taylor was opening a new "mourning store" to meet the pressing demand from grieving widows all across the North during the scourge of the Civil War. On offer for the women and girls of the North were variations of black crepe grenadines, black balzerines—a lightweight cotton and wool blend—and black bareges, sheer and gauzelike. Given the scarcity of appropriate mourning clothes, women went to great lengths to procure them. Women were eager—desperate—to find the clothing that felt as if it would help with the hard work of mourning.

This work was near endless. It is the subject of Drew Gilpin Faust's study of the American Civil War, *This Republic of Suffering*. "The number of soldiers who died between 1861 and 1865, an estimated 620,000, is approximately equal to the total American fatalities in the

Revolution, the War of 1812, the Mexican War, the Spanish-American War, World War I, World War II, and the Korean War combined," Faust wrote. "The Civil War's rate of death, its incidence in comparison with the size of the American population, was six times that of World War II. A similar rate, about 2 percent, in the United States today would mean six million fatalities."

In the American South, where the death rate was even higher—18 percent of enlisted white men died in the Civil War—the ritual of mourning clothes for the grieving women provided a form of coping. According to the social rituals of the era, the earliest and most intense period of mourning required that women grieving husbands or brothers who died in battle wear only black. During a middle phase of mourning, women were permitted to incorporate lighter shades of gray; lavender could be added later, especially at collars and cuffs. Jewelry was frowned upon unless it included a picture of—or a lock of hair from—the deceased. Most interesting to me, the length of time each phase lasted depended on how close the mourner was to the deceased. Black, gray, lavender; each of these phases would be longer for the loss of a husband, or brother, than for the loss of a cousin, or uncle.

I was moved by Faust's account of these poignant nineteenth-century mourning rituals—and struck by two elements, in particular. First, anyone who has experienced grief knows that the pain can feel endless. As a scientist, I couldn't help but wonder if people looking down to see that they were wearing gray might help them feel that there was hope that their grief might one day diminish. Did these sartorial codes of conduct serve as cues, reassuring mourners that others had followed them in the past and made their way through their pain?

I was also struck by the extent to which these Civil War mourning rituals combined elements of old and new. The practice of wearing mourning clothes for a designated period of time was well established. The mourners Faust portrayed in her book were no doubt practicing other well-established mourning rituals—prayer, church, visiting grave sites. Such time-honored mourning rituals can send important signals to us when we enact them. Grief leaves mourners wondering not only how to cope but how long. A clear ritual with a long history—such as sitting shiva in Judaism—can signal that grief is not never-ending and that it will pass. That people have been enacting this same mourning ritual, sometimes for thousands of years, proves that they recovered from their grief—offering us hope that, should we enact the ritual, we will recover, too.

But these Civil War mourners had also improvised new secular practices, taking established rituals and—faced with a grim new reality, an unprecedented loss of life in battle—made them their own. Why lavender? Why one length of time and not another?

I was perplexed by these questions. In my previous life as a ritual skeptic, I had conceived of rituals as necessarily religious, rooted in sacred beliefs and often dating back to the beginning of recorded history. (In the first work of literature on record, the *Epic of Gilgamesh*, from 2100 BC, its protagonist repeatedly makes offerings of flour to the sun god, Shamash.) But no holy book, no world religion, mandates lavender. Cultures vary astonishingly on the colors of mourning garments— from white (Japan and certain Native American cultures) to black (in Western/American culture and Hindu tradition), to yellow in Eastern Europe, or purple in South America. Time and again, people faced with loss have turned to color and clothing, and they have also shown remarkable creativity and diversity in how they go about it.

Many mourning rituals are public facing and highly regimented. In 2016, social scientists Corina Sas and Alina Coman interviewed a group of people who bear witness to mourning—psychotherapists— and asked them to share examples of patients' rituals that they felt had been therapeutically beneficial. From these descriptions, the researchers drew out several recurring elements—starting with the role that rituals play in embedding mourners in community.

When mourning is social and visible, it allows us to honor our connections with those we have lost. In some cultures, this mourning is even externalized and made legible through the performance of designated mourners. Take the professional mourners in Mani, Greece, as an example. The women, called moirologists, are paid to arrive at funerals dressed in black with their heads covered so that only their eyes and mouths are visible. At a precisely designated time, they let out a primal howl. It is not a song nor is it a scream. They externalize the emotional experience of grief and perform it at the funeral. This performance—designed to elicit a catharsis—provides those in genuine pain with a bit of distance from their experience. They are allowed to be spectators in the theater of grief.

Professional mourners are common in China and India, and the idea is catching on in England, where families now hire actors to come to the funeral to perform for the grieving community. For some families, the gesture is simply to give the appearance of more attendees at the service, but for others, these professional mourners are akin to the moirologists. They are present to help the ritual function, both by performing sorrow and as active listeners for the real guests. As Owen Vaughan, a professional mourner in England, put it in an essay, "People have been gathering to do this for as long as there have been people. Share stories, cry, get closure. I help people do that. It's why I took the job."

If professional mourners help to externalize grief, other collective rites bring a grieving community closer—bonding groups more tightly when they need it most. When a Navy SEAL dies, his fellow SEALs follow a distinct protocol:

SEALs approach a grave site one by one, remove the gold-colored pin from the left breast of their dress uniforms and pound them into the coffin of a fallen comrade. The living mourn, with the primary symbol of their brotherhood missing, to be replaced only after the dead have been buried. The dead take their comrades' SEAL pins with them to the grave.

Military units such as the Navy SEALs are intimately familiar with death, but that doesn't make coping with it any easier. The ritual enacted by SEALs allows them to honor bonds of shared service and sacrifice, and to feel a clear kinship with fellow SEALs, even those they may never have met.

When organ donors are officially declared brain dead, their altruism is commemorated in a similar way. Many hospitals will perform an "honor walk":

The double doors of the surgical intensive care unit opened into a hallway crowded with dozens of hospital employees. A hospital bed emerged, and we all fell silent. . . . People in street clothes trailed close behind the bed, unsure of where to look. These were the parents of the young woman in the bed, the one we had all come to honor. . . . The clothing in the crowd reflected the different jobs we'd been pulled away from: There were white coats and ties, crumpled blue scrubs, bouffant surgical hats and expensive pinstripe suits.

"Something solemn, even sacred, happens in those fifteen minutes in the hallway," Tim Lahey, a doctor at the University of Vermont Medical Center, recounted. "We wait and talk with people from all professions and all walks of life. Together, we honor a great sacrifice. We give thanks. We hope to help a grieving family in a moment of fathomless loss."

The honor walk channels everyone's attention and places people in a shared reality—even if for just a moment.

Mourning rituals with prescribed clothing, actions, schedules, and specific food and drink are occasions for shared attention, a way of channeling our feelings for the person we've lost, together. They provide a time and place for us to immerse ourselves in remembrance, to gather for a common purpose, to honor loss. Mourning rituals also offer a useful script, both for us to follow in coping with our own grief, and for others to follow in helping us. If people are wearing black, it signals their emotional state, offering guidance about how to interact with them.

Depriving Death of Its Strangeness

The French historian Philippe Ariès refers to the twentieth century as the age of "Forbidden Death," tracing how the modern practice of shielding the dying from the knowledge that they are dying led their loved ones to begin suppressing their own emotional reactions as well. Often, our instincts are to avoid thoughts of death, to shelter people from the specter of loss, to forget as quickly as possible and move on. Nowhere is this more true than in the practice of "protecting" children from the death of their loved ones by keeping them home from the funeral and excluding them from other community rituals of mourning. This, too, is a modern idea, and—like many other edicts of the current age—it reeks of delusion. As the Renaissance man of letters Michel de Montaigne wrote in his timeless *Essays*:

To begin depriving death of its greatest advantage over us, let us deprive death of its strangeness, let us frequent it, let us get used to it; let us have nothing more often in mind than death.

This is exactly what a journalist and songwriter named Mike Brick decided to do—"deprive death of its strangeness"—back in 2015. He had been experiencing fatigue and chest pain for months, so Brick, age forty, scheduled a doctor's appointment that he hoped would be merely a visit of due diligence.

Instead, Mike was diagnosed with stage 4 colon cancer and—although he pursued aggressive chemotherapy—he could do little to stop the cancer's spread. He started to make arrangements for his death with his wife, Stacy. Mike was devoutly Catholic and asked for a funeral mass—a gathering with the formality of suits and pews. Then they discussed a memorial service in the spirit of an Irish wake. As he was a songwriter, there would be good music—his own band could play in his honor—and lots of good stories, too. They chose a legendary musicians' haunt in Austin called the Hole in the Wall and sorted out the details of the near-future day.

As this vision came to life before them—this, the greatest party he would never actually get to attend—everything about it suddenly felt all wrong.

"You're here," Stacy told him. "You should be at your own wake."

Who says you have to be dead to attend your own funeral? In mere hours, the plans for a future night at the Hole in the Wall were scrapped, and instead Mike and Stacy nabbed a venue available later that week. Friends, family, former members of the band from all over the country—all flew in. The actions felt familiar—the mad rush and canceled plans we all make upon hearing that a loved one is dead—except that this time Mike would be there to experience it. He was about to play the greatest gig of his life.

On January 13, 2016, Mike stood up in a room full of loved ones and watched himself dying in their eyes. I discovered his brave act in the many published articles and tributes his journalist friends wrote to document the event. According to their accounts, Mike faced the hundred or so faces before him and told them all, "I've been lucky enough to choose the right people in my life, and I love you all." Then he and his band—the Music Grinders—tore the house down with a two-hour set while his dearest friends danced and his young children skipped in and out of the lights. The band ended with a six-minute-and-twenty-eight-second-long rendition of one of Mike's favorite songs before he stood and looked each and every person in the eyes. "I love you," he mouthed.

Why would you miss attending the most important event of your life? Mike died only weeks later, and days after his passing, Stacy and his family did lean on the legacy rituals they had originally put in place. What his children remember, however, and what Stacy holds dear to this day, was Mike's agency during an illness that so often felt disempowering.

"Mike knew he had to leave," Stacy told her friends. "He didn't want to leave. But he was so graceful about facing it that he just wanted to help everyone else get through. That's what this was."

Other groups are also trying to counteract our age of Forbidden Death. Death Over Dinner is a grassroots movement that brings people together over a shared meal to discuss the end of life. The invitations have fun with the seemingly somber topic—"Let's have dinner and talk about death"—while acknowledging that sharing a meal and sitting around a table is often the best way to connect over a discussion of our mortality. "We put forward this myth that we don't want to talk about death, but I think we just haven't gotten the right invitations," said Michael Hebb, who founded the organization to help address the crisis of end-of-life care in the United States.

Our cultural desire to shelter ourselves or to shy away from death can backfire, while opportunities to come to terms with death, however painful in the moment, can prove beneficial in our search for acceptance. Children who attend funerals of their departed parents, for example, have been shown to cope better with the loss than children who did not bear witness. And parents who undergo the devastating experience of delivering a stillborn child report being better able to cope with the loss if they can hold their baby before saying goodbye.

In Japan, a new movement is emerging to help an aging and isolated population find "friends" to share graves at death. These *hake tomos*, or grave friends, get to know one another and commit to buy adjacent plots of land in a burial ground. Rather than a friend for this world, the *hake tomos* are friends for the next life. They agree to accompany one another into death. Although this relationship might sound grim, anthropologist Anne Allison, who has studied the phenomenon, described it in more peaceful terms. *Hake tomos* is "a means of dying actively and not waiting to be homeless or lonely post-death."

Michel de Montaigne exhorts all of us to "frequent death." It isn't easy—it's often uncomfortable and leaves us feeling vulnerable—but rituals can step in and offer us support.

There Is No "Peak" Acceptance

Many of our honored legacy rituals are limited in time, sometimes to a single day (a funeral) or to a period of weeks. Rituals that once extended for longer, such as the sequences of colors in clothing rituals, have become rarer. When we marry, we celebrate our anniversary each year, but ceremonies to mark the anniversary of a loved one's death are less common. After a brief officially sanctioned period set aside for mourning, the communal aspect of grief abruptly comes to an end. Mourners often report experiencing an outpouring of condolences and concern immediately after a loss, but also describe how that outpouring shrinks to a trickle soon after. Once the funeral ends, after everyone drives and flies back home, we are left with our loss, and people expect us to head back to work. Literally. The United States has no law requiring bereavement leave.

As anyone who has experienced grief knows, this is not how the process works. In one study of 233 bereaved individuals followed for twenty-four months after the death of a loved one, disbelief peaked at one month after the loss, yearning peaked at four months, anger peaked at five months, and depression didn't peak until six months. Unfortunately, we often put pressure on ourselves to move on, to stop thinking about the person, to "get over it."

In 1969, Elisabeth Kübler-Ross, a Swiss-born psychiatrist, wrote a book documenting her work with terminally ill patients and the experience of dying. At the time of her research, the medical community tended to obfuscate or finesse patients' dying, assuming that the terminally ill did not want or need to know how sick they were. There were euphemisms and indirections: to talk about the reality of death was to admit defeat. Kübler-Ross pushed back against all of these assumptions with her massively influential book, *On Death and Dying*. She argued that patients were well aware of their condition and deserved the dignity of an honest medical assessment. "The patient is in the process of losing everything and everybody he loves. If he is allowed to express his sorrow, he will find a final acceptance much easier."

Kübler-Ross laid out her theory of five stages of dying for her terminally ill patients: denial, anger, bargaining, depression, and acceptance. This paradigm, originally conceived to correct the misguided assumptions of the medical community toward their dying patients, became a model for how people should grieve. Today, her terminology is so widely known that if mourners have not properly passed through each of their five stages, their family members are liable to tell them they have not completely processed the death.

I suspect that this linear aspect of Kübler-Ross's five stages—the sense that one stage will follow another in a sequence that culminates in a well-defined end point—accounts for its popularity. Yet, no proven science lies behind these stages of grief, no reason to think that everyone needs to pass through five stages—why not three or four? In many indigenous cultures where communicating with ancestors occurs every day and death is a transitional state, "acceptance" may never formally happen. Does that mean these cultures are getting grief wrong?

In one study of bereavement peer-support groups in Northern California, mourners who had lost a loved one within the previous three months were asked to rate which of twenty different goals they felt rituals had most helped them with. Two of the most highly rated outcomes were tightly related to a sense of acceptance: mourners felt that their rituals helped them to "accept grief as an ongoing process" and "accept the death of [my] loved one(s)."

Willie Nelson captures it best when he sings that loss isn't something we get over, it's something we get through. Grief subsides not by trying to forget and move on instantly, but rather by giving us fortitude to live through the acute pain after a loss. In the study of 233 mourners, the "acceptance" stage didn't peak at all—it just gradually increased over time.

The Man behind the Groucho Marx Glasses

In the fall of 2010, one of my intellectual heroes and a beloved member of the social psychology department at Harvard, Dan Wegner, was diagnosed with ALS. You might remember Dan as the researcher behind the ambitiously innovative study of thought suppression and white bears. In the academic world, Dan was known as a true original—an intellectual of fierce independence who was willing to chase down the weirdest, thorniest questions in the darkest corners of the field: What is free will? What is the psychological foundation of secrecy and obsession? But Dan's storied career as a psychologist doesn't even begin to do justice to all of the fun and playfulness he brought to aspects of the (sometimes) stuffy milieu of university life. To begin with, he was a giant—more than six feet, three inches tall—and he insisted on wearing a uniform of billowy and loud Hawaiian-print shirts. *Stylish?* Maybe not the right word. Authentic? Absolutely.

He also had a display case of meticulously collected Groucho Marx nose-and-glasses. When his first daughter was born, Dan brought out three and put one on himself, one on his wife, Toni, and one on the tiny head of his newborn daughter before snapping a picture. When his second daughter arrived, in keeping with the ritual, his family of four all put fake arrows on their heads.

When I heard that Dan died at age sixty-five in 2013, I joined the legions of devastated friends and colleagues in his community to mourn his loss. His family celebrated his life through the legacy ritual of a memorial service. But Dan had made a special request before he died. He asked that everyone in attendance wear both a Hawaiian shirt and their finest Groucho glasses. When we all looked around at one another during the crowded service, it was as if we were all channeling Dan. He was present in each and every one of us: the stagecraft had conjured him up. Forget black or even lavender. I suspect that no one has ever before—or ever since—charted grief and memory through folds of fabric in tropical patterns and topped by Groucho.

These externally legible manifestations of order—whether it is the instruction to wear a Hawaiian shirt or to put on a black crepe dress—bring some semblance of control back to the mourners' lives. This experience of lost control is, in and of itself, a predictor of the intensity of grief, and many assessments of grief zero in on this sense of disorder—measuring our worries about losing control of our emotions, feeling helpless, or crying uncontrollably. Joan Didion's description in *The Year of Magical Thinking* of her actions immediately after her husband's sudden death illustrate this need for control:

> I remember combining the cash that had been in his pocket with the cash in my own bag, smoothing the bills, taking special care to interleaf twenties with twenties, tens with tens, fives and ones with fives and ones. I remember thinking as I did this that he would see that I was handling things.

COVID and Mourning

One painful aspect of the COVID-19 pandemic was our inability to gather in person to mourn. As memorials, funerals, and celebrations of life returned to in-person gatherings, many people who lost loved ones during the pandemic were still waiting and yearning for more of a publicly legible ritual of mourning. In *Slate*'s Dear Prudence advice series, a woman wrote in asking for help with how to mourn well after her father's death in March 2020:

> I had frankly been holding on until he was gone to release that pent-up grief and pain via the "normal" rituals of funeral and

burial. But we couldn't have those, and for reasons that are inexplicable to me, my mom and siblings chose a two-sentence obituary when that was all we had to honor him publicly.

I need to mourn, I need the ritual. But I don't know how to do it so far past his death. I can't be the only reader of yours dealing with this issue—how did they honor their loved ones? How did they create a space for healing?

Her plaintive cry set off a wave of responses on Twitter as people wrote in to describe how they either adjusted their legacy rituals for mourning during COVID-19 or created new rituals better suited for these extraordinary circumstances. For three years, people gathered on Zoom to mourn, found ways to conduct socially distanced memorials, and instituted drive-through condolence caravans. It is moving to see how quickly and with such great variety people adjusted their behaviors to perform this final and profound rite of passage:

My grandpa died in Jan 2020 and we never got to have a funeral for him. My aunt planned a family lunch at one of his favorite places last year—everyone flew in for it and treated it like a low-key memorial service. We shared stories, gave speeches, cried, hugged.

June 2020. We're having a party and spreading his ashes in one of his favorite places this summer.

I'm a hospice chaplain. I see similar situations often. No judgment for the family who didn't choose to do much, although

I think the letter writer's outlook is ultimately healthier. But there's no statute of limitations for a funeral or memorial service.

The woman who wrote in, calling herself "Grief Is a Fanny Pack," said, "I need to mourn." But one of the respondents assured her that she was already mourning: "Your grief is now and has been and will continue to be valid. So don't feel as if you've wasted the past few years or somehow fallen behind."

I found these responses deeply revealing—both of our ability to find ways to mourn in whatever elements of behavior and stagecraft might be on hand, and also of our innate need for that work to be visible to others and acknowledged by a greater community.

A Reminder to Remember

Mourning rituals aren't simply about coping with grief. They are also about remembering and memorializing. They give us an occasion to focus shared attention on those we've lost. The world spins on, but we make the decision to stop. To linger. To remember. To honor. And when they work, mourning rituals can be magical. The Dinner Party is an organization that brings together complete strangers who have lost a loved one to share their grief while sharing a meal. One attendee wrote:

When my mom died, I felt achingly alone. It was an isolation that I had never experienced before. But as soon as I started attending dinners about a month and a half later, that loneliness abated. It was kind of a Dorothy from *The Wizard of Oz* moment—I was stepping out of a completely colorless world and back into something that was richer and more vibrant than before.

Even in the face of our worst losses, ritual has the power to animate and reenchant.

Family Lives On, a nonprofit dedicated to helping children who have lost a parent, developed a Tradition Program, in which they ask grieving children to describe the thing they most loved to do with their now-deceased parent. Family Lives On then helps children to reenact that event each year, often on a day that was meaningful to the family. This was the case for Matthew, who was four years old when his mother died from lung cancer. The organization helped create a fitting ritual: "Birthdays and Christmas were very special to her—she always enjoyed baking for her family. During her final stage in hospice care, Matthew and his mother decided together that his tradition would be to bake cookies/cupcakes every year to celebrate her birthday and honor her memory. Now, each year, Matthew and his dad bake and decorate either cookies or cupcakes in celebration of Mom."

People are endlessly inventive and—just as long-ago cultures decided which color to use for grief—they take what is in their environment, imbue it with meaning, then use it in a ritual that can help point them toward acceptance. One woman I encountered in my research described how she is using hydrangeas as memorials in her garden. Each time a good friend or beloved family member dies, she transplants a hydrangea from their garden into her own. Over many years, she has created an expansive hydrangea memorial in her backyard, and she knows exactly which plant is from her mother, her aunt, her best friend's mother, and her closest friend from college. Today she can step outside and spend a meditative afternoon enjoying her flowers or trimming her plants and feel she is connecting with a living embodiment of each of these important women in her life.

Maine resident Amy Hopkins was mourning the loss of both of her parents when she discovered solace and renewal in the ritual of cold-water plunges on the Maine coastline. "When your body is in that fight or flight, it's shocking," Hopkins told the *New York Times*. "That cold temperature immediately makes everything constrict and protect. Blood rushes to your vital organs."

In the intensity of this cold-water experience, Hopkins has found a way to breathe through the pain of her grief. Once inside the winter water, she can only live in the present moment. Breath by breath: this is how all of us survive grief. Hopkins has also found a community to support her through her organized dips in the frigid waters. On these outings—what she has dubbed Dip Down to Rise Up—she enters the near-frozen waves holding hands with her fellow dippers. They stand in the water together, often silent, for a few minutes, then embrace in a hug and return back to the warmth of coats, hats, and boots.

Mourning Our Ambiguous Losses

Rituals such as Hopkins's provide a sense of closure—and the importance of that feeling is not to be underrated. We've seen individuals invent breakup rituals to move on after relationships end badly, but on the whole, such rituals are rare. Many of us lack resources for grappling with the ways that our relationships change and end. The special form of grief that accompanies the end of a relationship—not just romantic, but with family and friends, too—is a potent loss when we know that person is just a text away. Read any advice column and you'll encounter a writer who is devastated by a loved one who simply stopped replying to calls and texts, with no explanation. It's called *ghosting* for a reason—it can *haunt* us. As one reader of the *New York Times* wrote in:

My younger sister died in a car accident 50 years ago. My older daughter estranged our whole family 9 years ago. In many ways the death of my sister was easier; I had loved her immensely, I grieved and eventually grew to accept her loss. My daughter, my firstborn, still walks this earth. My whole being grieves for her. I know that I will never accept her loss.

We hold funerals for those who pass away; we might burn pictures of our exes after a breakup; but we also need other ways to mourn the complicated relationships that haunt us. Psychologists have a name for this kind of loss: *ambiguous loss*. The loss is ongoing, it's uncertain, it's just not *final* enough for us to begin to move on. Ambiguous grief is a feeling that creeps up on us, and that often builds up unless there is an occasion—a ritual—to honor that loss.

This problem affects millions of people in different forms and hues. For instance, family members of people diagnosed with degenerative illnesses such as Alzheimer's are all too familiar with the feeling—that their loved one is both gone forever and yet still present. In one study on Alzheimer's, an interviewee reported the pain of that realization:

That afternoon my mother's eyes looked at me uninterested. There was no glance of happiness or connection. My mother didn't recognize me. When I tried to give her a hug, she looked frightened at me. At that point I couldn't keep my tears back; they just stood out of my eyes. [...] My mother died to me that day she didn't recognize me anymore.

Caregivers often report a particularly guilt-inducing desire to accept that their loved one is gone, even though the person is still present. It can feel deeply inappropriate to *do* anything to mark that sense of passing. The only widespread ritual to recognize such a loss is a funeral, but that's not fitting. Instead, for situations of ambiguous loss, the right approach is often to find our own rituals—which can be unique to our specific emotions and life situations.

When Lesley McCallister lost her first pregnancy at twenty-three weeks, people advised her it was best to move on quickly. Instead, she decided to honor the life that would have been, keeping her son as part of the family even while acknowledging his loss. Her two children mention their "big brother Will in heaven" in their prayers every night before bed, and the family celebrates his birthday each April with an ice cream cake. These rituals have helped Lesley cope with her loss; she now says, "As sad as it is and was, good has come out of it."

Rehearsing for Death

Most grief counselors and spiritual practitioners agree that it is only with the acknowledgment of death's inevitability that we achieve acceptance and peace. There is even an app, WeCroak, that sends messages to your iPhone at random times throughout the day. Each one says simply, "Don't forget, you're going to die." Its seventeenth-century equivalent might be the artwork of *memento mori*, which means "remember you must die." The paintings feature skulls, candles, fruits, and flowers. Like WeCroak, the paintings remind anyone looking that death is always on its way, serving as a rehearsal for death.

As soon as photography was invented in the mid-nineteenth century, mourners began using it to create memento mori of their loved ones—a last chance to capture an image of their deceased child or family member before burial. In Victorian England, the specter of death was so common—through the scourge of diseases such as measles, diphtheria, and tuberculosis—that the vision of these dead children posed and propped up like dolls did not strike anyone as excessively morbid. With the rarity and expense of cameras and film, the death of a child was often the first and last time a family would gather to have a photographer take their photo. Instead of a macabre spectacle, these photographs offered a last moment to look. This is what so many of these mourning rituals are designed to do—whether it's a moment of silence, an elegy, or our own living Irish wake. Look. Don't let this moment go unobserved.

Later in his life, the wonderful children's book author and creator of *Where the Wild Things Are*, Maurice Sendak, spoke plainly about death and grief: "I cry a lot because I miss people. They die and I can't stop them. They leave me and I love them more." In grief, Sendak found, there is also immense love. Mourning rituals are a key part of working through the pain of loss while keeping that love alive.

Part 4

Rituals at Work
and in the World

Chapter 11

How to Find Meaning at Work

Trust Falls and Other Team Rituals

When I'm asked to speak about rituals, I begin by coming to the front of the room or stage. I ask everyone to stand up. Without saying anything, I click to reveal this slide:

> Clap once. Stomp with your right foot. Clap once. Stomp with your left foot.
>
> Clap 3 times. Stomp with your right foot 3 times. Clap 3 times. Stomp with your left foot 3 times.
>
> Clap 5 times. Stomp with your right foot 5 times. Clap 5 times. Stomp with your left foot 5 times.
>
> Put your right hand in the air, and when I count to three, say, "Let's go!"
>
> Say it again, but louder.
>
> Say it one more time, even louder.

The same events unfold every time, without fail—whether I am speaking to an academic audience, to students, to an organization, really to *any* group. First, there is an awkward pause. Then someone claps, followed by other claps, then some scattered right-foot stomps . . . and then they're off and running. By the "clap three times" instruction, the room has fully synced up. Even when there are hundreds of people, somehow, magically, everyone starts clapping at precisely the same moments. Then, the people speed up. The claps get faster, the stomps get faster. I don't tell the people to speed up, they just do—and somehow, they manage to all speed up at the exact same rate, so the entire group stays in lockstep, as if they'd been practicing for weeks.

By the time they've shouted "Let's go" for the third time, they are really experiencing . . . something. I'm no cult leader, but at that moment I get the feeling that if I ran out of the room, they would follow me. When they finish the exercise, I remain silent, and slowly people snap out of it: that intense collective feeling subsides and they start to look at one another as if to say, "What just happened?"

This is the power of group rituals: they can spark the phenomenon Émile Durkheim called *collective effervescence*. Even a series of random actions, performed together, can turn a gathering of strangers into a meaningful unit. If we did run out of the room together, we'd do it with a strong sense of joint purpose—we'd *mean* it, whatever that *it* happened to be.

To be clear: I created this particular ritual from scratch. Yet time and time again, I've seen this series of basic actions become a ritual that is capable of turning a crowd of strangers in a random conference hall on a Wednesday afternoon into an ecstatic *we*.

No Strangers to Ritual

Ritual is a central part of the clockwork that makes communities and cultures tick. Think beyond that strange conference hall experiment to other mass rituals. National anthems and all the ceremony surrounding the American flag. Packed sports arenas where fans all wear the same jerseys and shout the same cheers. Religious services and symbols that remain constant across continents and centuries. These collective rituals can forge people from different backgrounds, across enormous distances, into a group. And not just a group, but often something more formidable: a people, a culture, a nation bound together by a shared sense of identity and belonging. "Every mind [is] drawn into the same eddy, the individual type nearly confounds itself with that of the race," explained Durkheim, using the term *race* to refer only to the group affiliation. Rituals can summon a sense of community out of simple, shared actions. This capacity to come together and bond over even the most seemingly insignificant shared actions appears to be a deep part of human nature. For those who have experienced or regularly engage in such rituals, that powerful sense of community and solidarity can be intensely meaningful.

Those same rituals can come with equally powerful social costs. Mass rituals have the power to divide us, encouraging us to identify strongly with some communities to the exclusion of others. This is ritual at scale and at its most sweeping: rituals have the ability to unite and divide us, and in some cases to repair the social rifts and fractures that can emerge along the way.

Research shows that the link between ritual and group bonding emerges early in human development. Nicole Wen, Patricia Herrmann, and Cristine Legare signed up seventy-one children aged four to eleven in an after-school program and gave them all a free wristband of a particular color—say, green. Three days a week for two weeks, they were given materials to make necklaces out of string and shapes of that same color. Some kids were given the materials and set loose, allowed to make necklaces in whatever manner and form they preferred. Other kids, though, were led through a necklace-making ritual (by a teacher dressed in the same color): "Hold up a green string. Then, touch a green star to your head. Then, string on a green star. Next clap your hands three times." The children did the same sequence for green circles and green squares, then repeated it all again.

When the two weeks ended, kids who'd enacted the ritual were less likely to want to exchange their wristband for a different color if given the option and were more likely to choose a free hat in the same color as their wristband. Moreover, they didn't just like their color— they also came to see the group that shared their color as *good*. They thought new students to the class would prefer to join the green group and were also more likely to recommend a student from the green group to be a special helper in another after-school program.

Even infants at sixteen months can recognize ritualistic actions and infer that people who engage in the same ritualistic action are likely to affiliate. In one study, infants who saw two people make the odd choice to turn on a light with their head (when they could have used their hands) expected those two people to get along.

The relationship between rituals and group affiliation runs deep. It also runs *wide*. Group rituals abound throughout our lives—in classrooms, barracks, arenas, and workplaces—anywhere that strangers come together for a common cause. Look at any championship-winning team (and, in fairness, most championship-losing teams) and you'll find that rituals make up the brick and mortar of their bond. New Zealand's star rugby team, the All Blacks, famously engage in the *haka*—originally a Maori ritual—which includes teammates slapping their thighs, stomping their feet as hard as they can, and shouting "Up the ladder" and "Up to the top." If you watch any professional sports teams before each game or at time-outs, you'll see them huddle and join together for a cheer. For instance, Drew Brees, the former quarterback of the New Orleans Saints, brought his team together for a ritual chant before each game. Drew says, "One." Saints say, "Two." Drew: "Win." Saints: "For you." Drew: "Three." Saints: "Four." Drew: "Win." Saints: "Some more!" (The ritual I use when I give talks deliberately echoes these team rituals.)

Only so many of us get to line up alongside Drew Brees on game day. For most of us, we use the word *team* most often in the office. Work has become the most prominent place where the average adult experiences the kind of group rituals meant to bring strangers together.

Some Wal-Mart employees enact a ritual at the start of each of their shifts: "Give me a *W*! Give me an *A*! Give me an *L*! Give me a squiggly! Give me an *M*! Give me an *A*! Give me an *R*! Give me a *T*!"—followed by "Whose Wal-Mart is it? It's *my* Wal-Mart." The instructions specify that when the "squiggly" moment arrives, all employees—in unison—must shimmy their hips. No wonder the meetings have been described as "two parts militaristic, one part kumbaya." You'd think that, in such a large and streamlined company, it'd be all efficiency all the time—with no extra room for weird rituals. Yet executives understand the importance of trying to build team spirit and how to foster it.

When Zipcar shifted to a mobile-first strategy, employees were given sledgehammers to smash their desktop computers. At Google, new employees wear beanie hats with propellers on top of them in the colors of the Google logo. Each hat has the word NOOGLER emblazoned across it: the name of a newbie to the tribe. At one annual shareholder meeting held by Starbucks in 2018, partners Fabiola Sanchez and Sergio Alvarez led a coffee tasting for all of the three thousand people in attendance, with careful instructions: smell the coffee, notice its unique notes, slurp it loudly, ensure the coffee covers the entire tongue to hit every taste bud. Why? In an effort to align attendees with the company's larger mission.

But let's be real. Are any of these work rituals effective? It's rare to find an employee (salesperson, consultant, customer service representative, *anyone*) who enthusiastically believes that the team rituals that managers enforce—from morning chants to trust falls—actually work. Can a shimmy and a squiggly really change employees' experience at work for the better?

Making the Team

People's desire to find meaning and purpose in their work has only increased in recent years. That desire is part of what has fueled the so-called Great Resignation, but those trends seem to have begun before the pandemic. One survey of more than two thousand American professionals found that, on average, people were willing to forgo 23 percent of their earnings for work that "offered you consistent meaning." We're also more likely to turn down higher-paying jobs when we see our current jobs as meaningful. As one *Harvard Business Review* piece put it, "Meaning Is the New Money." Most of us want to feel as if we're working as part of a functioning *team*, rather than off on our own, unsupported and going through the motions. My colleagues and I set out to figure out if workplace rituals had anything to do with how we feel about our jobs and our coworkers. Did they work, or did all that fuss just backfire, resulting in a massive, collective eye roll?

Take a moment to think about a group activity that you engage in at your workplace. What is the activity and what exactly do you and your coworkers do? When and how often do you do it? How do you feel about it, ultimately?

In research led by Tami Kim, we asked these questions, among others, of 275 professionals, and the range of responses was revealing. Many people report rituals involving lunch or drinks after work; potlucks are common, and so is exercising together. The majority of rituals are idiosyncratic to one work group or one organization, such as this one:

Every day my team (four members) and I order in lunch from a local restaurant (we cycle five restaurants per week with one restaurant per day). Since there are five of us, each one of us gets to pick a restaurant one day per week. I'm Monday, T is Tuesday, D is Wednesday, and so on. We always pay our share of the total of the order. We eat in the conference room, and it's nice because it breaks the monotony by making a regular lunch break exciting.

A few people we interviewed couldn't think of any ritual, such as this curmudgeon: "I don't participate in any such activity. I do my work, then go home."

By and large, though, the activities that people reported had common elements that we saw again and again. The rituals were often repeated. They seemed to enliven the mundanity and monotony of work—an experience described with words such as "exciting" and "fun"—and they brought people together, to "share" and "bond." Rituals allowed them to be more than cogs in a machine, automated to optimize every minute. They became team members instead, animated by a shared sense of purpose.

We also asked everyone in our survey to rate how meaningful they viewed their group activity, as well as, more broadly, how they felt about their work: How *meaningful* was their job to them? Two key findings emerged. First, the more the group activities were rated as ritualistic—everything from Friday drinks to walking meetings on Monday to mentoring sessions over lunch to afternoon yoga in the company gym—the more meaning employees found in that activity. Second, and most important, we found that the more ritualistic the activity, the more meaning people found in the work itself. Employees who reported an absence of ritual in their workplace simply weren't as emotionally engaged as those who told us that their job did feature elements of ritual.

Our survey was still open to interpretation. People who like their jobs and teams may simply be more likely to create rituals—in which case rituals are not a leading indicator but a lagging one. We wanted to get traction on this question. Do work rituals create meaning or just reflect meaning that already exists?

In an experiment we asked groups to collaborate on a creative task. We brought 360 people into our lab—all strangers to one another— and divided them into groups. We told all of them that they would be brainstorming in a group task, working together to generate as many uses for a six-sided die as possible.

But we first asked them to enact a group ritual together. We crafted this one ourselves, designing it to be similar to many of the rituals we've seen used in workplaces, with the following series of movements:

Step 1: With your left hand, pat your right shoulder three times.

Step 2: With your right hand, pat your left shoulder three times.

Step 3: Bend your knees; stomp with your right foot once and then again with your left foot.

Step 4:   Take the blank piece of paper on the table and crinkle
          it up. Hold it with your left hand.

Step 5:   Make a fist with your right hand and place it next to
          your heart for seven seconds.

Everyone performed this exact same ritual, except for one critical difference. Some groups *faced* one another while enacting the ritual, while others *faced away* from one another. This meant that the groups who were facing away from one another were in effect conducting something closer to an *individual* ritual. The groups who faced one another were conducting a *collective* ritual; they were experiencing it *together*—sharing attention and seeing the others doing the same thing and gauging their reactions.

After all the groups enacted their rituals, they got to work, brainstorming solutions. Not only did the groups facing one another report feeling closer to their teammates, but they also stated that they found both the ritual and the brainstorming task more meaningful. When we examined groups' performance on the brainstorming task, the meaning created by the ritual had transferred to finding more meaning in the task at hand: the exact same "work" began to matter more. In one of our studies, a group who had completed their collective ritual then asked if it was okay if they exchanged email addresses, so they could get together outside of the lab. Our ad hoc ritual had inspired the group to bond.

Researcher Douglas A. Lepisto wanted to investigate this phenomenon—ritual's effect on how employees perceive the meaning of their work—in an actual company. In 2022, he published a twenty-one-month field study of an unremarkable athletic apparel and footwear company—referred to as Fitco to preserve anonymity. During his time at Fitco, the company was introducing what it called Liven, a new exercise class offered to employees. To participate in Liven, employees had to walk down worn dirt paths to a building designated solely for this class. As the start time of the class drew closer, the music would swell, and the instructor counted down the clock—"Three, two, one, go!"—building the drama. The actual exercise activities varied from session to session, but they were always *intense*, to be completed as quickly as possible, sometimes in as little as five minutes, forcing employees to go all out. On the whole, employees liked it, so much so that some were rendered speechless after the experience, while others could only use profanities:

"We have unlocked something that is actually really fucking powerful and transformative for people," the communications manager at Fitco told Lepisto. "No one could really describe what it means to them," a customer-relations director added. "They all know how amazing it feels, everyone wants everyone else to feel it, but everyone struggles to articulate it."

One of the report managers said, "I think the organization became something different. . . . I don't know. I can't even explain it other than to say it [Liven] gave Fitco a purpose, and that purpose was being fulfilled not just in my life but in people's lives that I've known."

The Liven ritual changed something fundamental for those participating. Not only was the ritual effective on people's subjective states, but it changed employees' feelings about their work, their company, and their shared sense of meaning—underscoring for one employee that the company "existed for something bigger than shoes and T-shirts."

Do Trust Falls Actually Work?

Not every team ritual feels as transcendent as a Liven workout. Some rituals feel forced; some have us squiggling or rolling our eyes or worse.

Bloomberg News interviewed Christina Comben, a content manager at Day Translations in Valencia, Spain, who described a disastrous team-building exercise where her boss took the team paintballing. Yes, it went as badly as you're imagining. "I'm not a good shot," Comben wrote in her defense, "and I wasn't aiming for him, but my paintball went awry. The next thing I knew, [my boss] was on the floor. The game was stopped, the ambulance came, and people started talking about potential liver rupture and damage to his kidneys." Comben's boss turned out to be just fine—but Comben's career at the company did not. "I felt horrible," she wrote, "and left the company six weeks later."

Outright disasters aside, what *do* effective group rituals have in common—and how can we learn from them? When a group of strangers comes together in a cheer or a chant or a team-building exercise, what bonds them? What elements of the ritual create that sought-after sense of purpose and unity? My colleagues and I have found that it takes a surprisingly simple combination of elements to bring groups together. Even those clichéd trust-fall rituals can be sneakily effective.

Let's imagine a white-water rafting trip on the Yampa River in Colorado. When we arrive, we find ourselves in a group of strangers, all ready to brave the rapids. It's hard work. We wake up at sunrise, use the "groover" (a portable floating toilet created just for river rafting), and, in the morning chill, tie down gear in the raft. We spend the morning paddling, and the midday paddling, and the afternoon paddling. But in all this work, when do we—a collection of solitary people each holding an oar—transform into a cohesive team? To answer that question, researchers Eric Arnould and Linda Price analyzed how rafting-tour companies utilized rituals to bond groups to conquer the white water.

In one ritual, guides lead clients to a "kissing rock" that *everyone* must kiss to ensure safe passage through a treacherous segment of the river. At another transition, groups create a waterfall by using their bodies to block a stream. One respondent described the river rafters "hugging and having arms around people who I think under other conditions would be considered strangers. . . . It was a really wonderful shared moment."

Rafters on the tour reported that their excursion turned their bunch of strangers into a *group* that mattered to them. One person suggested that his group reunite the following year, even though "all of us were all so different from each other and come from different backgrounds and orientations."

What makes this kind of camaraderie possible? For one, as we saw in our laboratory experiment, synchrony, simply conducting the same actions *along with* a group of people, and shared attention, witnessing everyone do so in unison, builds trust. Second, many of the team-building rituals we've seen incorporate contact and physical movement. Similar to what we found with performance rituals, movement in group rituals helps us get out of our heads. Third, and perhaps most important, the camaraderie is built around the new identity work of the river rafters. They have all left their familiar contexts—comfortable affiliations and roles—for a situation fraught with risk where survival requires cohesion with the group.

These river rafters were open to trying most of the activities suggested by their guides. But even rituals that many people typically hate can still have a positive effect. Sometimes, having to go through a terrible team-building exercise together is the perfect way to grow closer. One of the most maligned of all group rituals still created meaning for those white-water rafters:

The next game we played was a trust game where we stood in a tight circle and the person went in the middle and went stiff and closed their eyes, and we then sort of rocked them around the circle. . . . This was sort of a turning point I think in terms of the creation of community on the trip.

That's right, even trust falls can work, exerting a positive effect on us. Why? In the workplace, even hated rituals can rebound to the company's favor, for a slightly surreptitious reason. Employees complain to one another, and all this grumbling accomplishes the very thing that their manager was aiming for: *making strangers into a team.* Eye rolling in lockstep with other employees during a particularly embarrassing, boss-mandated ritual is a synchronized group behavior that has many of the elements of an effective group ritual.

Just as rain dances can bring a community back together in a time of crisis, team-building rituals can give us that hard-won feeling of camaraderie—even if it's sometimes at the boss's expense. Group rituals—those we create and those mandated—can imbue our workdays, and our work itself, with greater meaning and purpose. Truly effective organizations also offer room for individuals to bring their own rituals and personalities to their work, leaving space for both types of rituals to thrive. We may have a group ritual such as a morning meeting to get everyone settled. But individuals also have their own rituals to prepare for it: a cup of coffee at one's desk while doing the crossword, a lap around the office to see who's in, the same seven-fifteen train every day, and a lucky tap on the company logo upon arrival. Each of these matter to the team as a whole.

Why Most of Us Hate Open-Floor Plans

Overengineering employee bonding can be to the detriment of individual employees—and to successful group bonding. The best evidence comes from the rage that accompanies any shift to an open-office plan. One headline in the *Guardian* proclaimed, "Open-Plan Offices Were Devised by Satan in the Deepest Caverns of Hell." Farhad Manjoo, writing about such offices as WeWork, noted, "Its rise is a sign that we have no good way, in modern life, to value and guard private, distraction-free spaces." Whether we are stretching, humming, foot tapping, or just taking three deep breaths, this lack of privacy can disrupt the little rituals we enact to help us through our days at work. It reduces our office life to an *Onion* headline: "Retail Employee Has Little Daily Ritual Where He Drinks Dr Pepper in Quiet Corner of Stock Room and Doesn't Kill Himself."

For corporations, the open-office plan is usually about economics: it's a more cost-effective use of the real estate. Often, however, the plans are sold to employees as intended to increase the casual and spontaneous conversations that lead to bonding. But open-office plans can have the opposite effect: rather than the openness *increasing* communication among employees, it often *decreases* it. Ethan Bernstein and Ben Waber tracked face-to-face interactions at the headquarters of two Fortune 500 firms in the weeks before and after they introduced their open-office plans. Face-to-face interactions didn't increase in the open-plan office; they fell by 70 percent. Bernstein wondered whether small privacy interventions might have big effects. He worked with managers in a factory in China to study the effect of introducing a little less openness—by literally curtaining off some work teams in their own private spaces. After putting up a trial curtain, Bernstein heard an employee react, "I wish they'd put those curtains up around the entire line. We could be so much more productive if they did that." So, they did just that, using curtains to divvy up the wide-open factory into smaller units. The curtain intervention led to a 10 to 15 percent performance improvement over the ensuing months.

Bringing Work Home

One possible solution to the open-floor plan's infringement on individual space and privacy is the trend that skyrocketed during the pandemic: working from home. But this solution presents its own set of challenges. When millions of professionals and students started working from their living rooms, it became a daily struggle to switch from "home self" to "work self" at the start of the day, and back again when the workday was over. Commutes, cubicles, and business casual—for all their headaches—made it simple to switch between the different roles we assume in our daily lives. Without them, many professionals found it hard to keep their priorities in balance.

When columnist Nellie Bowles started her new work-from-home life, she did everything she could to keep the workday ritual alive:

I'm hungry for ritual. Every day, I get dressed, put on shoes, make coffee, pour it in a mug and tell my two housemates that I'm heading to work and will see 'em later. Then I walk in a few circles and settle in at a desk in the corner of our living room, just a couple feet away. . . . It's how I help my bleary mind realize that the workday has begun.

In Toronto, Kyle Ashley developed a similar ritual that worked for him. He cycled to work every morning—until he, too, began to work from home. But something wasn't clicking. Then he had an epiphany—"One morning I woke up and said something has got to give"—and he started riding his bike from his bedroom to his living room, a commute of roughly seven feet.

As people returned to work, they were faced with yet another problem. How could they bring the rituals they'd developed in the privacy of their own WFH offices back into the open-floor plan? Like this one that someone shared with me:

When I started working from home in March of 2020, I had to begin the day by slipping on my Japanese house shoes every morning. It just felt so comforting. Now that we're back in the office most days of the week, I bought an extra pair online and I keep them tucked underneath my desk and slip them on as soon as I arrive. At first, I tried to hide the fact that I was wearing slippers at work, but now I know that no one cares. They all brought their creature comforts from home back, too.

As companies attempt to navigate both the possibilities and the pitfalls of designing more rituals into the day, the number of spiritual consultants and ritual designers has risen. Many of them are finding new ways to combine the language of the sacred and the social cohesion offered by religious communities with the edicts of a twenty-first-century management culture. Consider it McKinsey with candles. That these consultants exist at all is evidence of the relevance of rituals to today's corporate cultures, but time will tell if the increase in workplace rituals pays off, for employees or their employers.

Leaving Work Behind

The dizzying array of changes to work life in the last few years has many of us scrambling to juggle our individual identities with our work identities while logging in from home, the office, and everywhere in be-tween. This makes our ritualized transitions at the end of the workday even more important. Whether we are physically walking out of an office or a building or shutting down our laptop or closing our studio door, what can all of us do to leave work behind emotionally?

If you're still at home, you can give yourself distinct routines or areas of the house or even objects—such as mugs, pens, or a laptop— that you use *only* for work. Doing so lets us prime ourselves to begin working, and to draw boundaries when it's time to stop.

If you are leaving an office or an on-site job, it's important to find ways to mark an end to the day. This could be as simple as a brisk walk home, a splash of cold water before leaving the building, or a few minutes of classical music on the commute home. Without a ritualized transition of ending—a way to leave the stressors back at the office—all of us are vulnerable to burnout and distress.

In research led by Ben Rogers, my colleagues and I explored the end-of-day rituals of nearly three hundred nurses in North Carolina— most of whom experience hectic and stressful work almost daily. We discovered that many performed unique such rituals. As one nurse reported:

After clocking out for the day, I consciously take my badge off and put it in my work bag. As I do this, I tell myself, "I'm fin-ished," and I think about how I'm done being responsible for my patients for the day.

Another nurse turned showering into a complex ritual, right down to specific libations:

I get home and get a beer before getting into the shower. We have an old hot-water heater so I only get seven minutes of hot water. I do the hygiene portion of the shower and stretch afterward. I hold each stretch for thirty seconds, followed by a sip of beer until the hot water runs out, focusing on relaxing my body.

Tellingly, two common words that nurses used to describe the purpose and ultimate effect of their rituals were "decompress" and "unwind." That's something we all need—and if you're not finding it, even simple, repeated daily rituals like those practiced by these nurses can help you shed your work self at the end of the day and come back to your *real* self.

Even if hours of rituals every day are great for well-being, who has the time? The satirical website ClickHole captured the problem with constantly telling people what *else* they need to do to improve their lives: "Why Are You Not Already Doing This: 41 Things You Need to Be Doing Every Day to Avoid Burnout." Recognizing and honoring your existing workplace rituals can take no time at all—you're already doing them. The point is not to add forty-one new rituals to your life starting right now, but to find a handful of rituals that are right for you. Sometimes, this might mean small edits to meaningful rituals you've already been enacting. Other times, it may mean starting from scratch.

Chapter 12

How to Divide

When Rituals Breed Tension and Trouble

> *I hate so much about the things that you choose to be.*
>
> —Michael Scott to Toby Flenderson, *The Office*

For half a century, from the 1950s to the 2000s, Esther Pauline Lederer was America's go-to advice columnist. Under the pen name Ann Landers, she weighed in on countless sources of friction between family members, friends, and couples. Her wisdom was syndicated across the country, with daily readers nodding along. But one opinion in 1977 had her fans crumpling up their newspapers in outrage. What was it about? One uncelebrated household staple: toilet paper.

In an otherwise innocuous column, Lederer stated that she preferred hanging her toilet paper in the "under" orientation, rather than having the sheets unfurl "over" the roll. Little did she know, she'd just penned one of her most polarizing articles. More than fifteen thousand letters poured in expressing strong feelings and outright rancor on the issue. Many people admitted this was a topic of heated domestic debate—in one survey conducted on thousands of respondents, a full

40 percent claimed that toilet paper orientation had been a source of argument at home. The debate was far from settled. It stretched all the way to the farthest reaches of human habitation: researchers stationed in the cramped quarters of the Amundsen-Scott Research Station at the south pole reported their frequent clashes regarding . . ."over" versus "under." For decades afterward, Lederer never escaped "the toilet tissue issue," as she called it. It cropped up in letters to her and her columns for decades, until her death in 2002.

But why would something so innocuous be so deeply polarizing?

All the oaths and shibboleths and flag-waving of our different groups allow us to declare to the world, "I am a member of this tribe." But this enhanced sense of identity and ownership has the potential to cut both ways. If we feel our group is good, it's one small step to thinking that people outside our group are bad. Might our commitment to the correct execution, without deviation, of our rituals leave us pushing others away? Ritual can accelerate our ability to bond within a group, but can also accelerate division, distrust, and vindictiveness between groups.

Conflicts near and far, at our dining room tables and on the international stage, erupt over the smallest ritual "violations." In September of 1922, New York City was swept up in eight days of rioting, injuries, and arrests. The cause? Men continuing to wear straw hats after the traditional September 15 cutoff date (when men were supposed to switch to the seasonally correct felt or silk hats). In the ensuing chaos, "gangs of teenagers prowled the streets wielding large sticks, sometimes with a nail driven through the top, looking for pedestrians wearing straw hats and beating those who resisted." Among the resulting arrests, one A. Silverman was sentenced to three days in jail by Magistrate Peter . . . Hatting.

Both the custom and the conflict seem absurd to us now. But this headwear ritual signaled stability and tradition, a social order and structure within which a member's role and identity were clear. When that sense of social order was disrupted, someone woke up on September 16, 1922, shouting, "It's just not right! Something must be done!" At the tip of a hat—the *wrong* hat—a riot was born.

You may think you're immune: "I couldn't get worked up over something so small." That's why, when I speak to an audience, I always ask, "Does your partner load the dishwasher the right way?" The response is always audible. A staggering number of people believe that their partner's strategy is not only inefficient and hazardous to the machine, but also a sign of poor judgment and questionable morality: "How can he put bowls on the top rack!" Worse still, these feelings are often mutual, and mirrored: "Bowls on the bottom rack? Who does that!" For the record, many dishwashers come with a manual for the optimal method for loading dishes into each model. But, since many manuals go unread, both groups of people commonly load the *wrong* way. Yet that doesn't stop each of us from believing that our way is right and any other way is wrong. Which creates a perfect recipe for conflict.

The same practices that have the power to bond us together can become the battle lines that divide us. To keep the peace—in society at large, and on the home front—it's critical to understand when and why ritual becomes a hazard, and how we can retain the close bonds that our group rituals bring us without falling prey to their darker side.

Rituals and (Dis)Trust

When I've asked audiences to try out the "Clap once. Stomp with your right foot" activity, something interesting often occurs. As people start to sync up their actions, they begin to smile—but when someone claps at the *wrong* time, those smiles turn to frowns. When I ask what the problem is, people say, "Those people are doing it wrong." By "it" they mean the fabricated ritual they've never before done—but which they instantly see as having a correct implementation. And by "those people" they mean the people whose only offense was an errant clap.

I'd like to think that trivial differences in ritual wouldn't make much of a difference in how we feel about other people. But the reality is messier. Instead, small differences can be *the* key markers of the group boundaries we see as important. In research led by Nick Hobson, our team enrolled 107 people in a study whose goal was to put people into arbitrary groups and find out if small differences in ritual would affect how much they trusted—or distrusted—one another.

Our research team first divided people into groups using a "minimal groups paradigm"—or the most basic element of a group distinction—in which people are shown a screen filled with tiny dots and asked to estimate the number. This let us assign people to two different groups: those who overestimated the number, and those who underestimated. This is as meaningless as group distinctions can get—a culture of too many dots on a screen versus a culture of too few?—but we wondered if we could reinforce these group identities with a group ritual.

In their group ritual people enacted together the same sequence of actions every day for a week:

To start, take five deep breaths with your eyes closed, and bring your focus to rest on the sequences about to be performed. Gently bow your head, close your eyes, and make a wiping motion with your hands away from your body. Finish with your arms resting at your sides.

Ending with:

Bring your arms behind your back with your hands together. Slightly bend at the waist, and complete this movement five times: Bring your arms down. Bow your head, close your eyes, and make the wiping motion. Finish with your arms resting at your sides. Take five breaths. You are finished.

At the end of that week, everyone came into our laboratory and played the Trust Game, an experiment that uses real money to measure trust between participants. Some people played the Trust Game with someone from their own group, and others played with someone from the *other* group.

The ritual was sufficient to make people trust and reward "their own"—imbuing their arbitrary group identity with more meaning—and distrust and penalize the "other." Underestimators allocated more of their money to a fellow underestimator ($6.30 out of their $10) than to an overestimator ($5.29). A different set of people also played the Trust Game, but these people didn't enact a group ritual. The result? They were equally trusting of participants from both groups.

In a similar experiment, we asked people to observe others playing the Trust Game and used continuous electroencephalogram (EEG) to assess their brain activity. Our focus was a specific brain pattern—the feedback-P300—which tracks people's thoughts about reward and punishment. People who had enacted group rituals showed more positive processing when they observed members of their own groups, but more negative processing when they observed members of the other group. They liked their own group, but they were ready to punish the other.

The group ritual built trust within one group but generated distrust toward the other group. It's almost as if the ritual caused the group to close ranks, to say, "I know who I can trust, and it's not them."

We wondered whether we could glean anything about which aspects of the ritual were leading to this dual sense of trust and distrust. So, we developed a variation of the same experiment that involved several different rituals—one that was more involved and effortful, and another that was easier and quicker. Given our research on the role of effort in the IKEA effect—which showed that when we labor on something, we value it more—we theorized that effort might affect the intensity of our punitive streak toward people with the wrong ritual.

Effort is clearly a component of many existing group rituals. Researchers surveyed participants enacting two religious rituals during the annual Hindu festival of Thaipusam. One was *low ordeal* (involving singing and collective prayer), and one was *high ordeal* (involving body piercing with multiple needles and carrying heavy shrines on one's shoulders). After these rituals, the researchers measured people's devotion to their religion by asking them to donate to the temple. The high-ordeal ritual led to more giving (around 132 rupees) than the low-ordeal ritual (around 80 rupees). The pain people experienced was correlated with how much they gave: more pain, more giving, more loyalty to the group.

We couldn't go to such extremes in our own research, but we set up a final experiment to gauge the effects of effort. One group was assigned to enact a low-effort ritual (fewer actions, less repetition), and another conducted a high-effort ritual (more actions, more repetition). We then asked everyone to play the Trust Game twice—once with a member of their own group, and once with a member of the *other* group. Those who had enacted the low-effort ritual only slightly favored members of their group, giving them an average of $0.31 more than they gave to members of the other group. But for those who enacted the high-effort ritual, that gap between "us good" and "them bad" more than doubled, to $0.72.

Eating Our Own

When I ask audiences to enact a ritual, I can always predict one response like clockwork. One person, typically a male concerned with appearing smarter than everyone else, refuses to participate. (This person also refuses to raise a hand when I ask an audience a question like "How many people think A?" or "How many think B?" But when I ask, "How many people refuse to raise their hand?," this person's hand shoots up triumphantly.) Also, like clockwork, the people in the audience reserve a special kind of derision for these opt-outers. Because, with ritual, there are no bystanders. You're either doing it right and you're one of us—or you're wrong.

When we imbue our own rituals with deep meaning—when they become sacrosanct—straying from the path is a violation and must be met with consequences. A clear distrust arises when other groups have rituals that conflict with our own. A second strain of enmity evoked by rituals is a mirror image of this conflict: hatred not of *other* groups, but hatred directed at people in our *own* groups who are doing *our* ritual wrong. This is termed the *black sheep effect.* We are harsher toward members of our own group when they behave badly than we are toward members of other groups. You'd be angrier at your sister than your onetime colleague for skipping your wedding, or at your best friend than at a stranger for dating your ex. What about your best friend, a loyal Knicks fan with you from childhood, who does the unthinkable and roots for the Celtics after college. We expected more of these people—we expected that we could trust them.

Whenever I attend a religious service for a faith other than my own, I am always struck by how I compare *their* rituals to *my* rituals, looking for similarities but also noting differences: we stand during this part, and they shake hands before that other part, and we say that phrase like this, not like that. In a project led by Dan Stein, then a doctoral student at the University of California–Berkeley, my colleagues and I wanted to investigate reactions to violations of in-group rituals. Just how much can you change or tweak a ritual before outrage ensues? If we start with one tweak, then another, then another, when does our violation detector go off? What are we able to let slide—and when do the alarm bells start ringing?

To find out, we asked Jewish people to consider the following scenario:

Imagine you recently moved to an area and joined a new Temple congregation. The Temple hosts several Seders at the houses of different Congregation members. You sign up and you subsequently are invited to a local Passover Seder. When you arrive at the house for Seder, you are greeted by the host, who will be leading the Seder. The host walks with you to the Seder table.

We then asked our participants how they would feel if the host informed them some changes would be made to seder items. We told people to picture the host altering either one item, two items, three items, four items, five items, or six items—then told them what the replacement items would be. The egg (*beitzah*), for example, would be replaced with cheese, or the shank bone (*zeroa*) with a chicken bone.

We asked everyone questions about their level of anger at the changes, and their feelings about the (im)morality of the host. People in a control group were told to imagine that the host had made no changes at all.

One prediction would be a linear trend: each altered item makes judgments slightly more negative. But if rituals are sacrosanct—if our group knew better than to mess with tradition—then even a single change might be sufficient to engender anger and moral outrage comparable to that from reworking the whole ceremony. Our results supported the sacrosanct account: the biggest jump in feelings of anger and immorality occurs with the first modification, even just one substitution. After this, additional changes have only a slight effect; they do produce greater negative reactions, but the biggest damage is done by that initial change.

These harsh reactions toward ritual violators are not specific to Judaism. In another experiment, we asked Catholics to watch videos of people making the sign of the cross. Some videos showed people doing so correctly: using the right hand to touch (1) forehead, (2) chest, (3) left shoulder, and (4) right shoulder. Other videos showed people omitting some of these steps. We then asked Catholics to imagine that they were on a church committee planning a major holiday event and needed to allocate some unpleasant tasks for congregation members to complete—including cleaning toilets. Those who had witnessed a fellow Catholic screw up the sign of the cross were more likely to assign that violator to latrine duty.

These findings also offer some practical advice. When we craft private rituals just for ourselves, any changes we make affect only us. But when we try to alter rituals that others hold dear, even if we think that our own group members wouldn't mind, we enter far more turbulent waters. Often, if people are considering altering or giving up a ritual, they think about changing just small aspects of the ritual in order to appease the ritual stalwarts. "We'll just have ham instead of grandma's turkey recipe this year," you might think. But that one change is often just as anger provoking as a complete makeover.

There may be a different, bolder strategy. If alterations to *existing* rituals are what get us worked up, it might be better to start entirely from scratch, with a brand-new ritual. If the holidays without the kids at home isn't going to be the same no matter what you do—don't try to cling to rituals you cherished when you were all together. Try starting a new ritual from whole cloth—maybe it's time to get out of town this year and celebrate the holidays someplace warm.

The Elements of Hate

The evidence shows that even as group rituals bond us, they can also easily become the source of strife. What elements make us most likely to turn our rituals into points of conflict? Two related factors stand out: threat and belief.

When other groups question or threaten our beliefs and our rituals, we are more likely to react harshly toward them. Because of the identity work rituals do, we react as if others are trying to restrict how we express our identity as a group. We can see echoes of this feeling in phrases such as "the War on Christmas." In this case, some Christians feel that their way of life, and their rituals, are threatened—so much so that even a seemingly innocuous shift from "Merry Christmas" to "Happy holidays" triggers anger and outrage, an us-versus-them mentality. Another view is that, hey, other groups have different winter rituals and the phrase "Happy holidays" is more inclusive and covers more ground. Threat and belief are tied together—our beliefs make us feel threatened, and feeling threatened makes us even more sure that our beliefs are right.

Think back to the hat riot of 1922. The anger that day was undeniable. But the threat? In hindsight, that does seem pretty deniable. Keep in mind the way the ritual effect can warp our thinking. Rituals can bind us more closely together—they make us who we are—but this bond can be exclusive and costly. When rituals become not just what we do, but what must be done, they can shift from producing positive effects to engendering distrust, dislike, and punishment of those with conflicting rituals. If we demand that others adopt our rituals— or overlook that others have their own rituals—it inevitably leads to conflict. Sometimes the conflict is mundane—as with skirmishes over toilet paper or dishwashers—but it can also be profoundly devastating. Centuries of conflict have resulted from the hatred harbored by different religious groups. The Thirty Years' War essentially boiled down to a conflict over ritual—the question of whether eating a wafer and sipping wine in church is actually ingesting the body of Christ or metaphorically ingesting the body of Christ. The Catholics said real, the Protestants said metaphor. And so, Europe went to war for three decades.

Undoing Hate

We do have a built-in fail-safe for helping us keep our anger at *them* in check: we're members of many, many groups, and so who *they* are is constantly in flux. Think of a Democrat and a Republican, and what springs to mind is how different they are from each other—they believe different things, they enact different rituals (NPR versus Fox News first thing every morning). But when those two people are at a baseball game, rooting for their team, they don't stop to consider voting records before joining together to keep the wave going. Research shows that these kinds of cross-cutting affiliations have the potential to bridge seemingly irreconcilable group differences. In one study of more than twenty-eight thousand respondents in eighteen sub-Saharan countries, a win by the national team in a soccer match reliably shifted people away from identifying by their ethnicity and toward identifying by their country. The effect was especially true when the ethnic diversity of the national team was more representative of the ethnic diversity of the country as a whole. It is as if people say to themselves, "If they can understand each other well enough to play as an effective team, maybe we can, too."

In 2019, radio broadcaster Jad Abumrad hosted the podcast *Dolly Parton's America*. The premise was that, in a moment of intensely polarized politics and cultures, there was one thing—or rather one person—almost everyone could rally behind: Dolly Parton. By shifting the frame of identity to "Dolly Parton fans," Abumrad argues, we have an opportunity to share more of the same socially cohesive glue. And, maybe, a chance to listen more deeply to one another's grievances.

Rituals serve as social glue that coheres our group identities, for better *and* for worse. The good news is that these identities can be shaped and shifted to include a wider variety of people and practices. When we enlarge the tribe—shifting the frame from polarizing identities around politics, say, toward identities in sports, music, and other aspects of culture—we have an opportunity to defuse conflict, work toward productive change, and broaden everyone's experience of belonging.

Chapter 13

How to Heal

Rituals and Reconciliation

The Commissioners enter the hall in procession and this procession creates a sacred space for the victims. That sacred space contains reverential markers such as the Candle, the Litany for the Dead, and the Silence of Remembrance. Then the victims are led in to their allocated seats. While the victims stand at their seats, the chairperson and the whole Commission go over to greet them. They thank them for coming and they shake hands with each person. While everybody is still standing, the Candle is lit by the chairperson and the names of the victims and the dead are read out. This is followed by a moment of silence. The hearing is then opened with scripture, or a prayer, a song, or a time for silent prayer.

The ceremony described above marked the beginning of hearings held by the Truth and Reconciliation Commission in South Africa, as part of the country's efforts to come to terms with the soul-wrenching history of apartheid. The journalist Antjie Krog referred to these procedures as an effort to create a new "national ritual." The reading of names is an acknowledgment of the harms committed by the apartheid government, which systematically and brutally enforced white supremacy in South Africa for decades. Only through a grueling, drawn-out fight were activists led by Nelson Mandela and others able to bring the regime to an end. But, what then? How does a nation heal after blood and tears have been shed?

The Truth and Reconciliation Commission decided that it needed to start with a ritual, one that could at least serve as a symbolic reset, and a demonstration of comity after so much conflict. The procedures of that ritual are formalized and almost dramatic, but they are designed to *show* that peace and understanding are possible. It's not all just optics. Bishop Joseph Humper, chairman of Sierra Leone's Truth and Reconciliation Commission, made it clear that the national ritual needed to mark not just a new start, but remembrance and a national airing of the truth. Understanding and remembrance were both critical for reconciliation. Some criticized the focus on remembrance, preferring a "forgive and forget" viewpoint. But in defense of the process, Bishop Humper asked, "Why do we come and open the wounds again? Why do we come and recall the past? We have to reopen the wounds because they have not healed. Superficial healing will allow the wounds to explode again. We have to revisit the events so that we can heal properly."

Healing, in other words, can only happen when apologies are preceded by understanding.

Ripe for Apology

What do we do when we've messed up—when we've hurt a friend and we're in the wrong? Every parent, coach, or teacher who has ever encountered two warring children knows the drill. First and foremost, you have to apologize. Apologies are our go-to solution for parties in conflict.

But apologies are far more complicated to pull off than we often think. Simply saying "I'm sorry" doesn't get the job done. On the contrary, the most effective apologies take on the order and patterns of ritual. One taxonomy of apology used in the resolution of disputes between neighbors has no fewer than ten required elements: the statement of apology (this is where most of us stop); naming the offense; taking responsibility; attempting to explain the offense; conveying emotions; addressing emotions and/or damage of the other; admitting fault; promising forbearance; offering reparation; requesting acceptance—formally asking for the other party to accept the apology. An apology that begins with "I'm sorry if you were somehow hurt by my actions" is a failure to take responsibility and admit fault. It's not an admission that the behavior was wrong; it's an implication that the person offended is overreacting.

This distinction relates to one of the core aspects of a successful apology—the feeling that the other person understands you, and why you were hurt. Experts in conflict resolution use the word *ripeness* to describe how ready someone is for an apology—and for us to ripen, we need to feel that the other person understands the harm. In one study in which people were asked to recall times they'd been wronged, it was critical for the offending party, before apologizing, to fulfill other needs, such as "ask[ing] questions to understand what I was saying" and "understand[ing] my feelings and point of view." The preemptive apology, unfortunately, is all too common—in real life and in pop culture. When two very different television dads slipped up in trying to take responsibility, Tony Soprano was told, "You don't know what you're apologizing for," and Homer Simpson was told, "You don't even know why you're apologizing." Understanding is so important that when people apologize before understanding, the apology is often as ineffective as never apologizing at all.

A well-delivered apology can start us down the path of reconciliation, but it's often just the first step. This is likely why so many cultures have embraced action as a springboard to reconciliation. If one single action has become synonymous with understanding and goodwill, it's the surprisingly ubiquitous handshake. If you can apologize and shake hands—and mean it—that simple gesture often speaks louder than words.

Handshaking is one of our most widespread rituals—brief, but nonetheless psychologically potent—in domains ranging from meeting the in-laws to showing sportsmanship in intramural baseball games to both starting and ending negotiations. International politics can hinge on handshake drama—especially occasional violations of handshaking etiquette. In 2005, George W. Bush inadvertently insulted Slovak officials by failing to remove his gloves before shaking hands; in 2013, Hassan Rouhani's refusal to shake hands with Barack Obama was deemed a "historic non-handshake" that "irreparably damaged negotiations." On the other hand, successful completion of handshake protocol is often seen as evidence of amity. In 2014, Shinzo Abe of Japan and Xi Jinping of China agreed to meet for a single purpose—to shake hands—with the media noting that the "small gesture holds great importance."

How could such an unremarkable action come to be imbued with so much importance? As Margaret Atwood put it, "Touch comes before sight, before speech. It is the first language and the last, and it always tells the truth." The handshake is something anyone can do, in any setting, as long as people are face-to-face. The origins of the handshake are murky, but the two most common explanations reflect that simplicity and parity: it's either that the clasping of hands symbolizes a binding oath, or, less prosaically but more practically, that shaking hands dislodges any hidden daggers.

We tend not to have as many daggers up our sleeves these days. So why are we still shaking hands?

In a close relationship—such as in a family or a marriage—some trust is naturally present: I want to understand where you're coming from, and I trust that you are trying to understand where I'm coming from, too. That's not always obvious in strangers. But handshaking shows us that, even if we don't know these people, they're willing to engage. This can cut the tension enough to let a relationship start to form.

That said, before you start pumping hands with everyone you meet, you may want to practice on a friend, because the old adage that you need to have a firm handshake is true. In one study, students in mock job interviews shook hands before beginning, and those students whose handshakes were rated as having "poor grip" or "awkward duration" were evaluated more negatively by their counterparts. They were even seen to be less qualified for the position in question.

Handshakes are one mini-ritual we engage in to establish ourselves, but we turn to plenty of other simple actions when seeking understanding or reconciliation—each with its own underlying logic.

Consider the high five. Despite its widespread adoption, the high five is a recent ritual innovation, invented in 1977 by the baseball player Dusty Baker, who, after hitting a home run, saw a teammate with his hands up and decided to slap them. An arbitrary action at the time, it spread and deepened and has become a meaningful ritual.

Or the simple hug. When we hug a friend, the science of what's going on is deep and complex. We first employ "smooth and yielding movements with round transitions between muscular tensing and re-laxing"—but when the hug has gone on too long, we wrap it up quickly by stepping away or patting each other on the back.

Or an innocuous stroll. Why do world leaders go on walks to-gether? Why do U.S. presidents parade congressional leaders through the Rose Garden? Even simply walking next to another person can smooth interactions and facilitate cooperation. Research shows that when people walk next to each other, they naturally synchronize their movements, and they experience "shared attention" (looking at the same things), which can help them begin to understand each other's perspective.

Apologies, handshakes, and high fives all have their place. But many conflicts call for stronger medicine. Reconciliation rituals are central not just to our efforts to understand one another and reach ac-cord, but also to our goals of bringing together disparate groups. How do you bridge the divides that exist between groups with vastly differ-ent experiences?

Making One Plus One Equal One

Think of all the inside jokes you have with your friends—all the short-hand and nonsense phrases you've gradually loaded with meaning. Just a glance or a raised eyebrow can communicate entire worlds to your best friend. How much time did it take to build that level of understanding? When did it cross from friendship to a common cul-ture in miniature?

Psychologists and sociologists are perennially fascinated by how groups form, bond, and create their own cultures—and what happens when cultures collide. In the early 2000s, researchers Roberto Weber and Colin Camerer created a clever game to investigate these questions. The experiment is similar in spirit to a parlor game such as Celebrity, where each round gets more constrained and more hilarious as the two sides come up with shorthand words and gestures to signify the clues they originally solved in round one.

Imagine you're on a small team of just two people. You are the "manager" and your partner is the "employee." Each of you has a set of sixteen pictures, and each image captures a different scene of an office environment. The sixteen pictures have some shared features—people and furniture and shades of beige—but some features are varied, such as the gender, ethnicity, and clothing of the people, and their actions, such as conversing with others in the picture, talking on the telephone, or working at a computer. When the game starts, you as manager are given eight of the pictures, in a specific order, and are told to describe the pictures in any way you'd like so that your employee can guess which pictures you have, and in which order. You're asked to play this guessing game together for twenty rounds, and you both get paid based on how quickly you can identify the pictures.

Once they started, the pairs quickly developed idiosyncratic vernaculars that allowed them to get faster and faster at the task. For example, in the first round of the game, one pair referred to a given picture as "the one with three people: two men and one woman. The woman is sitting on the left. They're all looking at two computers that look like they have some PowerPoint graphs or charts. The two men are wearing ties and the woman has short blond hair. One guy is pointing at one of the charts."

But after several rounds, the pair referred to this picture succinctly as "PowerPoint."

Then the pairs were greeted with a surprise: their two-person "firm" was being merged with another two-person firm, and the game would continue for additional rounds, with these new partners. Now there was a problem. Remember the pair that efficiently got down to just

"PowerPoint" to describe a particular picture? Other pairs were just as efficient in capturing that same picture with minimal words, but they were not the same words. One pair used "Woman sitting, smiling" and another used "Guy hunching." The enlarged firms had to scramble to find a new common language.

What happened postmerger? The idiosyncrasies—that shared language developed by partners—had made the teams extremely efficient in the first segment of the game. But new team members with different languages slowed the new firms down in the second segment. Imagine the frustration of a manager shouting "PowerPoint!" over and over, while her new employee sits dumbfounded as to what picture the manager could possibly have in mind. The new folks haven't done anything wrong, but their failure to understand the idiosyncratic language (and culture) enrages the manager nonetheless. Employees who were acquired in the "merger" rated their new manager much more negatively than their old manager because their new manager was not a "strong communicator."

What was lacking was a sense of group identity and understanding. Feeling understood is linked to our emotional and even our physical well-being. In one study, people answered questions about their day, including "How satisfied are you with your life today?" and "During your interactions with others today, to what extent did you feel understood?" People who felt more understood were more satisfied—and even reported fewer negative physical symptoms such as headaches, stomachaches, or dizzy spells.

This study was a microcosm of why conflict comes so readily when we bring together different cultures. When two companies merge, when two families combine, when friend groups get together—each brings its own in-jokes and memories and rituals. This can lead to clashes. How do we turn two into one?

Researchers Dawn Braithwaite, Leslie Baxter, and Anneliese

Harper wanted to answer this question, specifically by looking at blended families. When trying to merge families, parents often want to build something new, but the children tend to want to continue the traditions of their birth family. To understand what works, and what doesn't, Braithwaite, Baxter, and Harper asked twenty stepparents and thirty-three stepchildren how they had managed the tension of combining old and new. It can go badly, as in the experience of this stepdaughter in their study:

In my original family, every Saturday night we used to go to the same restaurant. It's my mom's favorite restaurant. We'd have the same table, same waiter, every Saturday night. When my father got married again, we started to do it. We went to the [same restaurant] for a while, until one day I blurted out, "This is my mom's favorite restaurant!" And my stepmom said, "Well, we're not going to come here anymore." So we started going to this new restaurant. I don't even remember the name of it. It just wasn't the same. It was awful.

Holidays and celebrations can become a battle for loyalty: either you're with me (and *my* rituals) or you're against me (and for *their* rituals). An actual merger is more successful—a blend of two families coming together while retaining aspects of their uniquenesses—than a hostile takeover.

One move is to continue to honor existing rituals. One stepfather in the same study was willing to adopt a ritual of his wife's family but noted, "On New Year's Eve, they've got to eat pork and sauerkraut, and the sauerkraut's raw. I can't stand it. I hate it! But I do it." Despite his distaste, he does it because "it gives a feeling of togetherness, bonding."

Others make sure to fold new family members into existing rituals, such as the stepfather who chose personalized Christmas gifts for his stepdaughter in the same way that he did for his son, leading her to say, "It feels like I'm his daughter. . . . I'm not his stepdaughter, but just the same as his son."

Many families choose a third merging strategy: they jointly create new rituals. Often the best approach is to retain *some* elements of the old, as an acknowledgment of the importance of those past rituals, while giving the ritual enough originality that it feels like the family's own. For instance, one stepmother in the study spoke about her blended family's making of their own Christmas decorations every year, with each new ornament marking their years together as a (new) family:

It's a time of camaraderie and it's a time of teamwork and we find ourselves reminiscing about previous holidays and Christmases and holidays that we've had together. And when we finish, we're always amazed. "Gosh we made this and it looks good!" You know, everyone has made a contribution to it.

When parents divorce and marry new partners, children can feel pressured to choose between families, which only adds to their difficulty in processing the breakup. But when children's rituals from their original family are given a place, or when stepparents welcome children into existing rituals, or, finally, when families create new rituals that feel shared and distinctly theirs, children are relieved of some of this emotional work. Ritual cements the bonds of the new family; they own it together, and it makes them a new unit.

The same strategy that people use when blending families is also a best practice for merging companies. The most successful mergers result when companies use rituals to retain some of the old, to let some go, and to create new common touchstones that are unique to the new organization.

In one study exploring fifty mergers of companies based in the United States and Sweden, the effectiveness of each merger was rated on a scale ranging from "a successful merger" to "a very low level of acculturation," which was described as continued strong cultural clashes and almost no joint organizational culture. What was the difference between the winners and the losers? The researchers noted that "almost only one thing matters: involve the affected employees in such socialization activities as introduction programs, training, cross visits, joining retreats, celebrations and other such socialization rituals." That's right, it's important to use ritual to bring both parties into the fold. Doing so, and putting the employees at the forefront of those rituals, created a common sense of understanding that came from the bottom up. The benefits of ritual held up for many different kinds of mergers—for U.S. and Swedish firms, for smaller and larger firms. Notably, employee-generated rituals were more important than more "official" merger activities such as implementing transition teams or rotating personnel.

Executive coach Brian Gorman describes one corporate merger that perfectly captured that emphasis on merger rather than takeover—and it did so by successfully blending the old with the new. Employees were asked to take slips of paper and write down things they wanted to let go of after the merger, as well as the things that they wanted to carry forward to the new company. Employees then tossed their "letting go" slips into a fire. A few days later, the merged company gathered to define its new identity. Employees were encouraged to read their "holding on to" slips out loud, then post them on a wall. It was a way of forging a shared identity all at once.

Was it just a clever idea—or did it work? The answer lies in the employees' own actions. As part of the gathering the company took pictures of the "holding on to" wall and made them available to the staff. Even years later, some employees still had those photos as their desktop images.

The Healing Process

When two families or companies combine, it might look like a tinder-box at the outset—but no one has yet struck a match. What do we do when the fire has been lit, the blaze has been raging, and a thick smoke still sits in the air? How do we overcome scorched-earth conflicts: a marriage that partners have torn to shreds, a family dispute that has raged on for decades, or even a centuries-old injustice that spans continents and cultures?

In 1910, Eric Mjöberg committed a terrible crime. A Swede in Australia, he fled back home to Sweden with a trove stolen from aboriginal land. It wasn't artwork or bullion he made off with—it was worse. Mjöberg took fifteen skulls and other skeletal parts, which would soon end up in the collection of the Museum of Ethnography in Stockholm. That crime stood unaddressed for nearly a century, but in 2004, the museum finally responded to calls for justice. It was past time to repatriate the stolen skulls, and it was also time to reckon with the cultural cost.

The repatriation couldn't be a surreptitious exchange; there wasn't a simple way to heal the wound. How could there be? Members of the Australian aboriginal delegation and the staff of the museum co-created a ritual for a meaningful repatriation, one that honored the homecoming and made the Swedes understand the scope of the loss that had been inflicted. The resulting ceremony—commonly used for spiritual cleansing by aboriginal Australians—was a joint effort and meant to allow a connection between the two cultures, in stark contrast to the initial crime. One onlooker described it:

Soon, fragrant white smoke was billowing against the greenery: at that moment, it felt significant that it blended smoke from plants from different landscapes. A special kind of green twigs—"cherry tree," someone said—had been brought on the flight from Australia. Other sticks had been brought by one of the curators from an island in the Stockholm archipelago. The white-bearded leader of the [aboriginal Australian] delegation uttered some brief but kind words about how satisfying it felt to take the ancestors home to where they really belonged. A man began to play the didgeridoo. Then it was time to go through the smoke.

For the aboriginal Australian delegates, it was essential to fully represent their identity and to have their counterparts understand both that identity and the wrongs that were committed in the past through ignoring it. And, to acknowledge the weight of the crime, another important person attended: Lotte Mjöberg, a relative of Eric Mjöberg's. It was Lotte who screwed the lids onto the shipping crates, reversing the actions of her ancestor, as much as was possible. The offense was so great that, in this aspect of the ritual, it would be physically undone to be psychologically undone.

That the aboriginal Australians brought their Swedish counterparts into a ritual drawn from their own tradition—then altered it to incorporate Swedish elements—may seem surprising. But this is a common thread of healing rituals, which share many features with rituals to blend families or merge companies. The goal is to allow all parties to become involved and to take part together; sharing responsibility for the initial crime is crucial, but breaking down the barrier that lies between the two parties so there is mending is just as important. Think back to the postapartheid rituals in South Africa: they required truth and clarity, but also the creation of a new ritual that could be shared by the new nation, allowing a future with a possibility beyond the pains of the past.

Across all of these contexts, we cannot heal or see ourselves in community with another group unless we feel they understand us. In one survey that asked more than five thousand Scottish people whether they were for or against Scotland being an independent country, the Scots' answers hinged on whether they felt the English understood Scottish views and values. The best predictor of wanting to stay (or leave) was not so much how people said they liked the English, but instead how well they thought the English understood them. When people felt understood, they were more likely to want to try to make the union work, to want to remain a part of the larger nation.

Rituals that mend the rifts between groups are often about forging a joint identity—but they accomplish that by first acknowledging each group's individual identity. William Ury, the author of *Getting to Yes*, and the conflict-negotiation expert who worked on several Israeli and Palestinian mediations, argued that this individual respect is often missing from our most challenging negotiations. "It's the cheapest concession you can give as a negotiator—it doesn't cost anything—but it's amazing how often we don't give [it] to the other."

Ritual offers us a set of actions that we can all conduct together to confer that respect and understanding and establish a new start. This is true of nations and large organizations and is even key to healing long-held rifts on the domestic front.

Tom and Sagan Lewis, after twenty-two years of divorce, remarried in a ceremony exactly thirty-five years and one day after their first wedding. (They were fans of ritual in general; when they divorced in 1993, they held a Final Anniversary Party, telling guests, "If you must bring a gift, bring two.") Remarriages are rare, but according to marriage therapist Michele Weiner-Davis, when they do occur, it's often because both partners "come to the relationship with a new maturity and a willingness to learn how things got in disrepair to begin with. . . . They're more willing to take a look at what each person can do differently so that they don't find themselves in the same position again." Tom and Sagan had missed each other in the two decades of their divorce, but their remarriage was only possible because they owned that they were too busy being adversarial instead of collaborative in their initial marriage. They had to understand both what had held them back, and what they'd need to accomplish to make "happily ever after last." Their renewed pledge to be more understanding included this note on their (second) wedding invitation: "After 22 years, the divorce didn't work out."

We can use rituals to bond us together, creating meaning in our shared endeavors. We can also use rituals to divide, sowing distrust toward those whose rituals differ from ours. Fortunately, after the dust has settled, rituals can help reconcile. They encourage understanding—often by making it part of the ritual itself, by granting participants the opportunity to speak their truth, and to hear one another out. In our (re) marriages, in our (blended) families, in our mergers and acquisitions, in nations yearning to find peace, rituals of reconciliation help to turn the page and start a new chapter.

Epilogue

A Ritual Life

It's Monday morning. Before the sun rises, Flannery O'Connor is starting her day with morning prayers and a thermos of coffee, and Maya Angelou is opening the door to her motel room with all the art removed from the walls. Another woman living across the country lets her smartphone rest unattended at her bedside and, instead, draws back her curtains, takes a deep breath, and beholds the day. Meanwhile a man steps into his bathroom and turns the faucet to its coldest setting. Using three handfuls of freezing water—always three—he splashes it on his face and embraces the day with a jolt of vitality.

Sometime around 9:00 a.m., after Victor Hugo has stripped naked and instructed his valet to hide his clothes until he has met his daily writing goals, a chief marketing officer is meeting with her team and soaking in the Monday-morning "share" in which each member offers a highlight from the weekend. She drinks her second coffee—the second cup always at the office, where she keeps her mother's childhood mug stored in her desk drawer. She savors the coffee's fragrance and runs her fingers along the mug's chiseled ceramic ridges, an action that always evokes a memory of her mother's hands.

At exactly 3:30 p.m., the moment Immanuel Kant steps outside his door for his afternoon walk with his Spanish walking stick in hand, a fund manager might be starting to prepare for his biggest presentation of the fiscal year. He slips into his office and does his signature series of sun salutations, which always makes him feel more confident and relaxed. He steps outside his office—right foot always first—and gives three lucky taps to the sign above its door. Then it's time to enter the conference room filled with colleagues and clients.

When the workday is done, just about the time Agatha Christie slips into a bathtub and eats an apple, a third-grade teacher arrives back home, sloughs off her work clothes, and washes the stress of the day away with a long shower. She imagines her worries about a troubled student sliding off her body and circling down into the drain. At dinner, her son leads the family through "rose, thorn, and bud," where everyone lists a good thing and a bad thing from that day, followed by something the person is looking forward to tomorrow. She takes a deep breath and tells her family that her rose is the gratitude she feels for the simple beauty of their dinner together.

Our Monday is coming to an end. Charles Dickens is pulling out the compass he always keeps with him to confirm that his bed is facing north. A young mother is tucking in a child with the same two books and four songs, while a grandmother on the other side of the world is lighting a candle and giving thanks for good health. A teenager, exhausted after a soccer match, still finds the strength to put on his pajamas in an order that brings him comfort and calm—tops always first and then bottoms, left foot first and then right. Everywhere, all over the world, it's time to bring the day to its end in a way that feels "just right."

These simple actions might not be changing our outside world, but they do affect us—all of us—on the inside. Whether giving us a sense of ownership, an affirmation of identity and belonging, or an increased feeling of meaning, rituals are one of humanity's greatest tools for providing just the right emotional or psychological effect at just the right moment. Rituals are everywhere imbuing our ordinary actions with extraordinary power. All of us are living a ritual life.

Whether we are taking inspiration from the world's greatest performers, scientists, artists, and athletes and enacting unique rituals before a performance, sustaining our connections and commitment—at work and at home—or seeking out ways to cope with loss, the ritual effect is a reminder that these odd patterns of repetitive behavior exist because we, as humans, have always relied on them. They are available for all of us anywhere and at any time—we need only summon up their rough magic with a bit of effort and, even better, a dash of our individuality.

This is the great opportunity of rituals in the twenty-first century. Rituals offer all of us a way to enhance our lives with something more. Go out and experiment. In every one of your days, ordinary actions may transform into the extraordinary. What did you do today to love, appreciate, laugh, mourn, savor, *experience*, just a little bit more? And what more can you do tomorrow?

Acknowledgments

I want to express my thanks and gratitude to the following awesome people:

My many, many collaborators on all of our research on rituals. It's an unusual topic and I'm grateful to each of you for being willing to have it on your beloved CV.

My agents, Alison MacKeen and Celeste Fine, whose belief in the ideas in this book is the only reason I went forward with writing it.

My editors, Rick Horgan and Nan Graham, both of whom helped to guide the book to be both more compelling and more useful to readers.

Alison MacKeen, Campbell Schnebly, Jon Cox, and Ann Marie Healy, the people who helped to craft and shepherd the ideas in the book (in order of intellectual appearance).

Norma Hellstein for expert proofreading and Katie Boland for brilliantly wrangling the endnotes, Corey Powell and Peter Guzzardi for their helpful feedback in framing the book, and Chris McGrory for his assistance in tracking down compelling examples.

The students in the three freshman seminars I taught at Harvard for our many interesting discussions about how rituals play out in our lives (and without whom there would be no references to any cultural event this century).

And most of all, my mom, dad, siblings, and entire Irish Catholic extended family for the rituals you gave me, and Deals and the Tootch for the rituals we've created together.

Notes

Preface: Reenchanted

3 *Before the sun rises . . . and falls asleep:* Howard Thompson, "Quiet Murders Suit Miss Christie; Visiting Writer Still Prefers to Keep Crime in Family," *New York Times*, October 27, 1966, https://www .nytimes.com/1966/10/27/archives/quiet-murders-suit-miss -christie-visiting-writer-still-prefers-to.html; James Surowiecki, "Later," *New Yorker*, October 4, 2010, https://www.newyorker .com/magazine/2010/10/11/later; Emmie Martin, "14 Bizarre Sleeping Habits of Super-Successful People," *Independent*, April 26, 2016, https://www.independent.co.uk/news/people/14-bizarre -sleeping-habits-of-supersuccessful-people-a7002076.html; Mason Currey, *Daily Rituals: How Artists Work* (New York: Alfred A. Knopf, 2013).

4 *Keith Richards . . . a carefully arranged game of basketball:* David Sanderson, "Keith Richards Finds Satisfaction in Pre-concert Shepherd's Pie," *Times*, June 8, 2018, https://www.thetimes.co.uk /article/stones-find-satisfaction-in-pre-concert-shepherds-pie -qn80glfmh; "Chris Martin Gig Ritual," *Clash Magazine*, March 10, 2009, https://www.clashmusic.com/news/chris-martin-gig-ritual/; Nanny Fröman, "Marie and Pierre Curie and the Discovery of Polonium and Radium," Nobel Prize, https://www.nobelprize.org /prizes/themes/marie-and-pierre-curie-and-the-discovery-of

223

-polonium-and-radium/; Julie Hirschfeld Davis, "Obama's Election Day Ritual: Dribbling and Jump Shots," *New York Times*, November 8, 2016, https://www.nytimes.com/2016/11/09/us/politics/obama-election-day.html.

Chapter 1: What *Are* Rituals?

8 *what the philosopher Charles Taylor has called our "secular age":* Charles Taylor, *A Secular Age* (Cambridge, MA: Belknap Press of Harvard University Press, 2018).

9 *In the United States . . . by the year 2070:* Reem Nadeem, "How U.S. Religious Composition Has Changed in Recent Decades," Pew Research Center's Religion & Public Life Project, September 13, 2022, https://www.pewresearch.org/religion/2022/09/13/how-u-s-religious-composition-has-changed-in-recent-decades/.

9 *A 2022 Gallup poll showed Americans' trust in institutions . . . at an all-time low:* Jeffrey M. Jones, "Confidence in U.S. Institutions Down; Average at New Low," Gallup, July 5, 2022, https://news.gallup.com/poll/394283/confidence-institutions-down-average-new-low.aspx.

9 *German lawyer and economist Max Weber . . . world stripped of light and warmth:* Max Weber, *Economy and Society* (1922; repr., New York: Bedminster, 1968).

10 *Belief in God remains pervasive . . . some 81 percent in 2022:* Jeffrey M. Jones, "Belief in God in U.S. Drops to 81%, a New Low," Gallup, July 17, 2022, https://news.gallup.com/poll/393737/belief-god-dips-new-low.aspx.

10 *In China . . . 44 percent of unaffiliated adults:* "Religiously Unaffiliated," Pew Research Center, December 18, 2012, https://www.pewforum.org/2012/12/18/global-religious-landscape-unaffiliated/.

10 *starting with Burning Man . . . the Bombay Beach Biennale:* Penelope Green, "How Much Hip Can the Desert Absorb?," *New*

York Times, April 12, 2019, https://www.nytimes.com/2019/04/12/style/coachella-desert-hipsters-salton-sea.html.

10 *Orangetheory's "Hell Week":* Melissa Fiorenza, "Project: Hell Week—Preview & Expert Tips," Orangetheory Fitness, https://www.orangetheory.com/en-us/articles/project-hell-week.

10 *SoulCycle's candlelit rooms:* Julie Hirschfeld Davis, "A Beat and a Bike: The First Lady's Candlelit Habit," *New York Times*, January 10, 2016, https://www.nytimes.com/2016/01/11/us/politics/a-beat-and-a-bike-michelle-obamas-candlelit-habit.html.

10 *During the years of the COVID lockdown . . . move in synchrony with other humans:* Rachel Strugatz, "How SoulCycle Got Stuck Spinning Its Wheels," *New York Times*, May 27, 2020, https://www.nytimes.com/2020/05/19/style/soulcycle-peloton-home-exercise-bikes-coronavirus.html.

10 GYM IS MY CHURCH: Mark Oppenheimer, "When Some Turn to Church, Others Go to CrossFit," *New York Times*, November 27, 2015, https://www.nytimes.com/2015/11/28/us/some-turn-to-church-others-to-crossfit.html.

11 *"Digital Sabbath" rituals delineate a sacred space . . . "reveling in friendship":* Anand Giridharadas, "Exploring New York, Unplugged and on Foot," *New York Times*, January 24, 2013, https://www.nytimes.com/2013/01/25/nyregion/exploring-red-hook-brooklyn-unplugged-and-with-friends.html; Kostadin Kushlev, Ryan Dwyer, and Elizabeth Dunn, "The Social Price of Constant Connectivity: Smartphones Impose Subtle Costs on Well-Being," *Current Directions in Psychological Science* 28, no. 4 (2019): 347–52.

11 *members of the Luddite Club . . . if only for a few hours:* Alex Vadukul, "'Luddite' Teens Don't Want Your Likes," *New York Times*, December 15, 2022, https://www.nytimes.com/2022/12/15/style/teens-social-media.html.

11 *Seattle Atheist Church:* "Home," Seattle Atheist Church, https://seattleatheist.church/.

12 *corporate ritual consultants:* Nellie Bowles, "God Is Dead. So Is the Office. These People Want to Save Both," *New York Times*, August 28, 2020, https://www.nytimes.com/2020/08/28/business /remote-work-spiritual-consultants.html.

12 *quantifying the precise effect of spending our money . . . on our happiness:* Elizabeth Dunn and Michael I. Norton, *Happy Money: The Science of Happier Spending* (New York: Simon & Schuster, 2014).

12 *varying the type of information conveyed by political "spin doctors":* Michael I. Norton and George R. Goethals, "Spin (and Pitch) Doctors: Campaign Strategies in Televised Political Debates," *Political Behavior* 26, no. 3 (2004): 227–48.

12 *specific brain regions undergird the ubiquitous tendency:* Malia F. Mason et al., "Wandering Minds: The Default Network and Stimulus-Independent Thought," *Science* 315, no. 5810 (2007): 393–95.

16 *such as a twenty-first-century pandemic:* Sheryl Gay Stolberg, Benjamin Mueller, and Carl Zimmer, "The Origins of the COVID Pandemic: What We Know and Don't Know," *New York Times*, March 17, 2023, https://www.nytimes.com/article/covid-origin -lab-leak-china.html.

17 *"demo or die":* Lisa Guernsey, "M.I.T. Media Lab at 15: Big Ideas, Big Money," *New York Times*, November 9, 2000, https://www .nytimes.com/2000/11/09/technology/mit-media-lab-at-15-big -ideas-big-money.html.

18 *In her book* Talk of Love . . . *and Hollywood movie tropes:* Ann Swidler, *Talk of Love: How Culture Matters* (Chicago: University of Chicago Press, 2013).

19 *Kurt Cobain, who insisted on wearing plaid pajamas:* Lynn Hirschberg, "Strange Love: The Story of Kurt Cobain and Courtney Love," *Vanity Fair*, September 1, 1992, https://www.vanityfair.com /hollywood/2016/03/love-story-of-kurt-cobain-courtney-love.

22 *Brain-imaging research by my colleagues . . . observing other people perform rituals:* Nicholas M. Hobson et al., "When Novel Ritu-

als Lead to Intergroup Bias: Evidence from Economic Games and Neurophysiology," *Psychological Science* 28, no. 6 (2017): 733–50.

23   *In the 1930s, the self-styled "radical behaviorist" psychologist B. F. Skinner:* B. F. Skinner, "Operant Behavior," *American Psychologist* 18, no. 8 (1963): 503.

23   The Power of Habit: Charles Duhigg, *The Power of Habit: Why We Do What We Do in Life and Business* (New York: Random House, 2012).

24   *famously known as* nudges: Richard H. Thaler and Cass R. Sunstein, *Nudge: Improving Decisions about Health, Wealth, and Happiness* (New York: Penguin, 2009).

24   *"I've Optimized My Health":* Tom Ellison, "I've Optimized My Health to Make My Life as Long and Unpleasant as Possible," *McSweeney's*, March 3, 2023, https://www.mcsweeneys.net /articles/ive-optimized-my-health-to-make-my-life-as-long-and -unpleasant-as-possible.

25   *feeling sad might lead us to put on a favorite sitcom rerun:* Aaron C. Weidman and Ethan Kross, "Examining Emotional Tool Use in Daily Life," *Journal of Personality and Social Psychology* 120, no. 5 (2021): 1344.

25   *what we termed* emodiversity—*is associated with measurable benefits:* Jordi Quoidbach et al., "Emodiversity and the Emotional Ecosystem," *Journal of Experimental Psychology: General* 143, no. 6 (2014): 2057.

26   *Picasso famously did a lot with blue:* "Pablo Picasso's Blue Period—1901 to 1904," Pablo Picasso, https://www.pablopicasso .org/blue-period.jsp.

26   *Vantablack, which absorbs close to 100 percent of visible light:* Nicole Laporte, "How Hollywood Is Embracing the World's Blackest Black Paint," *Fast Company*, September 21, 2021, https://www.fast company.com/90677635/blackest-black-vantablack-hollywood.

27   *Paul Ekman:* Paul Ekman, "Basic Emotions," *Handbook of Cognition and Emotion* 98, no. 45–60 (1999): 16.

27 *twenty-seven or twenty-eight emotions:* Alan S. Cowen and Dacher Keltner, "Self-Report Captures 27 Distinct Categories of Emotion Bridged by Continuous Gradients," *Proceedings of the National Academy of Sciences* 114, no. 38 (2017): E7900–E7909; Carroll E. Izard, *Human Emotions* (New York: Springer Science & Business Media, 2013).

28 *from spending time with romantic partners:* Ximena Garcia-Rada, Övül Sezer, and Michael I. Norton, "Rituals and Nuptials: The Emotional and Relational Consequences of Relationship Rituals," *Journal of the Association for Consumer Research* 4, no. 2 (2019): 185–97; Övül Sezer et al., "Family Rituals Improve the Holidays," *Journal of the Association for Consumer Research* 1, no. 4 (2016): 509–26; Tami Kim et al., "Work Group Rituals Enhance the Meaning of Work," *Organizational Behavior and Human Decision Processes* 165 (2021): 197–212; Benjamin A. Rogers et al., "After-Work Rituals and Well-Being," working paper.

28 *Delhi on Diwali . . . Day of the Dead . . . ceremonial Passover seder:* Somini Sengupta, "To Celebrate Diwali Is to Celebrate the Light," *New York Times*, November 14, 2020, https://www.nytimes. com/2020/11/14/us/diwali-celebration.html; Oscar Lopez, "What Is the Day of the Dead, the Mexican Holiday?," *New York Times*, October 27, 2022, https://www.nytimes.com/article/day-of-the-dead-mexico.html; Elizabeth Dias, "'This Is What We Do': The Power of Passover and Tradition across Generations," *New York Times*, April 9, 2020, https://www.nytimes.com/2020/04/08/us/passover-seder-plagues-coronavirus.html.

29 *scientists call* identity work: Andrew D. Brown, "Identity Work and Organizational Identification," *International Journal of Management Reviews* 19, no. 3 (2017): 296–317.

Chapter 2: You Get Out of It
What You Put into It

32   *Thaler identified as the* endowment effect*:* Daniel Kahneman, Jack
     L. Knetsch, and Richard H. Thaler, "Anomalies: The Endowment
     Effect, Loss Aversion, and Status Quo Bias," *Journal of Economic
     Perspectives* 5, no. 1 (1991): 193–206.

33   *"One opens a box of cake mix": Living* (New York: Street & Smith,
     1956).

33   *In 1947, around $79 million of cake mixes:* Laura Shapiro, *Some-
     thing from the Oven: Reinventing Dinner in 1950s America* (Lon-
     don: Penguin Books, 2005); Emma Dill, "Betty Crocker Cake Mix,"
     *Mnopedia, January 23, 2019, http://www.mnopedia.org/thing
     /betty-crocker-cake-mix.*

33   *he called "focus groups":* Mark Tadajewski, "Focus Groups: History,
     Epistemology and Non-individualistic Consumer Research," *Con-
     sumption Markets & Culture* 19, no. 4 (2016): 319–45.

34   *"I like foods that are time-consuming":* Liza Featherstone, "Talk Is
     Cheap: The Myth of the Focus Group," *Guardian,* February 6, 2018,
     https://www.theguardian.com/news/2018/feb/06/talk-is-cheap
     -the-myth-of-the-focus-group.

35   *My colleague Ximena Garcia-Rada . . . "You give the XOXOs":* Xi-
     mena Garcia-Rada et al., "Consumers Value Effort over Ease When
     Caring for Close Others," *Journal of Consumer Research* 48, no. 6
     (2022): 970–90.

36   *willing to pay $0.78—a 63 percent increase:* Michael I. Norton et
     al., "The IKEA Effect: When Labor Leads to Love," *Journal of Con-
     sumer Psychology* 22, no. 3 (July 2012): 453–60.

36   *IKEA effect was featured on the television game show* Jeopardy!*:*
     Andy Saunders, "Today's Final Jeopardy—Wednesday, March 24,
     2021," Jeopardy! *Fan,* March 24, 2021, https://thejeopardyfan
     .com/2021/03/final-jeopardy-3-24-2021.html.

37 *The researchers found that five- and six-year-old children:* Lauren Marsh, Patricia Kanngiesser, and Bruce Hood, "When and How Does Labour Lead to Love? The Ontogeny and Mechanisms of the IKEA Effect," *Cognition* 170 (2018): 245–53.

Chapter 3: The Ritual Effect

41 *Rafael Nadal is widely considered:* Kurt Streeter, "GOATs Are Everywhere in Sports. So, What Really Defines Greatness?," *New York Times*, July 3, 2023, https://www.nytimes.com/2023/07/03/sports/tennis/greatest-athlete-of-all-time.html.

41 *"the most famous underwear adjuster in history"*: Ashley Fetters, "Catching Up with Noted Underwear Model (and Tennis Player) Rafael Nadal," *GQ*, September 20, 2016, https://www.gq.com/story/rafael-nadal-underwear-model-interview#:~:text=Not%20only%20is%20Nadal%20a,chronic%20underwear%20adjuster%20in%20history.

42 *"It's something I don't need to do"*: Rafael Nadal, *Rafa* (Paris: JC Lattès, 2012).

42 *he called it* operant conditioning: B. F. Skinner, "Operant Conditioning," *Encyclopedia of Education* 7 (1971): 29–33.

43 *sit back and enjoy the free lunch:* B. F. Skinner, "'Superstition' in the Pigeon," *Journal of Experimental Psychology* 38, no. 2 (1948): 168–72.

44 Magic, Science and Religion . . . *engaged in Kula:* Bronislaw Malinowski, *Magic, Science and Religion* (Redditch, England: Read Books, 2014).

44 *Southwestern Native Americans wore symbolic materials . . . Cat Parade:* W. Norton Jones Jr., "Thousands Gather to Entreat Their Gods for Water to Bring a Good Harvest to the Dry Mesas," *New York Times*, July 26, 1942, https://timesmachine.nytimes.com/timesmachine/1942/07/26/223791632.html?pageNumber=72;

"'Cat People' Parade in Uttaradit in Prayer for Rains," *Nation*, May 7, 2019, https://www.nationthailand.com/in-focus/30368970.

45 *success rate is a low 30 percent:* George Gmelch, "Baseball Magic," *Transaction* 8 (1971): 39–41.

45 *make sure to have their "lucky products":* Eric Hamerman and Gita Johar, "Conditioned Superstition: Desire for Control and Consumer Brand Preferences," *Journal of Consumer Research* 40, no. 3 (2013): 428–43.

46 *you see the sign of the cross as a way of honoring:* Robin Vallacher and Daniel Wegner, "What Do People Think They're Doing? Action Identification and Human Behavior," *Psychological Review* 94, no. 1 (1987): 3–15.

46 *One study showed . . . the children repeat this feather tap:* Derek E. Lyons, Andrew G. Young, and Frank C. Keil, "The Hidden Structure of Overimitation," *Proceedings of the National Academy of Sciences* 104, no. 50 (2007): 19751–56.

47 *the* ritual stance*:* Rohan Kapitány and Mark Nielsen, "Adopting the Ritual Stance: The Role of Opacity and Context in Ritual and Everyday Actions," *Cognition* 145 (2015): 13–29.

47 *Justice Ruth Bader Ginsburg with her lace bib . . . Charles Dickens at bedtime:* Vanessa Friedman, "Ruth Bader Ginsburg's Lace Collar Wasn't an Accessory, It Was a Gauntlet," *New York Times*, September 20, 2020, https://www.nytimes.com/2020/09/20/style/rbg-style.html; Marleide da Mota Gomes and Antonio E. Nardi, "Charles Dickens' Hypnagogia, Dreams, and Creativity," *Frontiers in Psychology* 12 (2021): 700882.

48 *When arranged marriages were more common:* Bess Liebenson, "The Traditions and Superstitions That Rule at the Wedding," *New York Times*, July 27, 1997, https://www.nytimes.com/1997/07/27/nyregion/the-traditions-and-superstitions-that-rule-at-the-wedding.html.

Chapter 4: How to Perform

54   *"Should he take the lobster onstage?":* Errol Morris, "The Pianist and the Lobster," *New York Times*, June 21, 2019, https://www.nytimes.com/interactive/2019/06/21/opinion/editorials/errol-morris-lobster-sviatoslav-richter.html.

54   *Tennis champion Serena Williams . . . soccer player Cristiano Ronaldo . . . baseball player Nomar Garciaparra?:* Serena Williams, "Mastering the Serve," MasterClass, https://www.masterclass.com/classes/serena-williams-teaches-tennis/chapters/the-serve-class-info; Jon Boon, "Very Superstitious Ronaldo, Messi, Bale and Their Bizarre Superstitions Including Sitting in Same Bus Seat and Drinking Port," *U.S. Sun*, November 25, 2022, https://www.the-sun.com/sport/349126/football-superstitions-messi-ronaldo/; Martin Miller, "Batter Up! Not So Fast . . . ," *Los Angeles Times*, September 20, 2006, https://www.latimes.com/archives/la-xpm-2006-sep-30-et-nomar30-story.html.

55   *average number of movements was an astonishing 83:* T. Ciborowski, "'Superstition' in the Collegiate Baseball Player," *Sport Psychologist* 11 (1997): 305–17.

55   *Ballerina Suzanne Farrell pinned a small toy mouse:* Suzanne Farrell and Toni Bentley, *Holding On to the Air* (New York: Penguin Books, 1990).

55   *The writer Joan Didion:* Paul Sehgal, "Joan Didion Chronicled American Disorder with Her Own Unmistakable Style," *New York Times*, December 23, 2021, https://www.nytimes.com/2021/12/23/books/death-of-joan-didion.html.

55   *Computing pioneer (and U.S. Navy rear admiral) Grace Hopper:* Walter Isaacson, "Grace Hopper, Computing Pioneer," *Harvard Gazette*, December 3, 2014, https://news.harvard.edu/gazette/story/2014/12/grace-hopper-computing-pioneer/.

57   *they spontaneously moved their hands in more specific:* Martin

Lang et al., "Effects of Anxiety on Spontaneous Ritualized Behavior," *Current Biology* 25 (2015): 1–6.

58 *"Keep calm and carry on":* Stephanie Clifford, "Calming Sign of Troubled Past Appears in Modern Offices," *New York Times*, November 22, 2009, https://www.nytimes.com/2009/11/23/business/media/23slogan.html.

58 *psychologist Dan Wegner also conducted research:* Daniel M. Wegner et al., "Paradoxical Effects of Thought Suppression," *Journal of Personality and Social Psychology* 53, no. 1 (1987): 5.

58 *anxiety is considered a state as well as a trait:* C. D. Spielberger and R. L. Rickman, "Assessment of State and Trait Anxiety," *Anxiety: Psychobiological and Clinical Perspectives* (1990): 69–83.

59 *Studies . . . show that telling ourselves to calm down:* Alison Wood Brooks, "Get Excited: Reappraising Pre-performance Anxiety as Excitement," *Journal of Experimental Psychology: General* 143, no. 3 (2014): 1144–58.

59 *people who are allowed to throw darts:* Marlou Nadine Perquin et al., "Inability to Improve Performance with Control Shows Limited Access to Inner States," *Journal of Experimental Psychology: General* 149, no. 2 (2020): 249–74.

59 *The evidence is decidedly mixed:* Jules Opplert and Nicolas Babault, "Acute Effects of Dynamic Stretching on Muscle Flexibility and Performance: An Analysis of the Current Literature," *Sports Medicine* 48, no. 2 (2018): 299–325.

59 *while antianxiety medications such as Xanax:* Samantha Stewart, "The Effects of Benzodiazepines on Cognition," *Journal of Clinical Psychiatry* 66, no. 2 (2005): 9–13.

59 *Yerkes-Dodson law:* Peter L. Broadhurst, "Emotionality and the Yerkes-Dodson Law," *Journal of Experimental Psychology* 54, no. 5 (1957): 345.

60 *"It's over":* Jeff Benedict, "To Bill Belichick, Tom Brady Beat Out Drew Bledsoe for QB Job in Summer 2001," *Athletic*, September 2,

2020, https://theathletic.com/2034943/2020/09/02/tom-brady
-drew-bledsoe-the-dynasty-excerpt/.

61   *one-week study to measure how they handled failure:* Nick Hobson, Devin Bonk, and Mickey Inzlicht, "Rituals Decrease the Neural Response to Performance Failure," *PeerJ* 5 (2017): e3363.

61   *the Stroop Color and Word Test:* Arthur R. Jensen and William D.
Rohwer Jr., "The Stroop Color-Word Test: A Review," *Acta Psycho-
logica* 25 (1966): 36–93.

62   *"You spend a good piece of your life gripping a":* Jim Bouton, *Ball
Four* (New York: Rosetta Books, 2012).

62   *Boggs had a spate of rituals:* Joe Posnanski, "The Baseball 100:
No. 47, Wade Boggs," *Athletic,* February 9, 2020, https://theathletic
.com/1578298/2020/02/09/the-baseball-100-no-47-wade-boggs/.

62   *"I don't know whether missing my pancake":* Joe Posnanski, "60
Moments: No. 43, Jim Palmer Outduels Sandy Koufax in the
1966 World Series," *Athletic,* May 17, 2020, https://theathletic
.com/1818540/2020/05/17/60-moments-no-43-jim-palmer
-outduels-sandy-koufax-in-the-1966-world-series/.

63   *"His mannerisms . . . the game often seems too fast for him":* Eric
Longenhagen and Kiley McDaniel, "Top 42 Prospects: Minnesota
Twins," *FanGraphs,* December 16, 2019, https://blogs.fangraphs
.com/top-43-prospects-minnesota-twins/.

Chapter 5: How to Savor

Getting the Most Out of Our
Cabernet and Cleaning

66   *The Ritual, as it's called:* "How to Pour Perfection," Stella Artois,
https://www.stellaartois.com/en/the-ritual.html.

67   fika, *or a break for coffee, tea:* David Nikel, "Swedish *Fika*: Sweden's
'Premium Coffee Break' Explained," *Forbes,* January 3, 2023, https://

www.forbes.com/sites/davidnikel/2023/01/03/swedish-fika
-swedens-premium-coffee-break-explained/?sh=556cb6be5ec1.

67 *If you are in India:* Rajyasree Sen, "How to Make the Perfect Chai,"
Wall Street Journal, June 17, 2013, https://www.wsj.com/articles
/BL-IRTB-19020.

67 *Or say you're in Italy:* Elisabetta Povoledo, "Italians Celebrate
Their Coffee and Want the World to Do So, Too," *New York Times*,
December 3, 2019, https://www.nytimes.com/2019/12/03/world
/europe/italy-coffee-world-heritage.html.

67 *American schools would serve their young students:* Tom Parker,
"Milk and Graham Crackers Being Served to Nursery School Children in a Block Recreation Hall," UC Berkeley, Bancroft Library,
December 11, 1942, https://oac.cdlib.org/ark:/13030/ft2k4003np
/?order=2&brand=oac4.

67 *the ritual pleasures of midmorning* pain au chocolat: Patricia
Wells, "Food: Time for Snacks," *New York Times*, September 25,
1988, https://www.nytimes.com/1988/09/25/magazine/food-time
-for-snacks.html.

70 *"Man feeds not only on proteins":* Claude Fischler, "Food, Self and
Identity," *Social Science Information* 27, no. 2 (1988): 275–92.

71 *In 2013, Rob Rhinehart:* Lizzie Widdicombe, "The End of Food,"
New Yorker, May 5, 2014, https://www.newyorker.com/magazine
/2014/05/12/the-end-of-food.

72 *Oenophiles consider their experience of what's in the glass:* Bruce
Schoenfeld, "The Wrath of Grapes," *New York Times*, May 28, 2015,
https://www.nytimes.com/2015/05/31/magazine/the-wrath-of
-grapes.html.

72 *In the movie: Sideways*, directed by Alexander Payne (Searchlight
Pictures, Michael London Productions, 2004).

74 *"I guess what I try to do":* Kathryn Latour and John Deighton,
"Learning to Become a Taste Expert," *Journal of Consumer Research* 46, no. 1 (2019): 1–19.

74 *Simply seeing the chef who is making our food:* Ryan Buell, Tami

Kim, and Chia-Jung Tsay, "Creating Reciprocal Value through Operational Transparency," *Management Science* 63, no. 6 (2017): 1673–95.

75 *"It took us six hours":* Clotilde Dusoulier, "Dinner at El Bulli," *Chocolate & Zucchini*, August 18, 2006, https://cnz.to/travels/dinner-at-el-bulli/.

76 *In 1997, Sue Ellen Cooper . . . the Red Hat Society:* Sue Ellen Cooper, *The Red Hat Society: Fun and Friendship after Fifty* (New York: Grand Central Publishing, 2004); Careen Yarnal, Julie Son, and Toni Liechty, "'She Was Buried in Her Purple Dress and Her Red Hat and All of Our Members Wore Full "Red Hat Regalia" to Celebrate her Life': Dress, Embodiment and Older Women's Leisure: Reconfiguring the Ageing Process," *Journal of Aging Studies* 25, no. 1 (2011): 52–61; "The Red Hat Society," https://redhatsociety.com/; Associated Press, "Marketers Flocking to Network for Older Women," *Deseret News*, February 20, 2005.

77 *"eat dessert first":* Emily Moscato and Julie Ozanne, "Rebellious Eating: Older Women Misbehaving through Indulgence," *Qualitative Market Research: An International Journal* (2019).

78 *learned, once again, how to have a conversation:* Setareh Baig, "The Radical Act of Eating with Strangers," *New York Times*, March 11, 2023, https://www.nytimes.com/2023/03/11/style/optimism-friendship-dinner.html.

78 *social networks decreased in size an average of 16 percent:* Balazs Kovacs et al., "Social Networks and Loneliness during the COVID-19 Pandemic," *Socius* 7 (2021).

79 *"People don't order chicken soup just because they're hungry":* Francine Maroukian, "An Ode to a Classic Grandma-Style Chicken Noodle Soup," *Oprah Daily*, April 15, 2022, https://www.oprahdaily.com/life/food/a39587412/chicken-soup-recipe-essay/.

80 *Behavioral scientists have identified four of the most successful strategies:* Jordi Quoidbach et al., "Positive Emotion Regulation

and Well-Being: Comparing the Impact of Eight Savoring and Dampening Strategies," *Personality and Individual Differences* 49, no. 5 (2010): 368–73.

81 *We decided to document and understand that experience:* Ting Zhang et al., "A 'Present' for the Future: The Unexpected Value of Rediscovery," *Psychological Science* 25, no. 10 (2014): 1851–60.

82 *nostalgic thinking can increase our feelings of:* Tim Wildschut et al., "Nostalgia: Content, Triggers, Functions," *Journal of Personality and Social Psychology* 91, no. 5 (2006): 975.

82 *In Sweden, a ritual called the* döstädning: Ronda Kaysen, "How to Discover the Life-Affirming Comforts of 'Death Cleaning,'" *New York Times*, February 25, 2022, https://www.nytimes.com /2022/02/25/realestate/how-to-discover-the-life-affirming-com-forts-of-death-cleaning.html.

82 khoneh takooni: Tina Lovgreen, "Celebrating Renewal at Nowruz," CBS News, March 20, 2021, https://newsinteractives.cbc.ca/long form/nowruz-rebirth-and-regrowth/.

83 *"It is a delight to go through things":* Margareta Magnusson, *The Gentle Art of Swedish Death Cleaning: How to Free Yourself and Your Family from a Lifetime of Clutter* (New York: Simon & Schuster, 2018).

83 *Less . . . is often more:* Jayne Merkel, "When Less Was More," *New York Times*, July 1, 2010, https://archive.nytimes.com/opinionator. blogs.nytimes.com/2010/07/01/when-less-was-more/.

83 *in the 1800s in the United States, spring marked the time:* J.K., "Spring Cleaning Is Based on Practices from Generations Ago," *Washington Post*, March 25, 2010, https://www.washingtonpost. com/wp-dyn/content/article/2010/03/23/AR2010032303492 .html.

83 *In 2022, 78 percent of Americans participated:* Derrick Bryson Tyler, "Spring Cleaning Was Once Backbreaking Work. For Many, It Still Is," *New York Times*, April 11, 2023, https://www.nytimes .com/2023/04/11/realestate/spring-cleaning-tradition.html#:~:-

text=The%20number%20of%20Americans%20who,from%20
69%20percent%20in%202021.

83   *"When tidying, the key is to pick up each object"*: Joanna Moor-
head, "Marie Kondo: How to Clear Out Sentimental Clutter,"
Guardian, January 14, 2017, https://www.theguardian.com/life
andstyle/2017/jan/14/how-to-declutter-your-life-marie-kondo
-spark-joy.

84   *the Oreo Dunk Challenge:* Mondelez International, "OREO Puts
New Spin on Iconic Dunking Ritual with Launch of OREO Dunk
Challenge," Cision PR Newswire, February 8, 2017, https://www
.prnewswire.com/news-releases/oreo-puts-new-spin-on-iconic
-dunking-ritual-with-launch-of-oreo-dunk-challenge-300404
389.html.

84   *The beverage ujji:* "Ujji—a Liquid Ritual," ujji, https://www.ujji.co/.

84   *true Cornhuskers fans squeeze their condiments down the Platte
River:* Joe Posnanski, "What the Constitution Means to Me," *Joe-
Blogs*, June 24, 2019, https://joeposnanski.substack.com/p/what
-the-constitution-means-to-me.

Chapter 6: How to Stay on Track

The Joy of Self-Control

85   *"I want to do right but not right now"*: Gillian Welch, "Look at Miss
Ohio," Genius, https://genius.com/Gillian-welch-look-at-miss-ohio
-lyrics.

86   *a weeklong study of temptation:* Wilhelm Hofmann et al.,
"Everyday Temptations: An Experience Sampling Study of Desire,
Conflict, and Self-Control," *Journal of Personality and Social Psy-
chology* 102, no. 6 (2012): 1318.

86   *intercepted people as they were about to enter:* David Neal et al.,
"The Pull of the Past: When Do Habits Persist despite Conflict with

Motives?," *Personality and Social Psychology Bulletin* 37, no. 11 (2011): 1428–37.

87   *Michael Walzer suggests that John Calvin:* Michael Walzer, *The Revolution of the Saints: A Study in the Origins of Radical Politics* (Cambridge, MA: Harvard University Press, 1982).

88   *religions' emphasis on effortful rituals:* Zeve Marcus and Michael McCullough, "Does Religion Make People More Self-Controlled? A Review of Research from the Lab and Life," *Current Opinion in Psychology* 40 (2021): 167–70.

88   sokushinbutsu*:* Ken Jeremiah, *Living Buddhas: The Self-Mummified Monks of Yamagata, Japan* (Jefferson, NC: McFarland, 2010).

89   *The monks at the monastery of Simonopetra:* Simon Critchley, "Athens in Pieces: The Happiest Man I've Ever Met," *New York Times,* April 3, 2019, https://www.nytimes.com/2019/04/03/opinion /mount-athos-monks.html.

89   *religious rituals can help people:* Sander Koole et al., "Why Religion's Burdens Are Light: From Religiosity to Implicit Self-Regulation," *Personality and Social Psychology Review* 14, no. 1 (2010): 95–107.

90   *Walter Mischel's "marshmallow test":* Walter Mischel, *The Marshmallow Test: Understanding Self-Control and How to Master It* (London: Bantam, 2014).

90   *set out to boost children's ability to delay gratification:* Veronika Rybanska et al., "Rituals Improve Children's Ability to Delay Gratification," *Child Development* 89, no. 2 (2018): 349–59.

90   *In one such game, called Drum Beats:* Shauna Tominey and Megan McClelland, "Red Light, Purple Light: Findings from a Randomized Trial Using Circle Time Games to Improve Behavioral Self-Regulation in Preschool," *Early Education & Development* 22, no. 3 (2011): 489–519.

92   *"A Plague of Tics":* David Sedaris, "A Plague of Tics," *This American Life,* January 31, 1997, https://www.thisamericanlife.org/52/edge -of-sanity/act-three-0.

92 the "need for order or symmetry": Orna Reuven-Magril, Reuven Dar, and Nira Liberman, "Illusion of Control and Behavioral Control Attempts in Obsessive-Compulsive Disorder," *Journal of Abnormal Psychology* 117, no. 2 (2008): 334; American Psychiatric Association, *Diagnostic and Statistical Manual of Mental Disorders*, 5th ed. (Washington, DC: American Psychiatric Association Publishing, 2013), 591–643.

92 OCD "is characterized by the individual striving": Richard Moulding et al., "Desire for Control, Sense of Control and Obsessive-Compulsive Checking: An Extension to Clinical Samples," *Journal of Anxiety Disorders* 22, no. 8 (2008): 1472–79.

93 "their foot is on the brake": Kara Gavin, "Stuck in a Loop of 'Wrongness': Brain Study Shows Roots of OCD," University of Michigan Health Lab, November 29, 2018, https://labblog.uofmhealth.org/lab-report/stuck-a-loop-of-wrongness-brain-study-shows-roots-of-ocd.

93 Alan Fiske suggests that the antecedents of OCD: Siri Dulaney and Alan Page Fiske, "Cultural Rituals and Obsessive-Compulsive Disorder: Is There a Common Psychological Mechanism?," *Ethos* 22, no. 3 (1994): 243–83.

93 People who experience OCD find it tremendously challenging: Catherine Francis Brooks, "Social Performance and Secret Ritual: Battling against Obsessive-Compulsive Disorder," *Qualitative Health Research* 21, no. 2 (2011): 249–61.

93 a ritual of eating a "150-calorie lunch": Deborah Glasofer and Joanna Steinglass, "Disrupting the Habits of Anorexia: How a Patient Learned to Escape the Rigid Routines of an Eating Disorder," *Scientific American*, September 1, 2016, https://www.scientificamerican.com/article/disrupting-the-habits-of-anorexia/.

94 These repeated rituals of nonconsumption: Edward Selby and Kathryn A. Coniglio, "Positive Emotion and Motivational Dynamics in Anorexia Nervosa: A Positive Emotion Amplification Model (PE-AMP)," *Psychological Review* 127, no. 5 (2020): 853.

94   *"habit reversal" training:* N. H. Azrin and R. G. Nunn, "Habit-Reversal: A Method of Eliminating Nervous Habits and Tics," *Behaviour Research and Therapy* 11, no. 4 (1973): 619–28.

94   *Drumming Out Drugs:* Michael Winkelman, "Complementary Therapy for Addiction: 'Drumming Out Drugs,'" *American Journal of Public Health* 93, no. 4 (2003): 647–51.

Chapter 7: How to Become

Rites (and Wrongs) of Passage

97   wabi-sabi: Andrew Juniper, *Wabi Sabi: The Japanese Art of Impermanence* (North Clarendon, VT: Tuttle Publishing, 2011).

98   *three distinct transitional phases:* Arnold van Gennep, *Les rites de passage* (Paris: Nourry, 1909).

98   *Rumspringa:* Tom Shachtman, *Rumspringa: To Be or Not to Be Amish* (New York: Macmillan, 2006).

99   *In Brazil's Sateré-Mawé tribe, thirteen-year-old boys:* Rachel Nuwer, "When Becoming a Man Means Sticking Your Hand into a Glove of Ants," *Smithsonian Magazine*, October 27, 2014, https://www.smithsonianmag.com/smart-news/brazilian-tribe -becoming-man-requires-sticking-your-hand-glove-full-angry -ants-180953156/.

99   *In Judaism, adulthood is marked by:* Michael Hilton, *Bar Mitzvah: A History* (Lincoln: University of Nebraska Press, 2014).

99   *In Norway, high school students participate:* William A. Corsaro and Berit O. Johannesen, "Collective Identity, Intergenerational Relations, and Civic Society: Transition Rituals among Norwegian Russ," *Journal of Contemporary Ethnography* 43, no. 3 (2014): 331–60.

100   Gautama Dharmasutra: Patrick Olivelle, *Dharmasutras: The Law Codes of Apastamba, Gautama, Baudhayana and Vasistha* (New Delhi: Motilal Banarsidass, 2000).

101   *the "betwixt and between" period:* Victor Turner, "Betwixt and Be-
       tween: The Liminal Period in *Rites de Passage,*" in *The Forest of
       Symbols: Aspects of Ndembu Ritual* (Ithaca, NY: Cornell Univer-
       sity Press, 1970).

102   *Cadets in Russia's cosmonaut program:* Jeffrey Kluger, "Here's the
       Russian Ritual That Ensures a Safe Space Flight," *Time,* February
       26, 2016, https://time.com/4238910/gagarin-red-square-ritual/.

103   *In the early 1990s . . . as a reminder of who they had been:* Nissan
       Rubin, Carmella Shmilovitz, and Meira Weiss, "From Fat to Thin:
       Informal Rites Affirming Identity Change," *Symbolic Interaction*
       16, no. 1 (1993): 1–17.

103   *As a person of faith . . . naming ceremony "was like coming home":* As-
       sociated Press, "Norwegian Church Holds Name Change Ceremony for
       a Transgender Woman," NBC News, July 20, 2021, https://www.nbc
       news.com/nbc-out/out-news/norwegian-church-holds-name
       -change-ceremony-transgender-woman-rcna1466.

104   *deadnaming:* Tim Fitzsimons, "News Sites Backtrack after 'Dead-
       naming' Transgender Woman in Obituary," NBC News, May 15,
       2020, https://www.nbcnews.com/feature/nbc-out/news-sites-back
       track-after-deadnaming-transgender-woman-obituary-n1207851.

104   *"Rebecca dipped below the surface":* Ari Kristan, "Opening Up the
       Mikvah," *Tikkun* 21, no. 3 (2006): 55–57.

105   *"It's called a second bar mitzvah":* Amy Oringel, "Why 83 Is the
       New 13 for Bar Mitzvahs," *Forward,* October 19, 2017, https://
       forward.com/culture/jewishness/384977/why-83-is-the-new-13
       -for-bar-mitzvahs/.

105   *"I feel like a woman":* Elodie Gentina, Kay Palan, and Marie-Hélène
       Fosse-Gomez, "The Practice of Using Makeup: A Consumption
       Ritual of Adolescent Girls," *Journal of Consumer Behaviour* 11,
       no. 2 (2012): 115–23.

105   *"The ability to exit . . . is the ability":* Sara Lawrence-Lightfoot,
       Exit: The Endings That Set Us Free (New York: Macmillan, 2012).

105 *"being fragile and in formation"*: Suzanne Garfinkle-Crowell, "Taylor Swift Has Rocked My Psychiatric Practice," *New York Times*, June 17, 2023, https://www.nytimes.com/2023/06/17/opinion /taylor-swift-mental-health.html.

105 *the increasing phenomenon of "extended adolescence"*: Bret Stetka, "Extended Adolescence: When 25 Is the New 18," *Scientific American*, September 19, 2017, https://www.scientificamerican.com /article/extended-adolescence-when-25-is-the-new-181/.

106 *an additional study in my investigation of the IKEA effect:* Michael I. Norton et al., "The IKEA Effect: When Labor Leads to Love," *Journal of Consumer Psychology* 22, no. 3 (July 2012): 453–60.

106 *"The primary work of a rite of passage"*: Ronald Grimes, *Deeply into the Bone: Re-inventing Rites of Passage* (Berkeley: University of California Press, 2000).

106 *Chief Justice John Roberts accidentally switched:* Samuel P. Jacobs, "After Fumbled Oath, Roberts and Obama Leave Little to Chance," Reuters, January 18, 2013, https://www.reuters .com/article/us-usa-inauguration-roberts/after-fumbled-oath -roberts-and-obama-leave-little-to-chance-idUSBRE90H16L 20130118.

107 *"a kind of inner illumination"*: Arnold van Gennep in a 1914 article on *The Golden Bough*, quoted in Nicole Belmont, *Arnold van Gennep: The Creator of French Ethnography* (Chicago: University of Chicago Press, 1979), 58.

Chapter 8: How to Stay in Sync

Why Rituals Help Relationships Flourish

111 This Is Us: *This Is Us*, season 1, episode 14, "I Call Marriage," directed by George Tillman Jr., written by Dan Fogelman, Kay Oye-

gun, and Aurin Squire, featuring Milo Ventimiglia et al., aired February 7, 2017.

114 *Would they take advantage of the upgrade:* Ximena Garcia-Rada, Michael I. Norton, and Rebecca K. Ratner, "A Desire to Create Shared Memories Increases Consumers' Willingness to Sacrifice Experience Quality for Togetherness," *Journal of Consumer Psychology* (April 2023).

114 *between 60 percent and 75 percent of people in relationships report:* Ximena Garcia-Rada, Övül Sezer, and Michael Norton, "Rituals and Nuptials: The Emotional and Relational Consequences of Relationship Rituals," *Journal of the Association for Consumer Research* 4, no. 2 (2019): 185–97.

115 *the simple act of sharing a plate when eating:* Kaitlin Woolley and Ayelet Fishbach, "Shared Plates, Shared Minds: Consuming from a Shared Plate Promotes Cooperation," *Psychological Science* 30, no. 4 (2019): 541–52.

115 *not able to eat the same meal:* Kaitlin Woolley, Ayelet Fishbach, and Ronghan Michelle Wang, "Food Restriction and the Experience of Social Isolation," *Journal of Personality and Social Psychology* 119, no. 3 (2020): 657.

116 *researchers examined saliva samples tracking cortisol:* Lisa Diamond, Angela Hicks, and Kimberly Otter-Henderson, "Every Time You Go Away: Changes in Affect, Behavior, and Physiology Associated with Travel-Related Separations from Romantic Partners," *Journal of Personality and Social Psychology* 95, no. 2 (2008): 385.

116 *the following personal ad:* Arlie Russell Hochschild, *The Outsourced Self: What Happens When We Pay Others to Live Our Lives for Us* (New York: Metropolitan Books, 2012).

117 *when relationships are reduced to transactions:* Tami Kim, Ting Zhang, and Michael I. Norton, "Pettiness in Social Exchange," *Journal of Experimental Psychology: General* 148, no. 2 (2019): 361.

118 *"shared reality":* Maya Rossignac-Milon et al., "Merged Minds: Generalized Shared Reality in Dyadic Relationships," *Journal of Personality and Social Psychology* 120, no. 4 (2021): 882.

119 *all couples "have their own weird cinematic universe":* Drew Magary, "'We Treat Our Stuffed Animal like a Real Child. Is That Whackadoodle Stuff?,'" *Vice*, March 3, 2020, https://www.vice.com/en_us/article/wxe499/we-treat-our-stuffed-animal-like-a-real-child-is-that-whackadoodle-stuff-drew-magary-funbag.

119 *"A couple's private language can develop":* Joshua Pashman, "Norman Rush, the Art of Fiction no. 205," *Paris Review* 194 (Fall 2010), https://www.theparisreview.org/interviews/6039/the-art-of-fiction-no-205-norman-rush.

119 *In the winter of 1975 . . . but whole, new, and united:* David Bramwell, "The Bittersweet Story of Marina Abramović's Epic Walk on the Great Wall of China," *Guardian*, April 25, 2020, https://www.theguardian.com/travel/2020/apr/25/marina-abramovic-ulay-walk-the-great-wall-of-china; Marina Abramović, *Walk through Walls* (New York: Crown, 2018).

121 *The iconic French intellectuals and existentialists*, "Stand By Your Man," *New Yorker*, September 18, 2005, https://www.newyorker.com/magazine/2005/09/26/stand-by-your-man.

123 *Olivia Wilde's "special salad dressing":* Carolyn Twersky, "Olivia Wilde Gives the People What They Want: Her Salad Dressing Recipe," *W*, October 19, 2022, https://www.wmagazine.com/culture/olivia-wilde-special-salad-dressing-recipe-jason-sudeikis-nanny.

123 *gift-giving rituals:* Lalin Anik and Ryan Hauser, "One of a Kind: The Strong and Complex Preference for Unique Treatment from Romantic Partners," *Journal of Experimental Social Psychology* 86 (2020): 103899.

125 *we simply stop noticing all the wonderful aspects:* Kennon M. Sheldon and Sonja Lyubomirsky, "The Challenge of Staying Happier:

Testing the Hedonic Adaptation Prevention Model," *Personality and Social Psychology Bulletin* 38, no. 5 (2012): 670–80.

126 *many couples believe that extraordinary experiences:* Ximena Garcia-Rada and Tami Kim, "Shared Time Scarcity and the Pursuit of Extraordinary Experiences," *Psychological Science* 32, no. 12 (2021): 1871–83.

128 *rituals to end relationships . . . provide opportunities for much-needed transitions*: Charity Yoro, "Why I Had a Closing Ceremony Ritual instead of a Breakup," *Huffington Post*, September 28, 2018, https://www.huffpost.com/entry/closing-ceremony-breakup _n_5b9bef57e4b046313fbad43f.

128 *"You take two bodies"*: Paul Simon, "Hearts and Bones," Genius, November 4, 1983, https://genius.com/Paul-simon-hearts-and-bones -lyrics.

130 *"socially controlled civility"*: Colleen Leahy Johnson, "Socially Controlled Civility: The Functioning of Rituals in the Divorce Process," *American Behavioral Scientist* 31, no. 6 (1988): 685–701.

130 *"Too often I see a ritual as an ending"*: Ardean Goertzen, "Falling Rings: Group and Ritual Process in a Divorce," *Journal of Religion and Health* 26, no. 3 (1987): 219–39.

130 *The philosopher and public intellectual Agnes Callard:* Rachel Aviv, "Agnes Callard's Marriage of the Minds," *New Yorker*, March 6, 2023, https://www.newyorker.com/magazine/2023/03/13/agnes -callard-profile-marriage-philosophy.

131 *"annivorcery"*: "Happy Annivorcery! The New Singles Parties," *Evening Standard*, July 19, 2010, https://www.standard.co.uk/life style/happy-annivorcery-the-new-singles-parties-6493345.html.

Chapter 9: How to Survive the Holidays

Rituals for the Ups and Downs of Kith and Kin

135 *Övül Sezer from Cornell University and I teamed up:* Övül Sezer et al., "Family Rituals Improve the Holidays," Special Issue on the Science of Hedonistic Consumption, *Journal of the Association for Consumer Research* 1, no. 4 (2016): 509–26.

137 *politically diverse Thanksgiving dinners were thirty-five to seventy:* Jeremy Frimer and Linda Skitka, "Political Diversity Reduces Thanksgiving Dinners by 4–11 Minutes, not 30–50," letter to the editor, *Science* 360, no. 6392 (2019).

137 *"The seating arrangement is more challenging than the cooking":* Michelle Slatalla, "The Art of Cramming People around Your Thanksgiving Table," *Wall Street Journal*, November 12, 2019, https://www.wsj.com/articles/the-art-of-cramming-people -around-your-thanksgiving-table-11573579298.

137 *"intensity and reactivity only breed more of the same":* Harriet Lerner, *The Dance of Anger* (Pune, India: Mehta Publishing House, 2017).

138 *Barbara Fiese . . . makes the distinction between family routines:* Barbara Fiese et al., "A Review of 50 Years of Research on Naturally Occurring Family Routines and Rituals: Cause for Celebration?," *Journal of Family Psychology* 16, no. 4 (2002): 381.

139 *"The school bus send-off transcended":* Jenny Rosenstrach, *How to Celebrate Everything: Recipes and Rituals for Birthdays, Holidays, Family Dinners, and Every Day in Between: A Cookbook* (New York: Ballantine, 2016).

140 *his family kinkeeper:* Carolyn Rosenthal, "Kinkeeping in the Familial Division of Labor," *Journal of Marriage and the Family* 47, no. 4 (1985): 965–74.

142 *"He is coming back to tradition":* Carolyn Rosenthal and Victor Marshall, "Generational Transmission of Family Ritual," *American Behavioral Scientist* 31, no. 6 (1988): 669–84.

142 *writer Rembert Browne describes his first Thanksgiving:* Rembert Brown, "Thank You God, for Black Thanksgiving," *Bon Appétit,* November 1, 2017, https://www.bonappetit.com/story/rembert-browne-thanksgiving.

143 *"I bet nobody else in the world is eating":* Julie Beck, Saahil Desai, and Natalie Escobar, "Families' Weird Holiday Traditions, Illustrated," *Atlantic,* December 24, 2018, https://www.theatlantic.com/family/archive/2018/12/families-weird-holiday-traditions-illustrated/578731/.

143 *88 percent of people reported having a family ritual:* Rosenthal and Marshall, "Generational Transmission," 669–84.

144 *one in five family meals are now consumed in a car:* Tara Parker-Pope, "How to Have Better Family Meals," *New York Times,* August 3, 2018, https://www.nytimes.com/guides/well/make-most-of-family-table.

144 *Fewer than 33 percent of American families:* Jill Anderson, "The Benefit of Family Mealtime," *Harvard Graduate School of Education,* April 1, 2020, https://www.gse.harvard.edu/ideas/edcast/20/04/benefit-family-mealtime.

145 *regular family dinners were linked to a decreased rate:* Mary Spagnola and Barbara H. Fiese, "Family Routines and Rituals: A Context for Development in the Lives of Young Children," *Infants & Young Children* 20, no. 4 (2007): 284–99; "The Importance of Family Dinners VII," Columbia University Report, September 2011.

145 *the benefits of mealtime rituals are particularly pronounced:* Yesel Yoon, Katie Newkirk, and Maureen Perry-Jenkins, "Parenting Stress, Dinnertime Rituals, and Child Well-Being in Working-Class Families," *Family Relations* 64, no. 1 (2015): 93–107.

145 *the Family Dinner Project:* Family Dinner Project, https://thefamilydinnerproject.org/.

Chapter 10: How to Mourn

Coping with Loss

149   *"It's not something you get over"*: Willie Nelson, "Something You Get Through," Genius, April 6, 2018, https://genius.com/Willie -nelson-something-you-get-through-lyrics.

149   *In 1863 . . . "The Civil War's rate of death . . . would mean six million fatalities"*: Drew Gilpin Faust, *This Republic of Suffering: Death and the American Civil War* (New York: Vintage, 2009).

151   *sitting shiva in Judaism:* Irwin W. Kidorf, "The Shiva: A Form of Group Psychotherapy," *Journal of Religion and Health* 5, no. 1 (1966): 43–46.

151   *its protagonist repeatedly makes offerings:* Andrew George, *The Epic of Gilgamesh: A New Translation* (London: Allen Lane, Penguin Press, 1999).

151   *Cultures vary astonishingly on the colors of mourning garments:* "Colours in Culture," Information Is Beautiful, https://information isbeautiful.net/visualizations/colours-in-cultures/.

151   *rituals that they felt had been therapeutically beneficial:* Corina Sas and Alina Coman, "Designing Personal Grief Rituals: An Analysis of Symbolic Objects and Actions," *Death Studies* 40, no. 9 (2016): 558–69.

152   *professional mourners:* William L. Hamilton, "A Consolation of Voices: At the Park Avenue Armory, Mourning the World Over," *New York Times*, September 11, 2016, https://www.nytimes .com/2016/09/12/arts/music/mourning-installation-taryn-simon -park-avenue-armory.html; Sarah Hucal, "Professional Mourners Still Exist in Greece," *DW*, November 15, 2020, https://www .dw.com/en/professional-mourners-keep-an-ancient-tradition -alive-in-greece/a-55572864.

152   *"People have been gathering to do this":* Evan V. Symon, "I'm Paid to Mourn at Funerals (and It's a Growing Industry)," *Cracked,*

March 21, 2016, https://www.cracked.com/personal-experiences
-1994-i-am-professional-mourner-6-realities-my-job.html.

152 *When a Navy SEAL dies:* John Ismay, "Edward Gallagher, the
SEALs and Why the Trident Pin Matters," *New York Times*, November 21, 2019, https://www.nytimes.com/2019/11/21/us/navy
-seal-trident-insignia.html.

153 *an "honor walk":* Tim Lahey, "Rituals of Honor in Hospital Hall-
ways," *New York Times*, April 2, 2019, https://www.nytimes.com
/2019/04/02/well/live/rituals-of-honor-in-hospital-hallways.html.

154 *the age of "Forbidden Death":* Philippe Ariès, *Western Attitudes toward Death: From the Middle Ages to the Present* (Baltimore: John
Hopkins University Press, 1975).

155 *"To begin depriving death of its greatest advantage":* Michel de
Montaigne, *The Essays* (London: Penguin UK, 2019).

155 *journalist and songwriter named Mike Brick:* Dane Schiller, "Michael Brick, Songwriter and Journalist, Remembered," *Chron*, February 9, 2016, https://www.chron.com/news/houston-texas/texas
/article/Michael-Brick-6815603.php; Bob Tedeschi, "A Beloved
Songwriter Wanted a Wake. He Got One Before He Was Gone,"
Stat, July 25, 2016, https://www.statenews.com/2016/07/25
/michael-brick-author-living-wake/.

156 *Death Over Dinner:* Richard Harris, "Discussing Death Over Dinner," *Atlantic*, April 16, 2016, https://www.theatlantic.com/health
/archive/2016/04/discussing-death-over-dinner/478452/.

157 *Our cultural desire to shelter ourselves:* Paul Clements et al., "Cultural Perspectives of Death, Grief, and Bereavement," *Journal of
Psychosocial Nursing and Mental Health Services* 41, no. 7 (2003):
18–26; Charles Kemp and Sonal Bhungalia, "Culture and the End
of Life: A Review of Major World Religions," *Journal of Hospice &
Palliative Nursing* 4, no. 4 (2002): 235–42.

157 *Children who attend funerals of their departed parents:* Mary Fris-
tad et al., "The Role of Ritual in Children's Bereavement," *Omega—
Journal of Death and Dying* 42, no. 4 (2001): 321–39.

157   *parents who undergo the devastating experience:* Kirsty Ryninks
      et al., "Mothers' Experience of Their Contact with Their Stillborn
      Infant: An Interpretative Phenomenological Analysis," *BMC Preg-
      nancy and Childbirth* 14, no. 1 (2014): 1–10.

157   *In Japan . . .* Hake tomos *is "a means of dying actively":* Anne Al-
      lison, *Being Dead Otherwise* (Durham, NC: Duke University Press,
      2023).

158   *The United States has no law:* Lisa Belkin, "A Time to Grieve, and
      to Forge a Bond," *New York Times*, January 14, 2007, https://www
      .nytimes.com/2007/01/14/jobs/14wcol.html.

158   *233 bereaved individuals followed for twenty-four months:* Paul
      Maciejewski et al., "An Empirical Examination of the Stage Theory
      of Grief," *JAMA* 297, no. 7 (2007): 716–23.

158   *In 1969, Elisabeth Kübler-Ross . . . "The patient is":* Elisabeth
      Kübler-Ross, *Living with Death and Dying* (New York: Simon &
      Schuster, 2011).

159   *related to a sense of acceptance:* Jason Castle and William Phillips,
      "Grief Rituals: Aspects That Facilitate Adjustment to Bereave-
      ment," *Journal of Loss & Trauma* 8, no. 1 (2003): 41–71.

159   *the "acceptance" stage didn't peak at all:* Maciejewski et al., "Em-
      pirical Examination," 716–23.

161   *loss of control is, in and of itself, a predictor:* Nancy Hogan, Daryl
      Greenfield, and Lee Schmidt, "Development and Validation of the
      Hogan Grief Reaction Checklist," *Death Studies* 25, no. 1 (2001):
      1–32.

161   *Joan Didion's description in* The Year*:* Joan Didion, *The Year of
      Magical Thinking* (New York: Vintage, 2007).

161   *a woman wrote in asking for help:* Jenée Desmond-Harris, "Help!
      I Never Got to Properly Mourn My Father's Death," *Slate*, March
      3, 2023, https://slate.com/human-interest/2023/03/pandemic
      -mourning-dear-prudence-advice.html.

162   *created new rituals better suited:* Elizabeth Diaz, "The Last Anoint-
      ing," *New York Times*, June 6, 2020, https://www.nytimes.com

/interactive/2020/06/06/us/coronavirus-priests-last-rites.html; Rachel Wolfe, "One Way to Say Good Riddance to 2020? Light Your Planner on Fire," *Wall Street Journal*, December 18, 2020, https://www.wsj.com/articles/one-way-to-say-good-riddance-to -2020-light-your-planner-on-fire-11608306802?mod=mhp.

163 *The Dinner Party . . . "When my mom died":* Alix, "About," Dinner Party, https://www.thedinnerparty.org/about.

164 *Family Lives On, a nonprofit:* "Why Traditions?: Healthy Grieving Isn't about Forgetting, It's about Remembering. Traditions Help Kids Maintain a Healthy Connection with the Parent Who Died," Family Lives On Foundation, https://www.familyliveson.org/tradition _stories/.

165 *Maine resident Amy Hopkins . . . warmth of coats, hats, and boots:* Greta Rybus, "Cold-Plunging with Maine's 'Ice Mermaids,'" *New York Times*, August 1, 2022, https://www.nytimes .com/2022/08/01/travel/cold-plunge-maine.html.

166 *"My younger sister died in a car accident":* David Brooks, "What's Ripping Apart American Families?," *New York Times*, July 29, 2021, https://www.nytimes.com/2021/07/29/opinion/estranged -american-families.html#commentsContainer.

166 *to mourn the complicated relationships that haunt us:* Holly Prigerson et al., "Inventory of Complicated Grief: A Scale to Measure Maladaptive Symptoms of Loss," *Psychiatry Research* 59, no. 1–2 (1995): 65–79.

166 ambiguous loss: Pauline Boss, *Ambiguous Loss: Learning to Live with Unresolved Grief* (Cambridge, MA: Harvard University Press, 2009).

166 *"That afternoon my mother's eyes":* Rikke Madsen and Regner Birkelund, "'The Path through the Unknown': The Experience of Being a Relative of a Dementia-Suffering Spouse or Parent," *Journal of Clinical Nursing* 22, no. 21–22 (2013): 3024–31.

167 *When Lesley McCallister lost . . . "good has come out of it":* Anna Sale, *Let's Talk about Hard Things* (New York: Simon & Schuster, 2021).

167 *even an app, WeCroak:* Ruth La Ferla, "Outing Death," *New York Times*, January 10, 2018, https://www.nytimes.com/2018/01/10/style/death-app-we-croak.html.

167 memento mori: Bethan Bell, "Taken from Life: The Unsettling Art of Death Photography," BBC News, June 5, 2016, https://www.bbc.com/news/uk-england-36389581.

168 *"I cry a lot because I miss people":* Terry Gross, "Maurice Sendak: On Life, Death, and Children's Lit," NPR, December 29, 2011, https://www.npr.org/transcripts/144077273.

Chapter 11: How to Find Meaning at Work

Trust Falls and Other Team Rituals

172 *the phenomenon Émile Durkheim called* collective effervescence: Tim Olaveson, "Collective Effervescence and Communitas: Processual Models of Ritual and Society in Émile Durkheim and Victor Turner," *Dialectical Anthropology* 26 (2001): 89–124.

173 *"Every mind [is] drawn into the same eddy":* Émile Durkheim, *The Elementary Forms of Religious Life* (1912; repr., Oxford: Oxford University Press, 2001).

173 *the link between ritual and group bonding emerges:* Nicole Wen, Patricia Herrmann, and Cristine Legare, "Ritual Increases Children's Affiliation with In-Group Members," *Evolution and Human Behavior* 37, no. 1 (2016): 54–60.

174 *Even infants at sixteen months can recognize ritualistic actions:* Zoe Liberman, Katherine Kinzler, and Amanda Woodward, "The Early Social Significance of Shared Ritual Actions," *Cognition* 171 (2018): 42–51.

174 *the* haka: Telegraph Sport, "How to Do the Haka: Master the Fearsome Maori Dance in 11 Steps (with Pictures)," *Telegraph*, November 6, 2014, https://www.telegraph.co.uk/sport/rugbyunion

/international/newzealand/11214585/How-to-do-the-Haka
-Master-the-fearsome-Maori-dance-in-11-Steps-with-pictures.html.

175   *the former quarterback of the New Orleans Saints:* Gregg Rosenthal, "Brees Reveals Text of Pre-game Chant," NBC Sports, February 10, 2010, https://www.nbcsports.com/nfl/profootballtalk /rumor-mill/news/brees-reveals-text-of-pre-game-chant.

175   *Some Wal-Mart employees enact a ritual:* Richard Metzger, "America circa 2013 in a Nutshell: The 'Wal-Mart Cheer' Is the Most Depressing Thing You'll Ever See," *Dangerous Minds*, July 3, 2013, https://dangerousminds.net/comments/america_circa_2013 _in_a_nutshell_the_wal_mart_cheer_is_the_most_depressing.

175   *"two parts militaristic, one part kumbaya":* Stephanie Rosenbloom, "My Initiation at Store 5476," *New York Times*, December 19, 2009, https://www.nytimes.com/2009/12/20/business/20walmart.html.

175   *employees were given sledgehammers to smash their desktop computers:* Soren Kaplan, "Zipcar Doesn't Just Ask Employees to Innovate—It Shows Them How," *Harvard Business Review*, February 1, 2017, https://hbr.org/2017/02/zipcar-doesnt-just-ask-employees -to-innovate-it-shows-them-how.

175   *NOOGLER:* Rachel Emma Silverman, "Companies Try to Make the First Day for New Hires More Fun," *Wall Street Journal*, May 28, 2013, https://www.wsj.com/articles/SB10001424127887323336I 0457850163147593485O.

175   *At one annual shareholder . . . to hit every taste bud:* "Complete Coverage of Starbucks 2018 Annual Meeting of Shareholders," *Starbucks Stories & News*, March 21, 2018, https://stories.star bucks.com/stories/2018/annual-meeting-of-shareholders-2018/.

176   *on average, people were willing to forgo 23 percent:* Jing Hu and Jacob Hirsh, "Accepting Lower Salaries for Meaningful Work," *Frontiers in Psychology* 8 (2017): 1649.

176   *"Meaning Is the New Money":* Tammy Erickson, "Meaning Is the New Money," *Harvard Business Review*, March 23, 2011, https:// hbr.org/2011/03/challenging-our-deeply-held-as.

177 *rituals involving lunch or drinks:* Tami Kim et al., "Work Group Rituals Enhance the Meaning of Work," *Organizational Behavior and Human Decision Processes* 165 (2021): 197–212.

179 *ritual's effect on how employees perceive the meaning of their work:* Douglas A. Lepisto, "Ritual Work and the Formation of a Shared Sense of Meaningfulness," *Academy of Management Journal* 65, no. 4 (2022): 1327–52.

181 *a disastrous team-building exercise:* Katie Morell, "CEOs Explain Their Most Awkward Team-Building Experiences," Bloomberg, April 5, 2017, https://www.bloomberg.com/news/articles/2017-04-05 /what-s-your-most-awkward-team-building-experience.

181 *analyzed how rafting-tour companies utilized rituals:* Eric Arnould and Linda Price, "River Magic: Extraordinary Experience and the Extended Service Encounter," *Journal of Consumer Research* 20, no. 1 (1993): 24–45.

184 *"Open-Plan Offices Were Devised by Satan":* Oliver Burkeman, "Open-Plan Offices Were Devised by Satan in the Deepest Caverns of Hell," *Guardian*, November 18, 2013, https://www.theguardian .com/news/2013/nov/18/open-plan-offices-bad-harvard-business -review.

184 *"Its rise is a sign that we have":* Farhad Manjoo, "Open Offices Are a Capitalist Dead End," *New York Times,* September 25, 2019, https://www.nytimes.com/2019/09/25/opinion/wework-adam -neumann.html.

184 *"Retail Employee Has Little Daily Ritual":* "Retail Employee Has Little Daily Ritual Where He Drinks Dr Pepper in Quiet Corner of Stock Room and Doesn't Kill Himself," *Onion,* September 19, 2019, https://www.theonion.com/retail-employee-has-little-daily -ritual-where-he-drinks-1838234948.

184 *Face-to-face interactions didn't increase:* Ethan Bernstein and Ben Waber, "The Truth about Open Offices," *Harvard Business Review,* November–December 2019, https://hbr.org/2019/11/the-truth -about-open-offices.

184　*The curtain intervention led to a 10 to 15 percent performance improvement:* Ethan Bernstein, "Privacy and Productivity," *Harvard Business School Newsroom*, March 25, 2014, https://www.hbs.edu/news/articles/Pages/privacy-and-productivity-ethan-bernstein.aspx.

185　*"I'm hungry for ritual":* Nellie Bowles, "God Is Dead. So Is the Office. These People Want to Save Both," *New York Times*, August 28, 2020, https://www.nytimes.com/2020/08/28/business/remote-work-spiritual-consultants.html.

185　*"One morning I woke up":* Jennifer Levitz, "Welcome to the Fake Office Commute (Turns Out People Miss the Routine)," *Wall Street Journal*, January 11, 2021, https://www.wsj.com/articles/welcome-to-the-fake-office-commute-turns-out-people-miss-the-routine-11610383617.

187　*end-of-day rituals of nearly three hundred:* Benjamin A. Rogers et al., "After-Work Rituals and Well-Being," working paper.

188　*"Why Are You Not Already Doing This":* "Why Are You Not Already Doing This: 41 Things You Need to Be Doing Every Day to Avoid Burnout," ClickHole, September 1, 2021, https://clickhole.com/why-are-you-not-already-doing-this-41-things-you-need-to-be-doing-every-day-to-avoid-burnout/.

Chapter 12: How to Divide

When Rituals Breed Tension and Trouble

190　*"over" versus "under":* Karl Smallwood, "What Is the Correct Way to Hang Toilet Paper?," *Today I Found Out*, April 25, 2020, http://www.todayifoundout.com/index.php/2020/04/what-is-the-correct-way-to-hang-toilet-paper/.

190　*"the toilet tissue issue":* David Rambo, *The Lady with All the Answers* (New York: Dramatists Play Service, 2006).

190   *one A. Silverman was sentenced to three days:* "The Straw Hat Riot of 1922," B Unique Millinery, https://www.buniquemillinery.com/pages/the-straw-hat-riot-of-1922.

192   *put people into arbitrary groups:* Nicholas M. Hobson et al., "When Novel Rituals Lead to Intergroup Bias: Evidence from Economic Games and Neurophysiology," *Psychological Science* 28, no. 6 (2017): 733–50.

192   *"minimal groups paradigm":* Henri Tajfel, "Social Identity and Intergroup Behaviour," *Social Science Information* 13, no. 2 (1974): 65–93.

193   *played the Trust Game, an experiment:* Joyce Berg, John Dickhaut, and Kevin McCabe, "Trust, Reciprocity, and Social History," *Games and Economic Behavior* 10, no. 1 (1995): 122–42.

193   *feedback-P300:* Yuan Zhang et al., "Brain Responses in Evaluating Feedback Stimuli with a Social Dimension," *Frontiers in Human Neuroscience* 6 (2012): 29.

194   *more pain, more giving, more loyalty:* Dimitris Xygalatas et al., "Extreme Rituals Promote Prosociality," *Psychological Science* 24, no. 8 (2013): 1602–5.

195   *the* black sheep effect: José Marques, Vincent Yzerbyt, and Jacques-Philippe Leyens, "The 'Black Sheep Effect': Extremity of Judgments towards Ingroup Members as a Function of Group Identification," *European Journal of Social Psychology* 18, no. 1 (1988): 1–16.

196   *reactions to violations of in-group rituals:* Daniel Stein et al., "When Alterations Are Violations: Moral Outrage and Punishment in Response to (Even Minor) Alterations to Rituals," *Journal of Personality and Social Psychology* 123, no. 1 (2021).

198   *When other groups question or threaten:* Frank Kachanoff et al., "Determining Our Destiny: Do Restrictions to Collective Autonomy Fuel Collective Action?," *Journal of Personality and Social Psychology* 119, no. 3 (2020): 600.

198   *"the War on Christmas":* Liam Stack, "How the 'War on Christmas' Controversy Was Created," *New York Times*, December 19, 2016,

https://www.nytimes.com/2016/12/19/us/war-on-christmas-controversy.html.

199 *The Thirty Years' War essentially boiled:* "Thirty Years' War," History, August 21, 2018, https://www.history.com/topics/european-history/thirty-years-war.

199 *cross-cutting affiliations have the potential:* Marilynn Brewer, "The Psychology of Prejudice: Ingroup Love or Outgroup Hate?," *Journal of Social Issues* 55 (1999): 429–44.

200 *The effect was especially true when the ethnic diversity:* Emilio Depetris-Chauvin, Ruben Durante, and Filipe Campante, "Building Nations through Shared Experiences: Evidence from African Football," *American Economic Review* 110, no. 5 (2020): 1572–1602.

200 *the podcast* Dolly Parton's America: Lindsay Zoladz, "Is There Anything We Can All Agree On? Yes: Dolly Parton," *New York Times*, November 21, 2019, https://www.nytimes.com/2019/11/21/arts/music/dolly-parton.html.

Chapter 13: How to Heal

Rituals and Reconciliation

201 *"The Commissioners enter the hall in procession":* Antjie Krog, "The Truth and Reconciliation Commission: A National Ritual?," *Missionalia: Southern African Journal of Mission Studies* 26, no. 1 (1998): 5–16.

202 *"Why do we come and open the wounds again?":* Rosalind Shaw, "Memory Frictions: Localizing the Truth and Reconciliation Commission in Sierra Leone," *International Journal of Transitional Justice* 1, no. 2 (2007): 183–207.

203 *taxonomy of apology:* Johanna Kirchhoff, Ulrich Wagner, and Micha Strack, "Apologies: Words of Magic? The Role of Verbal

Components, Anger Reduction, and Offence Severity," *Peace and Conflict: Journal of Peace Psychology* 18, no. 2 (2012): 109.

203 *the word* ripeness: Peter Coleman, "Redefining Ripeness: A Social-Psychological Perspective," *Peace and Conflict* 3, no. 1 (1997): 81–103.

204 *when people apologize before understanding:* Cynthia McPherson Frantz and Courtney Bennigson, "Better Late than Early: The Influence of Timing on Apology Effectiveness," *Journal of Experimental Social Psychology* 41, no. 2 (2005): 201–7.

204 *a "historic non-handshake":* Mark Landler, "Obama and Iranian Leader Miss Each Other, Diplomatically," *New York Times*, September 25, 2013, https://www.nytimes.com/2013/09/25/world/middleeast/obama-and-iranian-leader-miss-each-other-diplomatically.html.

204 *"small gesture holds great importance":* Martin Fackler, "For Japan, Small Gesture Holds Great Importance," *New York Times*, October 18, 2014, https://www.nytimes.com/2014/10/19/world/asia/for-japan-and-china-small-gesture-holds-great-importance.html.

204 *"Touch comes before sight":* Margaret Atwood, *The Blind Assassin* (Toronto: McClelland and Stewart, 2000).

205 *it's either that the clasping of hands:* Evan Andrews, "The History of the Handshake," History, August 9, 2016, https://www.history.com/news/what-is-the-origin-of-the-handshake.

205 *They were even seen to be less qualified:* Greg Stewart et al., "Exploring the Handshake in Employment Interviews," *Journal of Applied Psychology* 93, no. 5 (2008): 1139.

205 *Despite its widespread adoption, the high five:* Kelly Cohen, "Has the Coronavirus Ruined the High-Five?," ESPN, May 22, 2020, https://www.espn.com/mlb/story/_/id/29200202/has-coronavirus-ruined-high-five.

205 *Or the simple hug:* Sabine Koch and Helena Rautner, "Psychology of the Embrace: How Body Rhythms Communicate the Need to Indulge or Separate," *Behavioral Sciences* 7, no. 4 (2017): 80.

206 *"shared attention":* Christine Webb, Maya Rossignac-Milon, and E. Tory Higgins, "Stepping Forward Together: Could Walking Facilitate Interpersonal Conflict Resolution?," *American Psychologist* 72, no. 4 (2017): 374.

206 *Roberto Weber and Colin Camerer created a clever game:* Roberto Weber and Colin Camerer, "Cultural Conflict and Merger Failure: An Experimental Approach," *Management Science* 49, no. 4 (2003): 400–415.

208 *People who felt more understood were more satisfied:* Janetta Lun, Selin Kesebir, and Shigehiro Oishi, "On Feeling Understood and Feeling Well: The Role of Interdependence," *Journal of Research in Personality* 42, no. 6 (2008): 1623–28.

209 *how they had managed the tension of combining old and new:* Dawn Braithwaite, Leslie Baxter, and Anneliese Harper, "The Role of Rituals in the Management of the Dialectical Tension of 'Old' and 'New' in Blended Families," *Communication Studies* 49, no. 2 (1998): 101–20.

210 *"It's a time of camaraderie":* Ibid.

211 *employee-generated rituals were more important:* Rikard Larsson and Michael Lubatkin, "Achieving Acculturation in Mergers and Acquisitions: An International Case Survey," *Human Relations* 54, no. 12 (2001): 1573–1607.

212 *some employees still had those photos as their desktop images:* Brian Gorman, "Ritual and Celebration in the Workplace," *Forbes*, January 14, 2020, https://www.forbes.com/sites/forbescoachescouncil/2020/01/14/ritual-and-celebration-in-the-workplace.

213 *it would be physically undone:* Lotten Gustafsson Reinius, "The Ritual Labor of Reconciliation: An Autoethnography of a Return of Human Remains," *Museum Worlds: Advances in Research* 5, no. 1 (2017): 74–87.

214 *When people felt understood:* Andrew Livingstone, Lucía Fernández Rodríguez, and Adrian Rothers, "'They Just Don't Understand

Us': The Role of Felt Understanding in Intergroup Relations," *Journal of Personality and Social Psychology* 119, no. 3 (2020): 633.

214 *"It's the cheapest concession you can give"*: Roger Fisher, William L. Ury, and Bruce Patton, *Getting to Yes: Negotiating Agreement without Giving In* (New York: Penguin, 2011).

215 *"After 22 years, the divorce didn't work out"*: Abby Ellin, "You Married Them Once, but What about Twice?," *New York Times*, March 3, 2016, https://www.nytimes.com/2016/03/06/fashion/weddings/remarriage-divorce.html.

Index